Their Lives and Your Life

Their Lives and Your Life:
Children's Devotions on Bible Characters

Reformation Heritage Books
and
Youth and Education Committee, FRCNA

2007

© 2007 by Youth and Education Committee, FRCNA

Published by
Reformation Heritage Books
2965 Leonard St., NE
Grand Rapids, MI 49525
616-977-0599 / Fax 616-285-3246
e-mail: orders@heritagebooks.org
website: www.heritagebooks.org

and

Youth and Education Committee, FRCNA
29 Newcombe Rd.
Dundas, ON L9H 7B4
Canada
905-628-1211
e-mail: hdenhollander@yahoo.com
website: www.frcna.org

ISBN 978-1-60178-030-0

*For additional Reformed literature, both new and used, request a free
book list from Reformation Heritage Books at the above address.*

Contributors

C. Grandia: from January 1 through January 28; from June 24 through June 30

A. Karels: from January 29 through February 25

J. van der Meij: from February 26 through March 24

K. van Campen-Slappendel: from March 25 through April 21

R. D. L. Remmers: from April 22 through May 19

J. M. Strijbis: from May 20 through June16

J. Veldhuijzen: from June 17 through June 23; from July 1 through July 21

C. Ritmeester: from July 22 through August 4; from August 12 through August 25

A. J. de Bruijn: from August 5 through August 11; from August 26 through September 1; from September 9 through September 29

L. de Bruijn: from September 2 through September 8; from November 25 through December 22

C. F. van der Meij-Doorn: from September 30 through October 27; from December 23 through December 31

M. de Braal-Prins: from October 28 through November 24

Preface

It gives me great pleasure to introduce to you the first of what we hope will become a series of devotional books for children and young people. There is a great need for such material today; our children and young people need good, sound material to help them grow spiritually. We hope this book will help meet this need.

This book was originally published by Jongbloed in the Netherlands under the title *Hun Leven, Jou Leven*. It is part of a series of devotionals written by ministers from various conservative Reformed churches there. We would like to express our appreciation to Mrs. Ann Roth and her daughter-in-law, Mrs. Petra Roth, for translating the book, and to Mrs. Kate De Vries for doing the editing. Many thanks also to Dr. Joel Beeke, who first approached us about making this a joint venture between our committee and Reformation Heritage Books, and to Mr. Jay Collier for guiding us through the process. Our gratitude goes out to Jongbloed Publishing for granting us permission to publish the book in English.

We would especially like to thank Mr. Herman den Hollander for first presenting this idea to our committee and for overseeing the project from its inception. Without his efforts, this book would never have become a reality.

Rev. J. Schoeman
Chairman,
Youth and Education Committee,
Free Reformed Churches of North America

Adam — Genesis 1:26–31

Let Us Make Man

And God said, Let us make man in our image.
— Genesis 1:26

The sun was shining brightly, the wind moving softly through the treetops. The birds were raising their songs to heaven and everything was very good, for it was created by God. But there was no creature who thanked God for all these wonders and who would talk about His creation.

That is why God said, "Let us make man in our own image." God made Adam out of the dust of the earth. As a child of God, Adam could walk over the earth and rule the animals, the fish, and the birds. In all this, Adam resembled God and did as God wanted him to. It was all very good!

In the beginning, God made a human being like you and me, a person in His own image. Isn't this wonderful? It means that every person, including you, has been created for eternity. God gave you a soul and you are able to communicate with Him. Now you can live a life devoted to Him.

Adam was obedient to God. Are you?

1

Adam — Genesis 2:4–17

Paradise

And the LORD God took the man, and put him into the garden of Eden.
— Genesis 2:15

The earth was beautiful and good wherever you went, but the Garden of Eden stood out from everything else. Just think: a garden for Adam to live in. A lovely river wound its way through the garden where a rich diversity of plants and trees grew. It really was Paradise!

The Lord God designated two trees as very special: the tree of life and the tree of the knowledge of good and evil. Adam could eat all the fruit he wanted except the fruit of the tree of the knowledge of good and evil. He would surely die if he ate from that tree. God gave this test to the human race to see if they would be obedient.

How wonderful it was in Paradise—no pain, no anger, and no sorrow. But above all, God conversed with Adam just like a father does with his child. The Lord was good and kind. Would you not want to obey this God?

Some find keeping God's commandments a hard task. What do you think of the commandment God gave to Adam?

Adam — Genesis 2:18–24

A Great Miracle

And the rib, which the Lord God had taken from man, made he a woman.
— Genesis 2:22

Adam was very busy! All of the animals God created came to him to be named. They all received a name that suited that particular animal. God gave Adam the wisdom to do this.

Adam noticed that all the animals came in pairs, male and female; yet he himself was all alone. But God knew this, too, so when Adam was sleeping, the Lord performed a miracle! Without Adam realizing it, God removed a rib from his body. Then He made the rib into a woman and gave her to Adam. Just imagine: you go to sleep alone and when you wake up, there are two people!

Adam called the wife he had received from God "woman." Adam would take care of her as her husband, and she would care for him as his faithful wife. She and Adam belonged together. This was God's plan for them, as it is still today for husbands and wives. After marriage, a husband and wife belong together until death parts them.

Why did Adam name his wife "woman"?

3

Adam — Genesis 3:1–6

God as a Liar

And the serpent said....
— Genesis 3:4a

Adam and his wife were very happy. Every day they delighted in the pleasures God gave them. Their greatest joy was when God talked to them as a father and friend does.

Adam and his wife were determined to obey God and to live holy lives. But Satan, who once had been favored by God, came with a dreadful plan.

While the woman was walking through the splendid garden, she heard a voice. It was Satan speaking through a snake, one of the cleverest animals God had created. How wicked were his words! Satan turned upside-down everything that God had said to Adam. According to him, God was a liar. If they would eat the forbidden fruit, they would not die, but they would be like God!

And then, the terrible thing happened. Adam joined the woman in believing Satan and in disobeying God. We were created perfect, but now rebelled against God!

Satan turns everything upside-down. Do you notice this sometimes?

4

Adam — Genesis 3:7–15

Adam, Where are You?

And the LORD God called unto Adam, and said unto him,
Where art thou? — Genesis 3:9

As the wind blew softly, God came to talk with the people He had created. But this time, there were no happy faces waiting for Him. Adam and his wife hid themselves because they were scared and ashamed of their nakedness.

But God found Adam and called him by his name. "Why did you hide yourselves," He asked, "and who told you that you were naked? Did you eat the forbidden fruit?" Adam hung his head but immediately pointed his finger to his wife. "The woman thou gavest me gave me the fruit." The woman also hung her head, but pointed to the serpent, whom Satan used as his mouthpiece. They both blamed someone else.

God was angry with them, but also grieved. He pronounced His judgment. From now on, the devil would always try to make people sin and ruin what was good, and we would be punished as we deserve.

But God also had another message—a message of mercy! He promised that someone would come one day who would conquer the devil. I am sure that you know His name!

Have you observed that Satan wants to destroy that which is good? Do you fight against his temptations?

Adam — Genesis 3:16–24

Sorrow in Heaven and on Earth

Cursed is the ground for thy sake.
— Genesis 3:17b

God also told Adam and his wife that much sorrow would be experienced on earth. A mother would have much pain when a baby is born. Thorns and thistles would now grow on this earth, and you would have to work very hard to get a meal on your table!

Then, at the end of life, the terrible enemy, death, would come. People would die and return to the dust from where they had come.

Adam gave his wife a new name, Eve, because she was the mother of all the living. God told them they now had to leave Paradise. The fruit of the tree of life was forever out of their reach. God's image-bearers, who could have been His friends, had to leave Paradise behind them.

Two sad people and a grieving Creator in heaven—what an awful, distressing story. But, one day, there will be a new heaven and a new earth, without sin, pain, and sorrow. You can go there, too, if you receive a new heart and if you believe in the Lord Jesus, who was promised in Paradise. Then you will not die, but live.

Are you a child of the Lord Jesus?

Adam — Genesis 4

A Terrible Day

And it came to pass, when they were in the field, that Cain rose up against Abel his brother, and slew him.
— Genesis 4:8b

The earth had been created perfectly, but most of its beauty could not be seen anymore. The animals did not live in peace anymore and were afraid of each other. The earth was covered with thorns and thistles. God had said that man would die, and now it was fulfilled in a terrible way.

One day, as the sons of Adam and Eve were in a field, it happened. They were bringing a sacrifice to God; Cain was offering corn, and Abel, a sheep. Outwardly no difference could be seen, but they were certainly different!

Abel offered his sheep because he loved the Lord, but Cain offered his corn only because he had to. God, who knows and sees everything, let Cain know that He could not accept such an offering. God wanted Cain to love Him, just like Abel. But instead of asking for forgiveness, Cain became jealous and killed Abel! What a terrible day! People still kill each other over the smallest disagreement. Imagine how it would have been if sin had not entered the world.

Do you serve the Lord because you have to or because you love Him?

Noah — Genesis 6:1–8

A Dreadful Punishment

And the LORD said, I will destroy man whom I have created from the face of the earth.
— Genesis 6:7a

More and more people began to occupy the earth. It would have been wonderful if these people had served the Lord. But the opposite was true; they turned their backs on God more and more and sought their own pleasures. Partying and having a good time were the most important parts in their life.

Hardly anyone thought about God. Things became so bad that God repented of having made man. In the Bible it says that "it grieved the Lord at his heart," meaning He was so distressed that it caused Him great pain and He knew that this could not go on. He then decided to kill all of mankind, with all of the animals, as a punishment for their terrible sins.

But there was one family that served Him in truth. God saw Noah and his wife and his sons and their wives.

The Lord was grieved because almost no one served Him. Do you serve Him?

Noah — Genesis 6:9–22

Ridiculous!

Make thee an ark.
— Genesis 6:14a

God's plan was to destroy the earth, but He made a covenant with Noah: he and his family would be kept safe! For this reason, Noah was instructed to build an ark, a large boat. He had to build it in such a way that his family and many animals could survive in it. It had to be a boat with several stories and many rooms. God was making sure that after the flood there would be people and animals to occupy the earth again.

Noah started to build the ark in the middle of a field. People watched him and began to laugh and mock Noah. "Who builds a boat where no water is in sight? Are you going to sail in your field? Ridiculous!" Noah heard them mocking but carried on with his job of building the ark. He also gathered food for his family and all the animals. They would be safe living inside of the ark.

The people made fun of Noah but he kept working. How do you react when you are laughed at?

Noah — *Genesis 7*

The Door is Shut

...and the LORD *shut him in.*
— Genesis 7:16b

The ark was ready and the great judgment would come. But before God punished the earth, He sent into the ark every animal He had created. One pair of each unclean animal and seven pairs of each clean animal entered the ark. Noah gave each animal its own spot. Then God told Noah that he and his family had to enter the ark, and God Himself shut the door. No one else could enter in anymore!

For the people outside the ark, disaster struck. Big, dark clouds burst and the earth split open. The rivers turned into raging, foaming water, spilling over their banks. People fled as quickly as they could because the waters rose higher and higher, and the currents became fiercer.

Then it became very quiet on the earth: no bird chirped, no child played. Only the sounds of waves and wind were heard. The earth, once created perfectly, was again void and without form. All of the people that had not believed God's punishment had died, but in the ark was a family that served the Lord. God kept them and the animals all safe in the ark.

A child of God will be safe, even when the earth will be destroyed. Can you find another Bible verse that talks about the earth being destroyed again?

Noah — Genesis 8:1–19

The Door Has Been Opened

Go forth of the ark....
— Genesis 8:16a

The mockers had all died because what God had said had happened. Now the earth was one big ocean; even the tallest mountains were covered with water. For many months, the ark had been floating on the water, and it seemed endless.

But the Lord remembered Noah, his family, and all of the animals that were inside the ark! He sent a wind that dried up the earth. The clouds disappeared, the violent rains stopped, and the sun began to shine.

First Noah let out a raven and later a dove. How happy he was when the dove came back with an olive leaf in its beak. God would again take care of His creation. Everything would start growing and producing flowers. Soon they could start living on the earth. Noah opened the door. How gloriously the light was shining! People and animals could go outside again. How happy and joyful they were! In some ways it was like the first days of creation—only one family lived on the vast, wide world.

God always does what He promises to do. Can you think of some examples of this today?

Noah — *Genesis 8:20–22*

God Makes a Promise

...neither will I again smite any more every thing living, as I have done.
— Genesis 8:21b

Noah was very glad and thankful. To show his thankfulness to God, he built an altar and offered clean animals. When God saw and smelled the offering, He decided to do something wonderful. Even though the Lord knew that the people would sin again, He promised that the earth would never again be destroyed by a flood.

As long as the earth would continue, springtime would be followed by harvest. After the summer, winter would come, and the day would be followed by night.

What a great promise God gave! Do you think it's normal that the sun rises in the morning? Or that, after winter, spring arrives again? And that, after cold days, warm and pleasant days greet us? We receive all of this because God promised to do so. He is the One that sends it. Will you thank Him for all this? Do so, because this is what the Lord desires.

We often ask God for special things. But do you thank Him for your daily blessings?

Noah — *Genesis 9:1–17*

God's Rainbow

And I will remember my covenant.
— Genesis 9:15a

Everything looked gloomy with an overcast sky, rain, and wind. You would think that another flood was coming. But suddenly a miracle happened! The sun broke through the dark clouds and, while it was still raining, a rainbow appeared with its beautiful colors outlined against the dark sky.

God promised that the earth would never again be devastated by water and gave Noah the sign of the rainbow. Whenever a rainbow could be seen in the sky, the Lord would remember His promise.

What a wonderful thought: when you see a rainbow, God is remembering His promise to Noah. Next time you see a rainbow, think of the promise of God.

> *The earth will never be destroyed by a flood. But do you know what the Lord says will happen to this earth in the future?*

Noah — *Genesis 9:18–29*

Noah is Drunk

And he drank of the wine.
                    — Genesis 9:21a

Noah was busy making wine from his delicious, sweet grapes. Afterwards, he drank the wine—not a little bit, but far too much, so much that he became drunk. Unaware of what he was doing, Noah undressed himself and lay down naked in his tent.

At that moment, Ham, Noah's youngest son, entered his father's tent. With a mocking smile on his face, he saw his father. He quickly called his brothers, Shem and Japheth, to come and laugh at their father, too. But Shem and Japheth were wiser than Ham and honored their father. They took a rug, walked backwards into the tent, and covered their father with it so no one could see his nakedness.

When Noah awoke, a terrible curse was pronounced on Ham's son, Canaan. Shem and Japheth were blessed, and from the descendants of Shem the Savior would be born.

Should we ever mock others?

Abram — Genesis 11:26–12:4

God Calls Abram

Get thee out of thy country.
— Genesis 12:1

The earth was fully inhabited again, but were the people serving God? No, it was quite the opposite. Many were serving their own gods. Temples were being built, but not for the service of the living God.

Terah, the father of Abram, lived in Ur. He was one of the descendants of Shem, from whom the Messiah would be born. However, Terah's family also worshipped idols, and the moon was honored in the way that only God should be. It seemed impossible that the Messiah would be born from this family. But God will do what He promises, and He uses different ways from what we might expect. He called Abram and told him to go to a country God would direct him to. God was going to make a great nation from Abram, from which the Messiah would be born.

Abram went and left everything behind—his house, his friends, and much of his belongings. This must have been very difficult for him.

Do you listen to God, even when you don't like what He is asking you to do?

Abram — Genesis 12:5–13

Something Went Wrong

And Abram went down into Egypt.
                                        — Genesis 12:10

Abram obeyed God's call to leave, and after a long journey he arrived in Canaan. Under a big oak tree on the plain Moreh by Sichem, God told him that this was the country where his descendants would live. Abram believed God and gave the Lord a sacrifice to show his thankfulness.

But then famine entered the country. Instead of trusting the Lord, Abram decided to go to Egypt. In Egypt, there would be enough food for all of them. How sad that Abram went his own way without relying on God, because now things went wrong.

At times it is hard for us to understand God's ways. As with Abram, God's dealings with us can be so different from what we expect. Maybe you have a hard time at school or you have a quarrel with your friends. You may even think the Lord has forgotten you, or that it does not matter that you believe in Him. Whatever happens in your life, never forsake the Lord, but ask Him to give you strength. Maybe the Lord is testing you to see if you will obey Him.

> *What was Abram's fear? How did he try to solve his problems?*

Abram — Genesis 12:14–20

Rich and Yet Poor

And the woman was taken.
— Genesis 12:15b

Abram was afraid this would happen: his beautiful wife, Sarai, was taken by Pharaoh's servants. From now on, she would live in the Egyptian king's palace. Abram had received many gifts from Pharaoh—sheep, cows, camels, servants, and maids. He was rich but felt so poor without his dear wife.

But the Lord took care of Abram and Sarai. He sent great plagues on the house of Pharaoh, and Pharaoh realized that they were sent because of Sarai. He called Abram and asked him why he had lied about Sarai being his sister and not his wife! Sarai was allowed to leave the palace and Abram's life was spared. Together they went back to Canaan.

Even when Abram forgot to put his trust in God, the Lord did not forget him. At times, it can be difficult to trust in the Lord. You want to solve your own problems and forget to pray about them. But the God of Abram and Sarai still lives and cares about you. Will you remember this when troubles come into your life?

What do you do when you are scared or worried?

Abram — Genesis 13

Trouble

Then Lot chose him all the plain of Jordan.
— Genesis 13:11a

Abram's nephew, Lot, had left Ur of the Chaldees with Abram. He had traveled alongside Abram to Haran and from there to Egypt. As friends, they had gone back to Canaan. But then a quarrel broke out between the shepherds of Abram and Lot. It would be impossible for them to stay together.

Abram called Lot and let him choose in what part of the country he wanted to live. Lot looked around and chose the best part, right by the Jordan River. That part of the country was so beautiful that it looked like Paradise, but the people who lived there were very wicked. The beauties of nature were glorious but the people did not serve the Lord God. Lot chose by only looking at the outward appearance.

Abram was left behind, alone. But soon after Lot had departed, Abram's great Friend came to comfort him. God told him that the country to the north and the south, the east and the west, would one day belong to Abram and his descendants. God would be with him forever!

What part of the land would you have chosen? Why?

Abram — Genesis 15:1–6

Unable to Count

Look now toward heaven, and tell the stars.
— Genesis 15:5

Have you ever been outside at night? Did you see the stars shining in the clear, dark sky? Have you ever tried counting them? You know that it is impossible! The Lord told Abram that He would be his shield and would always guard and protect him. Abram believed God, but how was this going to happen? He was already old and had no children. Would the promise be for Eliezer, his most important servant?

God answered him that same night. Not his servant, but his own son would become the heir. Abram had to go outside and count the stars, and his descendants would be as numerous as them. Abram could not count the stars, and you cannot either, because there are so many. What seemed impossible to Abram would one day be given to him by God! The promise that Abram's descendants would become a great nation, with so many people you could not count all of them, would be fulfilled.

What did God mean when He said He would be Abram's shield? Where else is this mentioned in the Bible?

Abram — Genesis 15:7–21

A Fiery Torch

Behold a smoking furnace, and a burning lamp.
— Genesis 15:17

At the request of Abram, God confirmed His promise with a sign. Abram had to kill animals and lay them opposite each other. He waited for God to burn the offering, but day and night went by and nothing happened. It was as if God did not hear him. But then the Lord gave His sign. Abram saw a smoking furnace that went between the slaughtered animals.

It was a sign of what would happen to Abram's descendants in the future. They would be severely oppressed in Egypt, as though the furnace of affliction would suffocate them. But Abram also saw a burning lamp that would be the way out—through the smoke to a bright future. God would lead His people out of the misery of Egypt to the country He had given them.

Sometimes it can be dark in our lives—maybe in your life, too. Look to the Light because the Lord is willing to guide you through the darkness to the bright future of His eternal kingdom.

When you have troubles in your life, do you trust in the Lord?

Abram — Genesis 16

A Quarrel in the Tent!

I was despised in her eyes.
— Genesis 16:5b

God had promised a son to Abram, but it seemed like God would not fulfill this promise. Abram and Sarai were getting old and still had no child. Then Sarai thought that she had found a solution. She would help the Lord a little bit. Abram should take their servant Hagar as his wife, and maybe she would bear a son for them. Abram agreed to Sarai's plan. But, instead of joy, there was quarrelling in the tent. Hagar became proud and this angered Sarai. You can read this for yourself in the Bible.

Do you try to help the Lord in His work? We should never do that. But don't we act like Sarai more than we realize? Sometimes we totally disagree with God's ways; our plans are different and we would like to give God directions. Do not be as foolish as Sarai and Abram. Instead of joy, they received sorrow. You have to believe that God does what He promises, even if it turns out differently from what you had expected.

Did Abram ask a blessing from God before he took Hagar as his wife?

Abraham — Genesis 17:1–8

Abram Becomes Abraham

But thy name shall be Abraham.
— Genesis 17:5b

When Abram was ninety-nine years old, the Lord appeared to him again. God promised that He would not forget the covenant He had made with Abram, His friend. God would make Abram a father of many nations and His covenant would be for believers from all countries.

That is why Abram's name, which means "father of the faithful," was changed to Abraham, which means "father of many nations." Kings would come from Abraham's descendants.

The Lord also promised that His covenant with Abraham would be eternal. Christ would be born from Abraham's family one day. You probably have heard many times about the covenant the Lord made with Abraham. At every baptism service, the words are repeated: "I will establish my covenant between me and thee." The Lord wants to be your Father. He promised this when you were baptized, and His promise is sealed to your forehead. Go to the Lord and pray for Him to fulfill the promises of your baptism.

Where else in Scripture is this covenant mentioned?

Abraham — Genesis 17:9–27

God's Sign

And it shall be a token of the covenant betwixt me and you.   — Genesis 17:11b

Now that God had made His covenant with Abraham and his descendants, He wanted all the men and their sons to be circumcised. Every baby boy would from now on be circumcised on the eighth day. That would set them apart as children of God's covenant. If this did not happen, the covenant would be broken.

Not only was Abraham given a new name, but Sarai, whose name meant "my princess," would now become Sarah, meaning "princess of many." She would not only be Abraham's princess, but also a princess of many nations.

Abraham could hardly believe it, but Sarah would receive a son. What is impossible with man is possible with God! Abraham and Sarah would receive the promised son and his name would be Isaac.

Isaac would be blessed by God, but who else will receive a blessing from the Lord?

Abraham — Genesis 18:1–15

Important Guests

And the LORD appeared unto him....
— Genesis 18:1a

While Abraham was sitting in his tent one day, three men appeared before him. It was the Lord God with two angels. This was going to be a very important visit. When Abraham recognized them, he was filled with awe and delight, and bowed before them, asking, "Lord, if I have found favor in Thy sight, do not go, but stay for dinner." The Lord accepted Abraham's invitation and He and His two angels stayed for a meal. While they were eating, the Lord repeated His promise: in one year, their son Isaac would be born.

Sarah was outside the tent, listening to their conversation. When she heard that she would soon be having a baby boy, she burst out laughing. How can this be? What the Lord was saying was impossible. Scared of her own reaction, Sarah then lied to the Lord when He confronted her. But can we hide anything from the Lord?

How would you like it if the Lord walked past your house? Would you invite Him inside or would you not dare? Ask if the Lord will give you His Spirit to live in your heart. Ask that your heart would become pure in His sight so that the Most High God will make your heart His dwelling place.

Would you hide anything if the Lord came for a visit?

Abraham — Genesis 18:16–33

Troubled

Wilt thou also destroy the righteous with the wicked?
— Genesis 18:23

After the meal, the three men and Abraham walked in the direction of Sodom and Gomorrah. The surrounding area was beautiful, but it seemed as if the devil was in control of it. The two cities were very wicked and their sins were so many that God had decided to destroy them with everyone who lived there. They were on their way to do so when the Lord told Abraham this terrible news.

This message upset Abraham greatly. Who would not fear God's judgment? As the two angels walked on, the Lord stayed behind with Abraham. Abraham pleaded with the Lord to spare the cities, because maybe some of the people had not committed those horrible sins. Maybe there were fifty, or forty-five, or forty, or thirty, or twenty, or even only ten righteous people living there. Because the Lord is full of grace, He promised Abraham that He would spare the cities if there were only ten who served Him.

Do you pray for other children who do not know the Lord?

Abraham — Genesis 21:1–21

Mocked

And Sarah saw the son of Hagar…mocking.
— Genesis 21:9

A great celebration took place in the tents of Abraham and Sarah when Isaac, the son for whom they had waited so long, was finally born. For two years, everything was peaceful and harmonious. But then Ishmael, the son of Hagar, started teasing and mocking his younger brother, Isaac. Sarah saw this and became very angry; she would not tolerate it. Hagar and her son had to leave as soon as possible. Abraham must send them away. But Abraham did not want to do this since Ishmael was also his son.

Then the Lord told Abraham to follow Sarah's demand. Many years later, the Lord Jesus would be born from Isaac's descendants. This is why Isaac and Ishmael did not belong together.

It was difficult for Abraham to send Ishmael away, but God comforted him by promising that Ishmael would also become a great nation. Because of Sarah's meddling with the Lord's affairs years earlier, sorrow had entered their tents. Now Hagar and Ishmael had to leave.

Great nations did come from Isaac and Ishmael, but there was a difference between them. What was the difference?

Abraham — Genesis 22:1–14

Impossible

Take now thy son...and offer him there for a
burnt offering. — Genesis 22:2

The Lord had just told Abraham that the Lord Jesus would one day be born from the descendants of Isaac. But then God commanded Abraham to do something unbelievable: Abraham was to sacrifice his son. God had wonderfully fulfilled His promise and given Isaac, but now He commanded Abraham to kill him. How can this be? Abraham's heart was filled with sorrow and doubt. He did not understand. But one thing he was sure of: whatever the Lord asked him to do, he would be obedient.

Abraham prepared to offer up his son. He tied Isaac down with ropes. The sharp knife glittered in the sun as he raised his arm to strike. Then something marvelous and unexpected happened. A voice from heaven came: "Abraham, Abraham, do not do it, for now I know that you fear me!"

Abraham dropped his knife and loosened the ropes. Abraham and Isaac's sorrow changed into joy. Instead of sacrificing Isaac, Abraham sacrificed a ram as an offering to God. Abraham and Isaac are beautiful examples for us because they obeyed the Lord, even when they could not understand Him.

Are you obedient even when it is hard to understand why
we must obey?

Abraham — Genesis 22:15–19

A Wonderful Promise

And in thy seed shall all the nations of the earth be blessed.
— Genesis 22:18a

God spoke to Abraham from heaven again. Because Abraham was obedient, he would receive a great blessing. His descendants would be so many that you could not count them, and the country of Canaan would be theirs forever. What was even more wonderful was that the Messiah would one day be born from Abraham's descendants. Abraham and Isaac joyfully returned home to Beersheba, where they lived.

Centuries later, the Messiah, the Son of God, would be offered up at Calvary. When Isaac was about to be offered, a voice came from heaven, halting the sacrifice. But when God's Son was being sacrificed on the cross, no voice came from heaven; there was silence. God provided a ram, caught in the bushes, to take Isaac's place, but there was no one to take the Lord Jesus' place. The son of Abraham could live, but the Son of God had to die. Abraham joyfully took his son home, but the Father in heaven saw His Son in the grave. The Lord did all of this in order to take away the punishment of our sins. Doesn't this make you want to serve Jesus?

Of whom was Isaac an example?

Isaac — Genesis 24:4–7

Trust in God

Unto thy seed will I give this land.
— Genesis 24:7b

Abraham wanted his son to be married before he died. The people who lived in Canaan were heathens who did not belong to God's covenant people. How would Abraham be able to find a wife for Isaac?

It was probably his head servant, Eliezer, who was to go to Mesopotamia, where some of Abraham's relatives were living. Eliezer promised to search for a wife for Isaac there. Abraham was certain that the Lord would take care of him and Isaac.

Eliezer went on his journey by camel and took presents with him; after a while, he arrived at the well in Haran. Eliezer didn't know how to pick a wife for Isaac, but he believed that God would help him. He prayed, "Could it be this girl, who is giving me and my camels water to drink?" The Lord heard his prayer and answered him, showing him that, yes, Rebekah was the woman God wanted to be Isaac's wife. Eliezer gave Rebekah jewelry and asked whose daughter she was. She told him that her father's name was Bethuel. Eliezer knew that Bethuel and Abraham were brothers. He praised God for His guidance, for God had been faithful.

Did you trust God today? How does He guide you?

Isaac — Genesis 24:63–67

Isaac Marries Rebekah

And Isaac went out to meditate....
— Genesis 24:63a

Rebekah told everyone at home what had happened at the well. Her brother quickly went to Eliezer and invited him to stay at their house.

They took very good care of Eliezer, but Abraham's servant did not want to eat anything before he told them why he had come. He praised God's faithfulness and told them how God had been faithful in Canaan, on his journey, and again at the well. He then asked if he could take Rebekah back with him to be married to Isaac. Bethuel and Laban acknowledged God's providence and they agreed that she could go.

Do you think they stayed in Haran for a long time after this news? No, Rebekah decided that she wanted to go to Isaac right away. After the long journey, they arrived in Canaan. Isaac was in a field where he was praying for God's blessing. He was also waiting for Eliezer's return. The moment Rebekah saw her future husband, she climbed down from her camel and covered her face to show respect. The Lord remembered His covenant by bringing Rebecca to Isaac to be his wife.

How did the Lord keep his promise to Abraham?

Isaac — Genesis 25:30–34

Isaac Gets Esau and Jacob

Thus Esau despised his birthright.
— Genesis 25:34b

The Lord brought trials into Isaac and Rebekah's life. They had been praying for twenty years for the Lord to give them a child. They persevered in their prayers, and eventually the Lord answered them. They had twins boys and called them Esau and Jacob. The Lord told them that the oldest son, Esau, would serve the younger son, Jacob, because God loved Jacob.

Esau was a very hairy person and became a hunter, while Jacob stayed with his mother in her tent and took care of all the cattle. Isaac favored Esau, but Rebekah loved Jacob more. That was a sad situation and not according to God's will. Favoritism often brings jealousy and arguments. It is sin and will always cause grief.

Esau was a careless person. He didn't love the Lord. One day, Esau gave away his birthright to Jacob in exchange for a bowl of lentils. Esau even swore the birthright would now be Jacob's. He should have valued what God gave him, but he was so hungry he did not care. But Jacob's behavior wasn't right either, for he was supposed to wait for God's timing to bless him. Jacob had not yet learned that God fulfills His promises at the right time.

It is hard to be patient sometimes, but Jacob should have waited for the Lord to fulfill His promise. Can you think of times when you have to be patient? Why is it then better to wait?

Isaac — Genesis 26:22–25

Isaac is Tried

I am the God of Abraham thy father.
— Genesis 26:24a

There was a terrible famine in Canaan. God was testing Isaac. Isaac wanted to go to Egypt to live until the famine was over, but God came to him and commanded him to stay in Gerar, where he had to live among the Philistines.

Isaac listened to God and stayed, but he was afraid of Abimelech, the king of the Philistines, and his people. Isaac lied to them and said that Rebekah was his sister. He thought that they would not harm her then. What disappointing behavior! It showed that Isaac did not trust the Lord. But the Lord didn't forget Isaac; when Abimelech found out that Isaac had lied to him, the Lord still protected him.

God blessed Isaac with a good harvest and a lot of cattle. The Philistines became so jealous of all these blessings that Isaac had to leave. He was in need of water for his cattle but all the old wells were destroyed. The Lord blessed Isaac again when a shepherd found a well called Rehoboth, or "The Lord makes room." The Lord appeared again and promised Isaac that He would bless him. Isaac built an altar there and worshipped God.

How has God blessed you today?

Isaac — Genesis 26:26–33

Isaac and Abimelech

We saw certainly that the LORD was with thee.
— Genesis 26:28a

Isaac traveled with his family to Beersheba in the south. He didn't want to serve any other god than the God of his father Abraham. The Lord promised to make Isaac's seed into a great nation.

Abimelech, the king of the Philistines, paid Isaac a visit because he wanted to make a covenant with Isaac. Isaac was very surprised. God had told him to leave Gerar, and now Abimelech wanted to make peace with him there. Abimelech and his friends explained that they could tell that the Lord was with Isaac. Abimelech was jealous of all the blessings that came from the hand of the God of Abraham and Isaac. That was why he wanted to make a covenant of friendship with Isaac. You can be sure Isaac asked God first if that was a good thing to do. The next morning, Isaac and Abimelech made a covenant and then returned to Gerar.

Is jealousy always wrong? What about Abimelech's?

Isaac — Genesis 27:22–29

Isaac Blesses Jacob

The voice is Jacob's voice, but the hands are the hands of Esau.
— Genesis 27:22b

Isaac grew old and blind and he knew he would die soon. Isaac asked Esau to hunt some game and make a meal out of it for him. After the meal, Isaac would give him the blessing. That blessing belonged to the firstborn, but Isaac wasn't supposed to bless Esau. And didn't Esau also know that he had sold his birthright to Jacob? He didn't say anything about it to Isaac, which was dishonest of Esau.

Rebekah heard about the plans but she didn't say anything about it to Isaac. She came up with her own solution, one which didn't trust in the Lord. Jacob killed two goats and Rebekah prepared them for Isaac. Jacob put on Esau's clothes and also covered his smooth skin with the goat skins. Jacob agreed with his mother to be deceitful, and didn't ask the Lord for wisdom. That was sin.

Isaac wondered if the voice talking was really Esau's voice, and Jacob lied to him, claiming he was Esau. Isaac believed him and gave him the blessing. God would bless him and many nations would serve him.

Isaac, Jacob, and Esau's behavior was full of lies and deceit. The Lord, on the contrary, was still very merciful and good to them. The Lord Jesus would even be born from the descendants of Jacob.

What does the ninth commandment teach us?

Isaac — Genesis 27:38–41

Isaac Blesses Esau

Hast thou but one blessing, my father?
— Genesis 27:38b

Esau came to his dad with a deliciously prepared dish of venison. Isaac couldn't believe what had happened and told Esau that he had been betrayed by Jacob. The blessing that had been given to Jacob could not be taken back. Esau became very angry and cried. He didn't cry because he felt sorry about his own sin of trading his birthright, but he was sad that he didn't get the blessing.

Isaac still gave Esau a blessing, but not as wonderful as the one he gave to Jacob. Esau would not live in Canaan but in a barren land, and he would also have to serve Jacob. Esau hated his brother Jacob and planned to kill him. Rebekah heard about these plans and wanted to send Jacob far away to her family in Haran.

Isaac and Rebekah talked about finding a wife for Jacob. The women that lived in Canaan were all heathen women, so Rebekah tried to convince Isaac to approve of sending Jacob to Mesopotamia. There Jacob could search for a wife among her relatives.

Why are we not allowed to hate someone? How should Esau have responded when he heard what Jacob did?

Isaac — Genesis 28:1–5

Jacob Flees

Thou shalt not take a wife of the daughters of Canaan.
— Genesis 28:1b

Isaac called Jacob to come to him, and again Jacob received a blessing from him. He instructed Jacob not to marry a Canaanite woman, because that would be disobeying God. He had to search for a godly woman. He had to go to Paddan-Aram, where his uncle Laban lived. Rebekah's brother had two daughters and so Jacob could pick one of them to become his wife.

Jacob obeyed his father and went to Haran. By going to Haran, he was also fleeing from Esau. He traveled to Haran with the blessing of his father and the Lord. The blessing that was promised to Abraham would continue in Jacob's life. He would live back in Canaan and God would make him to be a great nation. The Messiah would be born from his descendants. This would happen because the Lord promised it, and His promises never fail. It is still like that today: the Lord will always keep His promises.

Can you think of some of God's promises to us?

Jacob — Genesis 28:12–15

Jacob in Bethel

The land whereon thou liest, to thee will I give it, and to thy seed.
                                                          — Genesis 28:13

Jacob traveled all by himself as a refugee. His journey covered hundreds of miles, all the way to Haran. After many more miles, he arrived in the town of Luz, where he had to sleep outside with a stone for a pillow. There the Lord appeared to him in a dream.

In his dream, Jacob saw a ladder that went from earth all the way up to heaven. Around that ladder were angels and at the top was the Lord Himself. The Lord spoke to Jacob and told him that his descendants would be as many as the dust of the earth, and that they would be blessed. The Lord Jesus would be born from his descendants. The Lord promised to protect and bless him on his journey. He also showed Jacob that one day he would return again to Canaan.

When Jacob woke up from his dream, he praised the Lord. From the stone pillow he made a stone memorial pillar, and on the top he poured some oil. Jacob made a promise that he would serve the Lord out of thankfulness. Jacob called this place Bethel, which means "the house of the Lord," because it was like the house of the Lord for him.

Can you remember times in your life when the Lord was especially good to you?

37

Jacob — Genesis 29:16–20

Jacob Serves Laban

And Jacob loved Rachel.
— Genesis 29:18a

Jacob's journey became much easier for him. He was happy now because the Lord had appeared to him and blessed him. Finally, after the long journey, Jacob arrived in Haran. Some shepherds tending their flock showed him the way to Laban's place. Just then, Laban's daughter, Rachel, arrived at the well to give her sheep some water to drink. It was clear to Jacob that the Lord was leading him. He greeted Rachel, his cousin, with a kiss. He also helped her remove the stone from the well and take care of her sheep. When they were done, they went to Laban's house together. There his uncle greeted Jacob and made him feel very welcome.

Laban had two daughters. The oldest one was named Leah and her younger sister was Rachel. After being with the family for a month, Laban asked Jacob to stay and work for him. Jacob gladly agreed to stay, and they agreed that he would get Rachel as his wife after seven years of work. Laban liked this deal, because this way he didn't have to pay Jacob for all his work. Laban didn't give Jacob a fair deal; he was stingy.

What commandment teaches us not to be stingy?

Jacob — Genesis 29:25–28

Jacob Marries Leah and Rachel

And he gave him Rachel his daughter to wife also.
— Genesis 29:28a

After working for seven years, Jacob asked Laban to give him his daughter, Rachel, to be his wife. He would like to marry her; that was the agreement they had made. So Laban organized a great wedding feast and Laban gave Jacob his bride. The face of the bride was covered with a veil, as was the custom.

When the wedding was over, Jacob discovered that the woman he had married was Leah, not Rachel! He talked to Laban about the trick, but Laban told him that the oldest daughter had to marry first, before the younger one could be married. That was unfair of Laban; he should have told Jacob about this custom seven years ago! Leah was also deceitful in pretending to be Rachel at the wedding.

Jacob had to promise to work another seven years for Laban. If he would do so, he would get Rachel as a wife one week after he married Leah. So Jacob ended up working as a very cheap servant for Laban. Laban sinned against the Lord. The Lord had commanded that a man should only marry one woman, but Jacob now had two wives. Everyone knew that Jacob liked Rachel better than Leah. This issue would bring problems and sorrow into their family.

Laban lied and persuaded Leah to lie, too. This was very wrong. Is the Lord willing to forgive when we lie?

Jacob — Genesis 30:1, 2 and 22–24, Genesis 35:18

Joseph and Benjamin are Born

But his father called him Benjamin.
— Genesis 35:18

Jacob loved Rachel more than Leah. Yet Leah was the one that received children from the Lord, and Rachel didn't. Rachel was jealous and angry and blamed Jacob for her lack of children. Jacob told her that he couldn't take God's place and bless her with children.

Receiving children is a blessing from the Lord. In the Old Testament times, every woman hoped to receive a son, for he could be the promised Messiah. People looked down on a woman who could not have children.

Finally, after quite awhile, Rachel brought all her sorrow and disappointment to the Lord. She prayed and the Lord heard her. He gave her the desire of her heart and blessed her with a son. She called him Joseph and said that she hoped she would be blessed with more children. Some years later, Jacob and his family lived in Canaan. There Rachel received another son and she called him Benjamin. While giving birth to Benjamin, Rachel died. Jacob buried Rachel close to Bethlehem. He set a pillar upon her grave as a memorial stone.

Why is it wrong to show favoritism? When people do not treat us well and we feel disappointed, what should we do?

40

Jacob — Genesis 32:29–31

Jacob at Peniel

I have seen God face to face, and my life is preserved.
— Genesis 32:30

Jacob became a very rich man. The Lord gave him many children, servants, and cattle. He was traveling back to Canaan with everything he possessed. They were almost there, and Jacob worried that Esau might take revenge. Jacob sent some of his servants ahead to Esau to give him some presents. When the servants returned, they told Jacob that Esau didn't say a word, but was on his way to meet Jacob with four hundred men. Jacob was very afraid, for he knew he would not be able to fight Esau and his men in his own strength. He prayed fervently to the Lord, for He alone could help him.

That night the Lord wrestled with Jacob at the ford called Jabbok. Jacob didn't dare go on without God's blessing. At the break of day, Jacob said, "I will not let thee go, except thou bless me." God did bless Jacob there, and gave him a new name. From now on his name would be Israel. It was a miracle that Jacob has seen God face to face without dying! That is why Jacob named that place Peniel; it means "I have seen God face to face, and my life is preserved."

Meeting Esau, his brother, turned out much better than Jacob imagined it would. Esau was friendly and they embraced each other and cried. Jacob then continued his journey and arrived in Shechem. Jacob built an altar to the Lord and confessed, "Israel's God is God."

When do you ask the Lord for a blessing?

41

Jacob — Genesis 35:11–15

Jacob Returns to Bethel

And Jacob called the name of the place where God spake with him, Bethel.
— Genesis 35:15

The Lord commanded Jacob to move to Bethel and serve Him there. Had Jacob forgotten his promise to the Lord when he dreamt about the ladder rising to heaven as he fled from Esau (Gen. 28:19–22)? He had promised to serve the Lord with all his heart.

Everyone who belonged to Jacob had to put away their idols. After taking all the idols, Jacob buried them under an oak tree in Shechem. His household also had to start dressing differently. They had to dress in a way that was pleasing to God.

On their way to Bethel the Lord protected them from their enemies. The enemies did not dare attack them and Jacob and his household arrived safely at their destination. Jacob built an altar at Bethel to serve the Lord and called the place Elbethel. Elbethel means, "The Lord of Bethel." There the Lord showed Himself again and repeated that Jacob would have a new name: Israel. The Lord God Almighty made a promise again to bless Jacob and his seed. They would live in the promised land. Jacob built a pillar of stone to remember that the Lord had spoken to him.

Have you ever forgotten about something you promised to the Lord?

Joseph — Genesis 37:6–11

Joseph and His Brothers

But his father observed the saying.
— Genesis 37:11b

Jacob's sons were in the fields taking care of their father's sheep. Joseph was one of the youngest and had eleven brothers. Joseph's brothers acted wickedly and he warned them not to behave so. He loved the Lord and knew his brothers were sinning against God. He also talked to his father about it. This made his brothers hate him even more. They already didn't like him because their father liked Joseph best of all his sons, and showed this openly. Joseph was the son of Rachel, whom Jacob loved dearly. The brothers were jealous because Jacob spoiled Joseph by giving him a special coat with many colors.

Some time later, Joseph had a dream. He dreamt that he and his brothers were binding sheaves in the field. The sheaves of his brothers bowed down before Joseph's sheaf. Joseph told his brothers about the dream and they hated him for it. In a second dream, Joseph dreamed that the sun, moon, and eleven stars bowed before him. He told his brothers and his father this dream. Even his father, Jacob, didn't like this dream, and Jacob saw that it made Joseph's brothers angry.

Why is it not good to spoil one person in the family?

Joseph — Genesis 37:27–33

The Brothers Sell Joseph

Thus his father wept for him. — Genesis 37:35b

Joseph's brothers were far away from home, taking care of a flock of sheep. Joseph was going to pay them a visit to see if they were all in good health. He thought they would be at Hebron, but they weren't; someone there said they had left for Dothan, so he headed there next. His brothers saw him coming from far away. They mocked him among themselves and called him "the master dreamer." They hated Joseph because their father favored him and because Joseph kept reminding them of their sins against the Lord. The brothers did not want to serve the Lord.

Before Joseph even arrived, they made an evil plan to kill him. Reuben, the oldest brother, intervened and persuaded the rest not to kill him, but to throw Joseph into a deep, dry pit instead. Then he would slowly die. It was Reuben's plan to rescue him later and return him to their father. The other brothers thought this plan was a good one. They took Joseph's coat and then threw him into the pit.

Reuben left for a little while. Meanwhile, Judah came up with a different idea. He wanted to sell Joseph to some traveling merchants. All the other brothers agreed and sold Joseph for twenty pieces of silver. When Reuben returned, he found Joseph gone, and he was angry with his brothers.

Joseph's brothers dipped his beautifully colored coat in blood and sent it to Jacob to trick him into thinking Joseph had been killed by a wild animal. Jacob was very sad and mourned for his son. No one was able to comfort him.

By hating Joseph, how did the brothers show their hatred for God?

44

Joseph — Genesis 39:2–6 and 9

Joseph with Potiphar

How then can I do this great wickedness, and sin against God?
— Genesis 39:9b

The merchants brought Joseph to Egypt where Potiphar, one of Pharaoh's officers, bought Joseph as a slave. He had to work in Potiphar's house. He proved to be a reliable and hardworking slave. Because the Lord was with Joseph, Potiphar's household was also being blessed. Potiphar decided to make Joseph the leader of all the other slaves in the house. Joseph was in charge of all the household duties except looking after the meals.

Potiphar's wife was a wicked woman who tried to get Joseph to love her as a husband. Joseph refused to do so and avoided her whenever she was around him in the house. Joseph loved the Lord and did not want to sin against God. He told the woman this, too. One day the woman grabbed Joseph by his coat. Joseph quickly pulled away and fled the room, but the woman still had his coat in her hands; she began screaming. She told everyone that Joseph had tried to touch her. That was a mean lie. Because she had Joseph's coat as false proof of her story, her husband sent Joseph to prison. But Joseph was innocent and the Lord knew that. The Lord took care of him there; Joseph was given the task of looking after all the other prisoners. The Lord made Joseph prosper in everything he did.

Can you think of someone else in the Bible who was falsely accused?

45

Joseph — Genesis 40:12–15

Joseph is in Prison

*Here also have I done nothing that they should put me
into the dungeon.*
— Genesis 40:15b

The chief butler and the chief baker of Pharaoh ended up in
prison with Joseph. One of them was guilty but no one knew
which one. They were put in prison until Pharaoh could
figure out who was the guilty one. Joseph was responsible
for taking care of them while they were in prison.

One night the butler and the baker both had a dream.
They didn't know what their dreams meant and they were
sad that no one in the prison could explain it to them. After
Joseph told them that his God was able to explain their
dreams, they told Joseph their dreams and he prayed to the
Lord for wisdom. The butler's dream was about a vine with
three branches. He pressed the grapes of the vine into a cup
and gave it to Pharaoh. Joseph explained that, in three days,
he would be back in the palace as Pharaoh's chief butler.
Joseph asked the butler to mention his name to Pharaoh, and
speak good things about him.

The baker's dream was about three baskets filled with baked
goods. The birds came and ate from the baked goods. The explanation for this dream was not good. In three days, the baker
would be hanged and the birds would eat from his body.

Both dreams came true as Joseph said. But when the butler
returned to Pharaoh's house, he forgot all about Joseph.

*Do you sometimes forget a promise you have made? Isn't
it wonderful that the Lord never forgets His promises?*

Joseph — *Genesis 41:25–31*

Pharaoh's Dreams

*…by reason of that famine following; for it shall be
very grievous.* — Genesis 41:31b

One night, Pharaoh had two dreams. In the first dream, he
was standing at the riverside where he saw seven fat, fine-
looking cows coming up out of the water. They were followed
by seven more cows, but these looked ugly and skinny. These
skinny, ugly cows ate the fat cows.

In the second dream, Pharaoh dreamed about seven good
and plump heads of grain coming out of one stalk. After that,
seven thin heads came out of another stalk, and these thin ones
devoured the good ones. Pharaoh needed to know the meaning of these dreams, but none of the magicians in Egypt could
tell him what they meant. Suddenly, the butler remembered
Joseph from the time he had been in prison. He told Pharaoh
about Joseph; they immediately got Joseph out of the prison
and brought him to Pharaoh. Joseph made it clear that it was
not him but God who would tell the meaning of the dreams.
He asked for wisdom from God and gave Him all the honor
and glory.

The Lord had a message for Pharaoh through his dreams.
Both dreams had the same meaning. There would be an
excellent harvest for seven years in all of Egypt, but those
years would be followed by seven years of famine. Joseph
advised Pharaoh to select a wise man who would collect part
of the good harvest during the seven years of plenty in order
to save food for the seven years of famine.

*How does the Lord speak to us today? Who made Joseph
wise enough to interpret the dreams? Who gives us all
of our abilities?*

Joseph — Genesis 42:8–11

Joseph's Brothers go to Egypt

Ye are spies. — Genesis 42:9

Jacob and his sons were hungry. The famine had spread to Canaan. Jacob heard that they could buy grain in Egypt, so he sent ten of his sons to Egypt. He kept his son Benjamin home because he was worried that something might happen to him.

When the ten brothers arrived in Egypt, they had to report to the governor. That governor was Joseph! Joseph recognized his own brothers, but they did not recognize him. They bowed down before him, just like Joseph had seen in his dream. Joseph accused them of being spies and put them into prison. Three days later, he told them he would let nine of them go home. Simeon had to stay in prison until the other brothers returned from Canaan with their brother Benjamin. Joseph was testing them to see if they were still evil men.

On the way home, they discovered money in one of the sacks of grain. They checked them all and found the money they used to pay for the grain in each of the sacks. Joseph had arranged for it to be there. They were nervous about what would happen when they returned to Egypt.

When the family had finished all the supplies they brought from Egypt, they went back to get more food. Jacob didn't want to send Benjamin along this time either. He was thinking about how he had already lost Joseph and Simeon; he felt like everything was going wrong for him.

Did Jacob really trust in the Lord? Why should we trust the Lord even when things are going wrong?

Joseph — Genesis 43:26–30

Joseph's Brothers Return to Egypt

And he said, God be gracious unto thee, my son.
— Genesis 43:29b

The brothers had no other choice than to return to Egypt to buy more food. The famine was very severe; they would die if they did not go back to Egypt. Finally, they convinced their father Jacob to send Benjamin along. Judah assured his father he would be the surety for his youngest brother and take care of him. Jacob gave his sons extra money and presents to give to the governor in Egypt.

When they arrived in Egypt, they were sent to Joseph's house. The brothers were very afraid. They told Joseph they had brought double the amount of money, but Joseph didn't even ask for the money. He was very friendly to them. Because they brought Benjamin with them, Simeon was set free and was able to join them. Joseph asked them many questions about Benjamin and his father. He also invited them to eat a meal together with him. He made an arrangement for the table setting and put them all in order according to their ages. They wondered how he seemed to know their birth order. And Benjamin received five times as much food as all the others! Again Joseph was testing his brothers. Were they still as jealous as before?

Who else is called a Surety in the Bible?

Joseph — Genesis 44: 18, 22 and 30–32

Joseph Tests His Brothers

…that he will die….
— Genesis 44:31

Filled with joy, the brothers began their return to Canaan. The trip had been very successful. Their father would be very thankful and happy that they all returned safely. But then, a servant of Joseph came after them and made them stop. He told them, "One of you is a thief, and has taken the governor's silver cup." The brothers were convinced that they were all innocent, so they agreed that whoever took the cup would have to die and all the other brothers would be slaves in Egypt. They knew for sure that no one had taken the cup!

The search started with Rueben's sack, then all the other brothers, and finally they opened Benjamin's sack. That was the last one and the brothers were relieved. The Egyptians hadn't found the cup! But oh, what terror suddenly filled their hearts, for there in Benjamin's sack was the silver cup! Benjamin and all his brothers had to return to the house of Joseph. They were terrified of what was going to happen to them. Judah offered to take Benjamin's place. He explained to Joseph that his father would surely die of grief if they would return without their brother Benjamin.

Would you be willing to take the place of your brother or sister, like Judah did?

Joseph — Genesis 45:14–18

Joseph Reveals Himself to His Brothers

And take your father and your households, and come unto me.   — Genesis 45:18

Joseph was unable to control his emotions any longer. He ordered all the servants out of the room. He started to cry out loud and told them who he really was. His first question was if everything was well with his father. His brothers were shocked at what they had just heard! They were convinced they would all be killed, but Joseph showed them that God had been in control of his life all these years. He told his brothers to go back to Canaan to get his father and all their loved ones and bring them all to Egypt. He would take care of them there. Then Joseph fell on his brother Benjamin's neck and cried. He also kissed his other brothers. Joseph's plan pleased Pharaoh and he sent chariots, food, and presents with the brothers. All of Joseph's family could live in Egypt.

When Jacob heard all that had happened to his sons, he couldn't believe it. It was too good to be true! In the end, he believed them and prepared to go to Egypt. He was so happy that he would be able to see his son Joseph again before he died.

The Lord takes care of His people, as you can see in Joseph's life. He is the same today; He still cares for every one of His children.

Do you think it was hard for the brothers to tell Jacob that Joseph was still alive?

Joseph — Genesis 46:28–30

Joseph Meets Jacob

Now let me die.
— Genesis 46:30

Jacob and all that belonged to him traveled to Egypt. In Beersheba, along the way, Jacob sacrificed to the Lord his God. The Lord spoke to Jacob that night, telling him not to worry about the future because God would go with him. He would make Jacob's descendants into a great nation, and this great nation would once again return to Canaan. These promises of the Lord were comforting. Knowing that Joseph would be with him when he died was also comforting to Jacob.

The travelers sent Judah ahead to ask if they could live in Goshen. When Joseph heard this, he knew they were on their way and he came out to meet them. They were all very excited; everyone was so happy to be together again! Joseph advised his brothers to tell Pharaoh that they were shepherds taking care of sheep. The Egyptians didn't really like shepherds, so Jacob's family would probably be asked to live separately in Goshen. Then they would have their own place to worship the Lord.

Isn't it amazing how the Lord directed everything?

Did the Lord separate you to serve Him? How?

Joseph — Genesis 47:5–8

Joseph Takes Care of His Family

How old art thou?
— Genesis 47:8

Joseph sent a message to Pharaoh that his family had arrived in Egypt. Five of the brothers paid Pharaoh a visit on behalf of the family. Pharaoh asked them what their jobs used to be. They told him that they took care of sheep. He wanted some of them to become the chief herdsmen of his own sheep, but all the others were allowed to live in Goshen.

Joseph also introduced his father Jacob to Pharaoh. Pharaoh asked how old Jacob was, and he told him that he was a hundred and thirty years old. Jacob shared some of his life's history and explained that he felt very old because of all the grief and hardship in his life. At the end of their visit, Jacob blessed Pharaoh. Then he and his family moved to Goshen. They lived there peacefully and Joseph took good care of them in the remaining years of the famine. It was the Lord, the God of Abraham, Isaac, and Jacob, who cared for him and his family. The Lord always keeps His promises.

The Bible says that "all things work together for good to them that love God" (Rom. 8:28). How did that occur in Joseph's life?

Joseph — *Genesis 47:25, 27, 29–30*

Joseph Saves Many Lives

I will do as thou hast said.
— Genesis 47:30b

The famine was getting worse and worse. Egypt and the countries around it struggled to have enough food. At first the people paid for food with money, but later on they had to trade their cattle and finally their lands in order to pay for the food. That is how Pharaoh became the owner of everything. The only people who could keep their lands and its fruits were the priests.

Then Joseph made an agreement with the people of the land that he would give them the seed they needed to start sowing again. In return, the people had to give back to Pharaoh one fifth of the harvest. The people did not really have any other choice and so they became slaves of their own king, but they saw Joseph as the one who saved their lives. Without the seed to sow, they would have starved.

In the meantime, Jacob's family kept growing. Just like God had promised, they became a great nation. But Jacob was old and knew he was going to die very soon. He asked Joseph to promise him that his bones would be carried back to Canaan and be buried there. Years later, Joseph kept that promise.

How was the sorrow in Jacob's life blessed by the Lord?
Has the Lord ever used sorrow in your life as a blessing?

Moses — Exodus 1–2:2

Forgetting the Lord

*And when she saw him that he was a goodly child, she
hid him three months.*
— Exodus 2:2

The children of Jacob had a good time in Egypt. They were
cared for by their brother Joseph, and food and drink were
plenty. They had no desire to go back to Canaan. Nothing
should change...but definitely it did!

Joseph died and another Pharaoh came to power. He did
not like the Israelites and was afraid that they were becoming
too powerful. He decided that they should become slaves. It
would weaken them and yet he could profit from their work.

The poor Israelites were enslaved to their new Pharaoh,
and the desire to return to Canaan rose up again in their
hearts. They needed the Lord in their terrible circumstances.
But would the Lord hear them? They had been feeling so
at home in Egypt that they had forgotten the Lord, and it
seemed as if the Lord had forgotten them. Things became
worse when Pharaoh decided that all the newborn baby boys
should be killed.

But God was already busy sending deliverance to His
people. Amram and Jochebed received a son. The Lord was
going to use this child to send the Israelites safely out of Egypt.
He had not forgotten them; He had heard their prayers!

*Do you long for the Lord with your whole heart? Is it
easy to forget Him when things are going well?*

Moses — *Exodus* 2:3–15

Moses' Choice

And I will give thee thy wages.
— Exodus 2:9

"Oh, Amram, what will become of our baby? Every day, the Egyptian soldiers pass our house and I get so scared."

"But Jochebed, don't you believe that the Lord has a special purpose with this child?"

"Yes, Amram, but when I see those soldiers I shiver with fright."

"Come, Jochebed; let us figure out what to do."

Amram and Jochebed decided that the baby, whose name was Moses, should be put in a basket made of reeds and placed by Jochebed in the Nile River. They trusted the Lord to take care of him. By faith, they handed their child over to God and how wonderfully did the Lord guide events thereafter!

Pharaoh's daughter found the basket and brought Moses home with her and adopted him. In the palace he learned so much; perhaps later he would become the king. But, deep in his heart, Moses had a different desire; he wanted to help the poor nation of Israel. He knew that he could only be happy if the God of Jacob was with him. This was worth more than all the treasures of Egypt.

What does Hebrews 11:24 say about Moses and what does it mean?

Moses — *Exodus* 2:16–25

This is God's Way?

And God remembered his covenant. — Exodus 2:24

Moses' wonderful plans all fell apart. One day, he saw an Egyptian hitting an Israelite, and he was very angry. When he looked around, he couldn't see anyone watching, so he intervened and killed the Egyptian. The next day, he found two Israelites fighting among themselves and he confronted one of them. The two men said to Moses, "What are you going to do about it? Will you kill us like you did that Egyptian yesterday?" Moses quickly realized that people had seen and heard about what he did. In fact, even Pharaoh heard about it, and Moses was forced to flee Egypt before Pharaoh punished him and put him to death.

Moses fled to the desert of Midian. The wise prince became a shepherd. For hours on end, he wandered with his sheep through the wilderness. "Is this God's plan?" he wondered. But do not forget that God's way is always the best way. The Lord knows what is good for us.

Moses needed this time to prepare for a great task and to become acquainted with the wilderness. He also gained a deeper knowledge of the Lord. In God's time, he would lead the people of Israel out of Egypt.

God had heard the cry of His people, but they also had to learn that they did not deserve God's help. The Lord answered them because He had promised to do so in His covenant, which you can read about in Exodus 2:24, 25.

What does God promise in Psalm 81:12?

59

Moses — Exodus 3:1–14

Moses Called by the Lord

I AM THAT I AM.
— Exodus 3:14

What is your attitude toward the Lord and His service? Are you reverent when the Bible is being read? We read that Moses hid his face when He met with God. Because God is holy, Moses did not dare to look at Him!

Moses was confused when he walked up to the burning bush; how strange that the fire did not consume the bush! Then he heard God's voice: "Moses, I am the God of Abraham, Isaac, and Jacob, the God of the covenant. My time has come, and I have a task for you. You have to go to Pharaoh and lead My people out of Egypt." Do you see how God calls His servants?

But Moses was not happy with this call. Forty years earlier, he had thought he wanted to lead Israel, but God did not think he was ready then. Now that Moses was ready in God's eyes, Moses did not want to go. But Moses had to realize that he was not going alone; the Lord would be with him. The Lord revealed His name to Moses: Jehovah, "I AM THAT I AM." He was telling Moses, "I do as I say in My judgments and in My promises. I am all powerful."

How blessed are God's people on earth! Are you one of His people? Do you have a new heart? Ask for it often!

How old was Moses when God called him?

Moses — *Exodus 3:15–22*

The All-Knowing God

And I am sure that the king of Egypt will not let you go.
— Exodus 3:19

Moses received instructions from the Lord to go and talk to the elders of Israel. They were the leaders and rulers of the people, the decision makers. "Make known to them My name," God told Moses, "and tell them everything I have told you; they will listen to your words."

The Lord knows all things and rules the hearts of men. Forty years before, these men would not listen to Moses, but now they will. The Lord warned Moses that Pharaoh would not listen and would not let the Israelites go to the wilderness to offer sacrifices to the Lord. But the Lord says, "But I will defend My people. For many years they have slaved for Pharaoh, and I will make sure they get their wages."

Even if Pharaoh would not consent, God would lead His people out of Egypt. He ruled and would show that He was almighty.

Do you recognize the power of Satan and do you struggle with it? Does it seem that he will win at times? Remember that the Lord is almighty; He can deliver you just like He delivered the children of Israel.

What is the difference between mighty *and* almighty?

61

Moses — *Exodus* 4:1–17

Unwilling

...and will teach you what ye shall do.
— Exodus 4:15

God had a lot of patience with Moses. His words should have encouraged Moses, but Moses was unwilling and afraid to go to Egypt. He did not think he was a good enough speaker to bring God's message.

Are you unwilling or afraid to obey God sometimes? Are you afraid that your friends won't believe you or will make fun of you? You can go to the Lord with all of your sin, anger, and troubles. Ask Him to give you an obedient and loving heart that wants to do His will.

The Lord gave Moses signs so the elders would not only hear but also see that God had sent Moses. He would also send Aaron along to help Moses. We can see how the Lord takes care of everything.

"Moses, take the staff in your hand and go!" Moses no longer refused. He now did not trust his own strength and went in God's strength. Now God would receive all the honor, and that is how it should be.

What signs did the Lord give to Moses?

Moses — *Exodus 4:18–31*

Circumcision

...and did the signs in the sight of the people.
— Exodus 4:30

Do God's people, those who have a new heart, still sin? And are they punished for their sin? Maybe these are questions you have wondered about. You can read the answer in the section of the Bible you just read.

Because Moses did not have his second son circumcised, the Lord was ready to kill him. Circumcision was instituted by God as a sign of the covenant. But why had Moses not done it? It could be because his wife, Zipporah, was not an Israelite and did not want it done. The little baby boys often became sick and suffered pain after the circumcision.

But Moses should have listened to the Lord instead of his wife. When Zipporah realized Moses was going to be killed, she had their son circumcised, and everything turned out well. Instead of circumcision today, we have baptism. Girls, as well as boys, can be baptized. Baptism means the same thing that circumcision did for Moses' son.

What does baptism mean?

Moses — *Exodus 5*

Joy and Disappointment

Neither hast thou delivered thy people at all.
— Exodus 5:23

When the elders heard the news of God's deliverance from Moses and Aaron, they were very happy and thanked the Lord. But what a disappointment soon came! Angry Israelites knocked on the elders' door and asked, "What have you done? Now we have to work even harder; what caused this?"

They blamed Moses and Aaron for all their troubles. Had they forgotten God's words, and the signs that Moses showed them? Where was their trust in the Lord?

Moses responded far better by going to the Lord in prayer and asking Him for advice. When everything seems to go wrong in your life, go to the Lord for counsel. When you are in distress and don't have a solution, go to the Lord. Ask if He, for Jesus' sake, will deliver you. He is always listening and He is almighty. No request is too hard for Him.

How did Pharaoh punish the Israelites?

Moses — Exodus 12:29–39

A Hard Heart

And they spoiled the Egyptians.
— Exodus 12:36

Nine plagues had gone over Egypt, and still Pharaoh would not bow before God. He hardened his heart and chose to make his own decisions. God had no place in his life.

Do you harden your heart, or do you listen to the Lord? When we don't listen to God's warning voice, our hearts become hard and nothing scares us. But if we do not know the Lord Jesus as our Savior, we will be lost forever and go to hell because we did not listen to the Lord's commands.

The tenth plague came, and what sorrow it caused in Egypt. Had Pharaoh only listened, this horrible event would not have taken place! This time, Pharaoh gave in. The Israelites were finally allowed to leave, and gold and silver were handed out freely. The Lord took care that they received their wages for their years of slave labor.

We all deserve death because of our sins; therefore, do not harden your heart like Pharaoh, but seek the Lord.

What was the tenth plague? Would this horrible thing have happened if Pharaoh had obeyed the Lord's first command?

Moses — *Exodus 13:17–22*

God Shows the Way

By day in a pillar of cloud...and by night in a pillar of fire....
— Exodus 13:21

The Lord took great care of His people. They walked in rows of five. They could look up and see a pillar of cloud above them. This was a sign that the Lord was with them and was showing them the way. At night, there was the pillar of fire to give them light and to keep the wild animals at bay. In the daytime, the pillar of cloud protected the Israelites from the burning sun.

How strange that the pillar of cloud did not take the shortest route. But as a Father, the Lord looked after His children. If they had taken the shorter route, they would have had to fight the Philistines. They had just come out of Egypt where they did such heavy work as slaves and they did not have the strength to fight.

The Lord knows exactly what we need and what the best way is for us.

Who is he that fears Jehovah,
Walking with Him day by day?
God will lead him safely onward,
Guide him in the chosen way.

Can you put this psalm into your own words?

Moses — Exodus 14

Through the Red Sea

And the pillar of the cloud...stood behind them.
— Exodus 14:19

What a different, strange route the Israelites had to travel. The pillar of cloud moved back a little and, when they looked around, they saw mountains on each side. The Red Sea was in front of them and behind them was the road to Egypt.

Suddenly, glittering weapons were seen and noisy army chariots were heard among the dust clouds! "Here comes Pharaoh with his army!" someone screamed. "What do we do?" Pharaoh regretted letting the Israelites go, and now he was coming to bring his slaves back. Would he succeed?

There was only one way for the Israelites: the way of the Lord. The Lord opened a path right through the Red Sea and they arrived safely on the far shore. When Pharaoh and his army tried to follow, they all were drowned.

What about us? If you begin to serve the Lord, Satan will not want to let you go, just as Pharaoh wanted to take the Israelites back. But there is a way out. God is willing to help you in your greatest troubles!

What does Exodus 14:19 say about the pillar of cloud?

Moses — *Exodus* 16:1–17

Unthankful

It is manna.
— Exodus 16:15

With angry faces the Israelites stood before Moses and Aaron. What had happened? Listen to what they said: "Oh, that we had died in Egypt when we sat at the fleshpots." Were the Israelites dying? This was impossible because the Lord had promised to bring them to Canaan. But the food they had taken from Egypt was gone and they were shouting at Moses.

Where was their trust in the Lord now? They were insulting Him even though He had already done many miracles for them. What was the Lord's answer to all this? Did He punish or kill them? No, He helped them and showed great patience with the children of Israel.

Around their tents lay the manna, bread from the Lord. He also sent them quails, birds that could be eaten. And now the Lord was waiting to see how they would react. You can read this in verse 4.

"Will they obey My law or not?" Will the Israelites listen to the Lord because He is good and kind? The Lord also looks at us. He gives us so much that we do not deserve. Are we truly thankful?

Do you think the Israelites had a good time at the flesh-pots of Egypt?

Moses — *Exodus 17:8–16*

The Power of Prayer

Jehovah-nissi [The LORD is my banner].
— Exodus 17:15

Do you pray often? Do you realize that you need the Lord's guidance in everything you do? Do you pray for your pastor, elders, and deacons? It is important that we pray for them. They have a serious and difficult task, showing people the way to God and warning against sin.

Moses also prayed. He stood on the hill, holding his staff up to heaven. Down below, Joshua and his soldiers were fighting the Amalekites. Like cowards, they had attacked the Israelites from behind.

Up on the hill, Moses was fighting with the help of Aaron and Hur. He was fighting by praying to the Lord. Prayer is a mighty weapon! Amalek was losing the battle because the Lord fought for Israel! Moses needed the help of Aaron and Hur to hold his arms up so long. Just as they helped Moses, we should help each other by praying for each other. Ask the Lord, "Lord, teach me how to pray!"

What happened when Moses' arms dropped?

Moses — *Exodus 18*

The Lord is God

Blessed be the LORD, who hath delivered you.
— Exodus 18:10

Moses was happy because Jethro, his father-in-law, had come to visit. He brought Moses' wife and two children along, too. They were so glad to see each other again. When Moses had to go to Pharaoh, Zipporah had come along with the children, but later Moses had sent them back to Jethro, Zipporah's father. Now they were finally together again. Moses had many things to tell them. He told about the plagues, the journey through the Red Sea, and the war with the Amalekites. The Lord had delivered them every time; how good He had been for the Israelites.

"Oh Moses, now I know that the Lord is God," Jethro cried. "The other gods are idols and cannot help us. They are just pieces of wood or stone." Jethro thanked the Lord for all He had done.

If you are a child of God, difficulties will come in your life. But like the Israelites, you will receive help—and how happy you will be!

What are the names of the sons of Moses?

Moses — Exodus 19

Our God is a Consuming Fire

And Moses went up unto God.
— Exodus 19:3

Mount Sinai was a mountain covered with thorny bushes. It was where a very special message came from the Lord. God told Moses that He wanted to make a covenant with the children of Israel. The Israelites did not ask to make a covenant with God, but God came to enter into a covenant with them. This was a good thing, because how could a fallen sinner make a covenant with God and keep his promises?

The Israelites all had to wash their clothes, which would remind them that their hearts also had to be cleansed from sin. The people said, "We will be obedient to the Lord in all things." But would they succeed?

A fence was put up around the mountain because anyone who touched the mountain would die. Then the blast of a trumpet was heard, and Moses led the people to the mountain. The sermon began while it was thundering and lightening.

Because of our sins, we are like a thorn bush before God. When fire touches the bush, it will burn. God's holiness is as pure and strong as fire. We need a mediator who will go between God and us, one who can restore the relationship between God and us so that our thorny hearts are not consumed by the fire of God's holiness.

Who is that mediator? Read the answer in the Heidelberg Catechism, question 18.

71

Moses — *Exodus* 20 *and* 31:18

The Mirror of the Law

I am the LORD *thy God.*
— Exodus 20:2

How often do you look in the mirror? And what do you want to see? Spending too much time gazing in the mirror at ourselves can make us vain or proud, but there is a mirror that we should spend a lot of time looking at. That is the mirror of God's law.

When you take a good look at yourself in the mirror of the law, it will frighten you. You do not look beautiful in this mirror, but ugly. You can see that you are full of sin.

How do you react? Many say, "I don't like the mirror—get rid of it." But we should not try to run and hide like that. When you look into the mirror of God's law, you will find the way back to God, and that will bring true happiness.

In Paradise, the people looked beautiful because they were still perfectly created in God's image. But through sin, that image was shattered. We now resemble the devil. Have you learned this? Do you see who you are before God? Flee to the Lord Jesus; He is the only one who can deliver and renew you. You will be clean and without sin in heaven, forever praising Him.

What are the ten commandments of the law?

Moses — *Exodus 32: 1–15 and 30–35*

A Good Shepherd

And if not, blot me, I pray thee, out of thy book which thou hast written.
— Exodus 32:32

The children of Israel danced around the golden calf and shouted: "These gods are our gods; they have delivered us out of Egypt!" These were the same people who had once confessed: "We will do everything the Lord has commanded us." How did this happen? Even Aaron said that this was a feast of the Lord. But Aaron should have known better. God would not be served in this manner, and He would surely send His punishment. Although Moses was still on the mountain and did not know what had happened, God knew.

God always looks into our hearts; we cannot hide anything from Him. Moses left the mountain immediately and, as a good shepherd, prayed for his sinful nation. He pleaded the promises God had made to Abraham, Isaac, and Jacob, and also pointed out that God's honor was at stake. What would the Egyptians say if God would destroy His own people?

The golden calf was broken into pieces and God's commandments, engraved on the stone tablets, were also in pieces. The Israelites needed to repent and follow the Lord again.

Ask the Lord Jesus to reconcile you to God and to forgive your sins. Pray for the Lord Jesus to become your Good Shepherd.

Were the Israelites punished for this sin?

Moses — Exodus 34:27–35:1

The Lord is Longsuffering

I have made a covenant with thee and with Israel.
— Exodus 34:27

Again Moses stood at Mt. Sinai with the two tables of stone. But the people were frightened when they saw him. His face was shining and they wondered whether it was Moses or an angel standing in front of them.

No other idol had been made and yet the people were afraid. A few weeks ago, three thousand people had been killed. Remembering their sins, they realized that they were no better than those Israelites that had been killed. But God delays punishment, just as He does for us. We still live in the day of grace. We can still ask the Lord to convert and change us. The Lord says the same thing to us that He said to the Israelites: "I have no desire in your death but that you should live."

An angel was not standing before the children of Israel; it was Moses. His face was shining because he had been with the Lord. Heavenly peace radiated from his face. Do you wish that you could be in the Lord's presence like that? Do you want to know Him more and more? How miserable you are if you do not feel your need of Him!

What do we mean when we say that we "live in the day of grace"? How can we learn more about the Lord?

Moses — Numbers 21:1–9

The Brazen Serpent

And Moses made a serpent of brass.
— Numbers 21:9

When the children of Israel looked around them, they saw fiery snakes everywhere. Fathers, mothers, and children were falling down dead to the ground, bitten by the snakes! What had happened?

The Israelites had complained about the manna they were receiving every day. "It's disgusting," they said. They were being punished for being so ungrateful Now they confessed that they had sinned and they pleaded with Moses: "Oh Moses, pray that the snakes will go away."

Then a large, brass serpent was lifted up, raised so high that everyone could see it. "Look at the serpent and you will be saved," the Lord said. Some did look and were healed. Others refused to look and died in their unbelief.

What about you and me? We were attacked by the serpent in Paradise; we have the incurable disease of sin. We are not friends of God, but enemies. The Lord Jesus hung and died on the cross. He can deliver us from sin and evil and give us eternal life. Do you look to Him for your salvation from sin?

What does John 3:14–16 speak of?

Moses — Deuteronomy 3:18–29

Does God Answer Prayer?

And I besought the LORD at that time.
— Deuteronomy 3:23

When someone prays for a new heart, will the Lord answer him? In Psalm 81:10, we read, "Open thy mouth wide, and I will fill it." When we seek Him with all our heart and with all our might, He will show Himself to us.

But does the Lord answer all the prayers of His children? No, not always, as we can also read in this portion of Scripture. In Numbers 20, we read how Moses had been angry and unbelieving. Therefore, he was not allowed to enter Canaan. Moses' prayer had not been answered because he had to learn to say: "Thy will be done, for what Thou doest is good; I don't deserve anything."

The Lord was still good to Moses and so Moses is satisfied. Is the Lord not always good to His children? When they submit themselves to His will, He will comfort them. Has the Lord been your refuge? With Him, you will be blessed and safe.

Why was Moses not allowed to enter Canaan?

Moses — Deuteronomy 34:1–12

The Death of Moses

And he buried him in a valley.
                    — Deuteronomy 34:6

Do you remember when Moses was a young prince in Egypt? Do you remember the choice he made there? Read Hebrews 11:24–26. Moses would rather belong to the despised children of Israel than to be a rich and honored Egyptian prince. Moses saw that those who had God as their Help and Refuge in times of trouble were blessed. What if you die and have no refuge for your soul? You will need a redeemer to pay your debt.

Moses was not allowed to enter Canaan, but the Lord did show it to him. The Lord was with Moses until the end of his life, and when he died, Moses entered the heavenly Canaan.

Do you enjoy worldly pleasures, doing what you want even if it is against God's will? The Lord can give you the same desire He gave to Moses when he was young. You will never be sorry about this choice!

What do we mean when we say that Moses entered "the heavenly Canaan"?

Moses — Leviticus 8:1–24

Dedicated to the Priesthood

And he poured of the anointing oil upon Aaron's head.
— Leviticus 8:12

In the middle of the people's tents stood the tabernacle. The tabernacle was the place where the Lord was willing to live with His people. This was a special day; all the people were required to gather in the outer court. Moses called Aaron and his four sons. He was going to dedicate Aaron to the office of high priest and his sons to that of priests.

First, they are washed with water from the basin. After this, they are anointed with holy oil and they put on the holy clothing. What will happen next? Three animals are offered to the Lord. Moses takes blood and dabs some on Aaron's right ear, thumb, and toe. This was also done to the sons of Aaron. This was done to show the priests that they could not do this holy work by themselves. They needed the blood of Jesus Christ in all they did. Only through His sacrifice could the Lord live with His people.

Aaron and his sons stood before the Israelites. They had not been appointed by Moses but by God Himself. They would offer sacrifices and pray for the people. Aaron spread his arms heavenward and pronounced the priestly blessing.

The High Priest, Christ Jesus, is far greater than Aaron. He lives forever to pray for His people.

What is the content of the priestly blessing? Read it in Numbers 6:24–26.

Aaron — Leviticus 9:1–24

The Offering

Aaron therefore went unto the altar.
— Leviticus 9:8

The offering services had started; Aaron came forward. He first had to sacrifice for himself, because he was also a sinner and needed forgiveness. After this, he would sacrifice for the children of Israel.

A devout Israelite was standing beside the animal that had to be offered. It was tied down and the man looked at it. He laid his hand on the head of the animal and said, "I deserve death because of my sins, but now you have to die instead of me so that I may live." A serious expression is on his face as he thinks in amazement of the great sacrifice the Lord Jesus would one day make. How the Israelites longed for Him!

Aaron, the high priest, had to offer for himself, but the Lord Jesus did not have to do this when He gave Himself for others. This is a miracle that is hard to understand. Do you long for the forgiveness of your sins, or do they not bother you? Ask the Lord to show you how terrible sin is. "How blessed is he whose trespass has freely been forgiven!"

How do you know if the Lord accepted the offering? Read Leviticus 9:24.

Aaron — Leviticus 10:1–7

Strange Fire

And offered strange fire before the LORD.
                              — Leviticus 10:1

The fire at the altar of burnt offering was burning. This fire had been ignited by the Lord Himself. The priests were only allowed to offer sacrifices with this holy fire. But now we see two priests, Nadab and Abihu, entering the holy place while only one was allowed to enter. They carry their censors and walk to the altar of incense. The fire from their censors is put on the altar and the incense on top of it.

In a little while, a wonderful aroma fills the air. But something dreadful happens: Nadab and Abihu fall down dead! Why did this happen? Nadab and Abihu had not obeyed the Lord, for their fire had not been from the altar of burnt offering.

The lesson from this sad history is that we cannot serve God our own way. We have to listen to what God says in His Word, for the Lord will punish sin. Ask the Lord, "Teach me Thy ways and show me Thy paths."

Did Aaron become angry when he heard that two of his sons had died?

Aaron — Leviticus 16

Without Shedding of Blood
There is No Forgiveness

And offer him for a sin offering.
— Leviticus 16:9

It was the Day of Atonement and the children of Israel had to come to the outer court. They come with sorrow in their hearts because of their sins. An animal was slaughtered and offered to the Lord. The blood of the animal was caught in a bowl. It was precious because, without blood, there was no forgiveness of sin. The people knew that they deserved to die instead of the animal.

But what was done with the blood? Well, once a year the high priest entered the Holy of Holies. There he took some blood on his finger and sprinkled it on the mercy seat. The blood was also sprinkled on different places, for this is how the Lord commanded it.

By the shedding of blood, sins would be taken away. We can see God and live only when our sins are forgiven. The Lord Jesus is the Great High Priest who offered Himself on the cross. He did not enter heaven with the blood of an animal, but with His own blood. This blood tells us that we need to be reconciled unto God.

What does the word "atonement" mean?

Aaron — Leviticus 24:1–9

In the Holy Place

For it is most holy unto him.
                    — Leviticus 24:9

The altar of incense stood in the back of the holy place. On the left side was the golden candlestick, reaching about a yard and a half high. It burned day and night but never burned out. The thickest part of the candlestick was in the middle, and on each side three thinner arms reached out. Altogether it had seven arms. This candlestick shed enough light to illuminate the holy place.

The golden candlestick was symbolic; the middle arm pointed to the Lord Jesus and the side arms to His children. They are connected to Him, for without Him they can do nothing. The Lord Jesus is the Light of the World. When He shines His light in your heart, you will see your sins and you will see that Satan rules your life. When you realize this, it will drive you to the Lord Jesus. You will seek Him day and night until you have found Him. You will want to live for His honor and to bear His light.

At the right side of the holy place stood the Table of Showbread. Twelve loaves were placed there to represent each of the tribes of Israel. When God saw these loaves, He saw His people. He would take care of them in good and in bad times and never forsake them.

What did the twelve tribes represent?

Aaron — Numbers 17:1–13

The Budding Rod of Aaron

And the rod of Aaron was among their rods.
                                    — Numbers 17:6

There were twelve families in Israel, and they were all descendants of the children of Jacob. Moses asked for a rod from each of their families. Why? In Numbers 16, we read that a rebellion broke out among the children of Israel. Some of the Israelites had complained that they were just as important as Moses and Aaron were. A severe punishment followed: the ground underneath them opened, and Korah, Dathan, and Abiram sunk alive into it with their families.

The people were frightened; they could clearly see that God sides with His children. We should never make fun of God's servants or God's children, for the Lord will surely punish us for that.

The Lord wished to show the children of Israel again whom He had chosen for His service. The twelve rods were laid before the ark in the Holy of Holies. As Moses gathered the rods the next morning, the people observed a great miracle. The rod of Aaron was full of blossoms! How could a dead piece of wood bloom? Only the Lord could have done this miracle, and the children of Israel were duly impressed. The rod was put back into the ark where a jug of manna and the stone tablets, engraved with the law, rested. The rods were kept safe in the ark as a memorial of God's great deeds.

What were the names of the twelve families?

Aaron — Numbers 20:22–29

The Death of Aaron

They mourned for Aaron thirty days.
— Numbers 20:29

Some men were walking up Mount Hor. Higher and higher they climbed. What were they doing on this mountain? Something special was going on. Aaron was going to die. He did not look sad because he was ready to die. He knew that all his sins were forgiven and a heavenly joy filled his heart.

Moses took the holy garments from Aaron and gave them to Eleazar, the son of Aaron. He would become the new High Priest, for God's work would continue after Aaron's death. Aaron was very blessed; his death would be glorious, for now he would see his Lord and King in all His glory!

Moses, Eleazar, and the elders come down the mountain. The Israelites realized that from now on Eleazar would be their High Priest. God's work would continue, even until today. Pray that the Lord will send more pastors to work in His kingdom and that He would make you willing to work in His service.

Why are the sacrifices no longer necessary?

Joshua — Joshua 1:1–9

I Am With You

I will not fail thee, nor forsake thee.
— Joshua 1:5

After Moses' death, Joshua became the new leader of the Israelites. This was a difficult task. He wasn't looking forward to it. Fortunately, he didn't have to do it all alone. The Lord encouraged him. "Be strong, Joshua, and be of good courage!" That is what the Lord said to him. He encouraged Joshua that way three times. The Lord encouraged him further by saying, "I will be with thee: I will not fail thee nor forsake thee." Those were amazing words that Joshua would remember. God would give him everything he needed for his new task—courage and strength.

The Lord is still the same today. Maybe you are going through hard times. There can be many different reasons for difficulties. Maybe you are bullied at school, you are sad, or you can't seem to understand how to do all your homework. Maybe you don't know how you can carry on because of trouble at home. Tell the Lord all your worries in prayer. He will listen to you. He is telling you today, "Be strong and of a good courage. I am with you. I will never leave you. I will help you." Our God is a help in times of need. He will help you just like He helped Joshua!

How does God help you?

Joshua — Joshua 3:9–17

The Israelites Cross the Jordan River

And all the Israelites passed over on dry ground.
— Joshua 3:17

The people of Israel were almost in the Promised Land. Everyone was ready to enter. The only thing left to do was to cross the Jordan River. But the Jordan was a wide and dangerous river; the people knew that only a miracle of God could help them cross over.

The priests went in front of all the other people. The priests carried the ark so everyone could see it. The ark was the sign that the Lord was present with His people. The ark reminded the people that their God was faithful, and that He was able to perform miracles. The mercy seat was on top of the ark. On the Day of Atonement, the High Priest sprinkled goat's blood on the mercy seat. It was a sign that there was forgiveness with God and that He wanted to be their God.

The people followed the priests, anxious to see how they would cross the river. As soon as the priests' feet touched the river, God did a marvelous miracle: the river stood still on either side of them! The people could go straight across as long as the priests stood in the river, holding the ark.

The ark points to Christ. His blood cleanses from all sins. Through faith in Him, miracles can happen, even in your life or my life. He will bring us safely to the Promised Land, just like He did with the Israelites at the Jordan. He brought his people straight through the rough water to the other side.

Why is the ark so important in this story?

Joshua — Joshua 4:19–24

Speaking Stones

When your children shall ask their fathers in time to come.
— Joshua 4:21

Can you imagine the question a little boy would have asked his dad? "Dad, why are all these stones here?" His father answered, "It is a memorial." They were standing together looking at the twelve stones. They were at Gilgal, the exact spot where the Israelites crossed the Jordan River. From wandering in the desert, the Israelites crossed the river to enter the Promised Land.

God had made a pathway for them across the river. The priests with the ark stood right in the middle of the river. When all the people had passed them, Joshua commanded that a heap of stones be put there as a memorial to the Lord. But those were not as visible as the ones this boy was looking at. These stones were a reminder to the people that God had performed a miracle here. These stones told a story.

Did you know that there are signs in your life that tell a story, too? Just think of the water in baptism. It is a sign and reminder that God wants to be your Father. He wants to be there for you every day, and is willing to forgive your sins, for Jesus' sake! The Holy Spirit teaches us more and more about this sign. We should not forget about it as we grow up. Ask your parents sometime and they can tell you even more about it. We should never forget the wonderful works of God. We have to keep telling the story to every new generation. These stones at the Jordan River teach us that.

Could you name some more "stones" or signs that tell a story about the work of the Lord?

87

Joshua — Joshua 5:13–6:5

An Unexpected Encounter

But as captain of the host of the LORD am I now come.
— Joshua 5:14

Joshua led the people of Israel to Jericho. Jericho would be the first city they had to capture. But when the Israelites looked at those walls, they were shocked: the walls were so wide that even houses were built on top of the wall! Looking at those immense gates at the entrance, it seemed to be impossible to capture Jericho.

Suddenly, a Man appeared in front of Joshua. The sword that He carried was drawn. Who was this? Joshua asked, "Are you a friend or an enemy?" The answer was, "Nay, but as captain of the host of the Lord am I now come." Filled with reverence, Joshua fell with his face to the ground for it was the Lord Himself coming to him to encourage him. The Lord told Joshua how to defeat the people of Jericho. There would be no fighting, no swords. The Lord would fight for them.

God never forsakes or leaves His servants. Sometimes you and I can face impossible circumstances like the great wall of Jericho. Our worries and problems seem to tower over our heads. What can we do? Tell the Lord everything. Trust in Him and He will help! He knows us and will help us in times of distress.

Why does the Lord visit Joshua? What can we learn from this?

Joshua — Joshua 6:8–17

An Example of Faith

Shout; for the LORD *hath given you the city.*
— Joshua 6:16

Look at all those Israelites! The people of Jericho watched the great procession of Israelites pass by, marching around their city. In front, they saw heavily armed soldiers. Following right behind them were seven priests, carrying seven trumpets of rams' horns. The ark was immediately behind the priests. And finally they saw all the Israelites. For six days, they walked around the city very quietly every day. They did not talk at all.

But on the seventh day, they walked around the city seven times. Then they heard Joshua's voice calling, "Shout; for the Lord hath given you the city!" They shouted and the priests blew the trumpets and, miraculously, the walls of Jericho started falling! Everyone living in Jericho died as their city collapsed—everyone except one family, that is.

The house where Rahab and her family were was the only one saved. A red cord was hanging from one of her windows. She had chosen to hide the messengers of the Lord a few days earlier, and that is why she and her family survived. From now on, she would belong to God's people. The Bible tells us that the faith of this woman sets an example for us because she risked her own life to help God's messengers.

Is it obvious to the people that know you that you belong to the Lord? If we speak honorably of God's work in our lives, the Lord will honor us, too. How else can we show that we love the Lord?

89

Joshua — Joshua 9:3–16

A Wrong Decision

…and asked not counsel at the mouth of the LORD.
— Joshua 9:14

Joshua received foreign visitors who wanted to make a covenant with him. They had heard about the God of Israel, how mighty He was. They heard how the Lord brought the Israelites out of slavery in Egypt. They also heard of the defeat of the Kings Sihon and Og. They told Joshua that they had traveled very far. When they left, they were wearing new sandals, and in their bags was fresh water and bread. But look at them now! Their clothing and water bags were torn and their bread had become moldy. What would Joshua do?

Joshua listened to them and made a covenant with them, promising to do them no harm. Joshua forgot one important thing, though. He didn't ask counsel of the Lord.

Maybe you wonder if that is really very important. Do you have to ask the Lord for counsel for everything? The answer is yes. The Lord requires us to ask Him what we should do. When you have questions, bring them to the Lord. Are you in difficult circumstances? Go to the Lord. He is willing to show you the way. It would be foolish to figure it out on our own. You can see that in Joshua's life.

Joshua soon discovered that the travelers had told him a lie. These men were not from a far away country, but were men from Gibeon! He had walked into their trap. He should have asked the Lord what to do. We can be kept from many wrong decisions by praying every day, "Lord, what wilt Thou have me to do?"

How does the Lord answer when you ask Him for help?

Joshua — Joshua 24:13–15

Joshua's Choice

But as for me and my house, we will serve the Lord.
— Joshua 24:15

The Israelites were finally living in Canaan. Now they had a place to call their own. Every tribe had its own part of the country to settle. At this important new start for the Israelites, Joshua asked them a crucial question. "Who will you serve in the future? Will you serve the heathen gods or the Lord God?" He told them that he had already made the decision for his household. "As for me and my house, we will serve the Lord."

What about you? Have you already chosen? Or do you think that idols and heathen gods do not exist in our time? There are more idols today than maybe you can imagine. We might not put sculptures or wooden images in our houses to worship. But perhaps our idols are money, sports, or music. An idol can be anything that takes a more important place in our lives than God.

Or maybe we try to pretend it exists besides serving the Lord. The people of Israel often worshipped other gods besides the Lord. They tried to have the best of both worlds. But that is impossible. The Bible tells us we have to make a choice. Whom do you serve? Do you serve the Lord with all your heart? This is the most important question in your life.

Some children say they will make a choice of whom they will serve when they are older. What do you think about that?

91

Gideon — Judges 6:1–10

Gideon and His People

I am the LORD your God.
— Judges 6:10

A prophet traveled throughout Israel, bringing a message from God. This is the message God gave him to pass on: "I am the Lord who has delivered you from slavery to the Egyptians. I have given you this country. I always took good care of you. This have I told you: Serve me only, and not your idols. You have disobeyed me, and that is the reason that you are unhappy now."

Things will always go wrong if we do not continue to serve the Lord and serve our idols instead. Our Lord is a jealous God and He desires our whole heart. We hurt Him if we turn to others besides Him. If we continue to go our own way, He will punish us. The Israelites experienced that again and again, including here in this story. What happened?

For seven years already, the Midianites invaded the country. They oppressed the people of God. Along with the Amalekites, they plundered the harvest. They stole the cattle, oxen, and donkeys. They took whatever else that could get their hands on, and so the Israelites became poor. They hid themselves in holes in the ground and in mountain caves. Who would come to help them?

Does the Lord always punish us for our sins immediately?

Gideon — Judges 6:11–16

Gideon's Task

The LORD is with thee.
                    —Judges 6:12

While Gideon was secretly grinding wheat so that the Midianites would not find out, the angel of the Lord appeared to him. The angel greeted Gideon with these words: "The Lord is with thee, thou mighty man of valour." Gideon shrank back, thinking, "The Lord is with us?" He did not believe it. The Lord had forgotten and forsaken them! For seven years, the Midianites had plundered the land

But the angel continued, "You will deliver Israel." Gideon couldn't believe his ears. He answered, "Me? I come from a very small family and I am the youngest." The angel answered, "Because I am with you, you will defeat the Midianites."

Everything becomes easy when the Lord is with you, even a difficult task such as Gideon received. Maybe you find it very hard to serve the Lord. But He is willing to help you. He will give direction and guidance in your life; He promises this in His Word. The Lord is reliable and you can trust Him. We will see that in the coming week in the life of Gideon.

Do you find it hard to serve the Lord?

Gideon — Judges 6:33–40

Gideon's Fleece of Wool

And God did so that night.
— Judges 6:40

Again the Midianites and Amalekites came. They pitched their tents in a valley by Jezreel. It was harvest time and they were ready to start their plundering. Gideon blew a trumpet and called an army together. Many men came and volunteered to fight, but there was doubt in Gideon's heart. He was not convinced in his heart that God would help him in the battle. Could he really trust in Him? He knew that his enemies were strong and cruel.

Sometimes we doubt, too. Is God really able to do what He promises in His Word? Would He be willing to help me? If you have doubt in your heart, pray to the Lord to take it away from you. Pray for faith and trust in Him.

Gideon prayed, too, asking the Lord for a sign. He put a fleece of wool on the ground. His request was that the next morning the fleece would be wet but the ground dry. And the next morning, the miracle happened exactly that way. Gideon wrung the dew out of the fleece, and collected a bowlful of water. But there was still doubt in Gideon's heart. He prayed, "Lord, let me test Thee once more with the fleece—make it dry in the morning and the earth wet with dew." Again the Lord granted him the request. Gideon was now ready for battle. The doubt was gone and courage was with him. He was ready for his task.

Should we ask the Lord for signs?

94

Gideon — Judges 7:1–7

Gideon's Army

By the three hundred men that lapped will I save you.
— Judges 7:7

Gideon had been told by the Lord that his army was too big. He couldn't fight the Midianites like this. If the Israelites won, they would brag that they had gained the victory because of their own strength. They would not give God the glory. The Lord told Gideon to send away all the men who were afraid. After they left, Gideon had an army of ten thousand men, but still the army was too big. The Lord said, "Bring your men to the brook and tell them to drink of the water." The men who knelt down and drank the water quickly, like a dog, were set apart. The biggest group of men knelt down to drink like that. Gideon sent all of those men home and was left with a small group of three hundred men. It was difficult for Gideon to believe that he would succeed in defeating the enemy with this tiny army! The army of the Midianites was large.

But the Lord keeps His promises. The Bible is filled with examples. He asks us to completely trust in His Word. The victory is sure, but it sometimes comes in a totally different way from what we think or expect. Our God works in wondrous ways. Gideon and his men trusted that the Lord would give them the victory. What about you?

The Bible is filled with miracles of God. Do miracles still happen today?

Gideon — Judges 7:9–15

Encouragement for Gideon

For the Lord hath delivered into your hand the host of Midian.
— Judges 7:15

That night, Gideon went down to the camp of the Midianites. His servant Purah had come along with him. Gideon had to go there; it was part of God's plan to encourage him. God knew that Gideon needed encouragement right then, for at any time the fight could start. What would be in Gideon's heart then? Would he be scared?

God knows exactly what we need and when we need it. We can often dread something—a test at school or a scary situation. But something can suddenly happen that reminds us again that our God is almighty. He can help us. That gives us courage to continue.

Gideon and Purah were sneaking past the tents of the enemy's camp. Suddenly, they heard someone talking. The man said, "I had a dream. There was a loaf of barley bread that came rolling into the camp of Midian. It struck a tent, and the tent collapsed." They heard someone else answer, "That doesn't sound very good. The Israelites will defeat us." That is all Gideon needed to hear. He understood why the Lord sent him here. He knelt down and worshiped the Lord. All his fear was gone, for the Lord would give them the victory.

How does the Lord encourage us today?

Gideon — Judges 7:16–21

Gideon's Victory

When I blow with a trumpet....   — Judges 7:18

Gideon divided his army into three groups. Every man received a trumpet, a pitcher, and a torch. They would approach the enemy's camp from three different directions. Gideon told them exactly what they had to do. When all three groups had reached the camp, Gideon would blow his trumpet. The well-instructed men followed the orders. Three hundred trumpets sounded through the valley. Three hundred pitchers smashed at the same time, and three hundred torches lit the sky. From all different directions, they shouted, "The sword of the Lord and of Gideon!"

It seemed like a huge army surrounded the Midian camp! The Midianites awoke in a panic. What was going on? Were they surrounded by the Israelites? Hardly realizing what was happening, they tried to flee as fast as their feet would carry them. They killed everyone who crossed their path. They didn't realize they were killing their fellow soldiers. Remember how the Lord said that the Israelites would win without using swords? The Lord was fighting for them! They didn't need any weapons. The Lord was giving them the victory.

The Lord is still victorious today. Do you know why? It's because of what the Lord Jesus did. He conquered all our enemies. Whoever believes in Him will not lose, but will overcome.

Why is it so hard for us to let the Lord fight the battle for us?

Gideon — Judges 8:22,23, 32–35

Gideon's Death

And Gideon the son of Joash died in a good old age, and was buried in the sepulchre of Joash his father, in Ophrah of the Abiezrites.
— Judges 8:32

The people of Israel were ecstatic. They had gained the victory! They were so thankful that Gideon helped them that they wanted to make him king. But Gideon couldn't be their king, nor could his son become their ruler. He explained to them, "The Lord will rule over you. You should direct your thanks to God." Gideon didn't want to take the honor for the victory which belonged to the Lord.

For many years, the Israelites lived in peace. Gideon was an old man by now. After he died, something terrible took place: the Israelites forgot Gideon, but what was worse, they forgot the Lord. They served idols again. What a grievous thing to do.

There are a lot of things we can learn from Gideon's life. Aren't we often like the Israelites in forgetting about the Lord when everything is fine, even if the Lord delivers us in hard times? Do you thank the Lord often for all the blessings that come from Him? The Lord is very compassionate. Do you have a desire in your heart to serve the Lord? Do not wait another day to ask the Lord to teach you. Ask Him to teach you how to remember His good gifts. Ask Him to show you how to live for His honor and glory every day.

Make a list of five ways to show thankfulness to the Lord.

Samson — Judges 13:1–5 and 24

A Servant of the Lord

For the child shall be a Nazarite unto God from the womb.
— Judges 13:5

Manoah and his wife were expecting a baby. The Angel of the Lord had told them so. It would be a very special child—not like any of the other children born in Israel. He would be a servant of the Lord with a special mission. He would be set apart from the others when he was growing up, so his hair should never be cut. Samson would deliver the Israelites out of the hands of the Philistines. That would be this boy's task, given by the Lord.

Did you know that the Lord has a task for everyone who serves Him? Not just adults, either; children have a task, too. Some people became missionaries, working far away in other countries. But most people receive a task closer to home. Perhaps these examples will help you understand your task better. Do you play with that girl who sits in a wheelchair? Do you make friends with the boy who has no friends in your class? Maybe you can send a postcard or a letter to someone who has been sick for a long time. Show others that you love the Lord. Doesn't that make you happy, living for Him? Stay close to the Lord. That is very important when serving the Lord. We will learn just how important it is as we study the life of Samson.

What other tasks could the Lord give to children?

Samson — Judges 14:1–6

Samson Goes to Timnath

And the Spirit of the LORD came mightily upon him.
                                        —Judges 14:6

Samson was in love with a girl. He and his parents traveled to Timnath, where his girlfriend lived. She was a daughter of the Philistines. But didn't Samson know the law of God? Did the Lord not tell them explicitly not to marry a heathen, because heathens do not know the Lord? How can you serve the Lord in your marriage if your spouse doesn't know Him? Was there no woman among the Israelites for Samson? Samson's parents asked him questions like these and warned him because he should have known better. They tried to change his mind, but it made no difference. He refused to listen to their pleading.

It is very foolish not to listen to your parents when they try to give you good advice. You should especially listen when their advice is based upon the Word of God. Samson is not a good example for us that way. Isn't it marvelous to see how the Lord turns Samson's disobedience to a miraculous deliverance? Our Lord is the Almighty and His ways are wonderful. He is able to use sinful people to fulfill His promises.

What can you learn from the story of Samson about your attitude towards your parents?

Samson — Judges 14:10–20

A Wedding with a Sad Ending

And Samson's wife wept before him. — Judges 14:16

Samson returned to Timnath a little while later. The wedding day had arrived! His parents accompanied him. It was the custom to have a wedding feast that lasted seven days. During the party, Samson gave thirty of the male guests a riddle to solve. If they could solve it before the party was over, they would receive beautiful clothes. This is the riddle: "Out of the eater came something to eat, and out of the strong came something sweet."

That was a difficult riddle to solve. The Philistine men couldn't solve it. They went to Samson's wife and asked if she knew the answer, but she didn't know it either. They threatened her, "You better find out what the answer is, or else we will burn you and your father's house." No wonder Samson's wife kept asking him for the clue! She even cried to get him to tell the answer. Finally, Samson gave in and told her. On the last day of the wedding, the men told Samson the answer. They said, "What is sweeter than honey? And what is stronger than a lion?" Of course, Samson realized that his wife had told them. Samson went to Ashkelon and the Spirit of the Lord came upon him. He killed thirty Philistines there and gave their clothes to the Philistine men at the wedding. He was so angry with them that he decided to return home with his parents. The wedding feast ended on a bad note. Do you know why it ended without happiness and joy?

Were these Philistine guests good friends for Samson? Why or why not?

Samson — Judges 15:1–8

Vengeance or Love

Now I shall be more blameless than the Philistines.
— Judges 15:3

Samson regretted returning home after the wedding and decided to head back to Timnath. The woman he married there was his wife, after all. But an unpleasant surprise awaited him. The woman had been given by her father to become someone else's wife. Samson was furious! He went out and caught three hundred foxes and bound together the tails of every two foxes. Every pair of foxes had a torch tied to their tails. Then Samson set all the torches on fire and chased the foxes into Philistine fields and vineyards. Nothing was left of their harvest; everything burned down to the ground!

Now it was the Philistines' turn to be furious and they took vengeance. Samson's wife and her father were burned to death by them. That made Samson so angry that he killed many more Philistines. So one evil caused many other evils, and it kept getting worse.

Perhaps something like this has happened to you. Someone tries to get you back. You get very angry with him or her and want to get even. The Bible tells us not to do so. In Proverbs 20:22 we read, "Say not thou, I will recompense evil; but wait on the Lord, and he shall save thee." That is the solution. Do not start or continue a fight; it just makes everything worse. Even the Lord Jesus taught us this when He said, "Love your enemies; bless those who curse you."

Do you agree with the idea of "the survival of the fittest"?

Samson — Judges 15:9–20

Bound

But God clave an hollow place....
— Judges 15:19

Samson was living in a cave in the rocks. One day, three thousand Israelites paid him a visit. They wanted to bind him and deliver him to the Philistines. What was going on? Wasn't Samson one of them?

Here is what had happened. The army of the Philistines had come to Judah to capture Samson and, if the Israelites wouldn't cooperate, they would start a war against them. Samson's countrymen decided to capture him, for they were afraid of the Philistines. They bound Samson with brand new ropes and brought him to the enemy. When they arrived at the Philistine camp, the ropes fell off Samson's hands as if they were just thread! The Spirit of the Lord was working mightily again in Samson. He picked up the jawbone of a donkey and used it to kill a thousand Philistines.

Centuries later, the Lord Jesus was also bound by His enemies. But there is a difference. The Lord Jesus could have freed Himself, just like Samson, but He didn't. He chose the way of suffering. He ended up hanging on the cross at Calvary, where He died. Do you know why He died? To free us of everything that keeps us in bondage. Our sins keep us in their grip. Bad habits bind us, but Jesus gave His life to set us free.

Could you name a few things that bind you and keep you away from God?

Samson — Judges 16:16–21

A Dangerous Game

There hath not come a razor upon mine head.
— Judges 16:17

Samson was visiting another Philistine woman at her house. Her name was Delilah, and Samson liked her very much. Delilah was amazed at how strong Samson was. She would love to find out how he got this strong! Some of the Philistine nobles offered Delilah money in exchange for finding out Samson's secret. She asked Samson time and again, but he never told her. He continued his visits to her. Didn't he see how this woman was trying to deceive him? He was playing with the gifts he had received from God.

Finally one day, Samson gave in and told the woman his secret. His hair had never been cut. If anyone would cut his hair his extraordinary power would leave him.

While Samson was sleeping at Delilah's house, someone came in and shaved off all of Samson's hair. Delilah called out, "The Philistines are upon you, Samson!" Samson had no power in him. His game was over. The Bible says, "But he did not know that the Lord had departed from Him." The Lord had left Samson to himself.

It is still possible for the Lord to leave us to ourselves. If we continue to sin against God knowingly and willingly, a moment could come that the Lord withdraws Himself. That would be the worst thing that could ever happen to us. Where would we be without the Lord? Pray every day, "Lord, keep me from sin. Keep me close to Thyself."

Can you give an example of how we can play games with the love of God? Why is that a dangerous thing to do?

104

Samson — Judges 16:22–31

Samson's Death

O Lord God, remember me.
                    — Judges 16:28

A big feast was taking place. It was a feast to honor the god Dagon. The Philistines gathered to bring sacrifices to their god. They thought that it was because of Dagon that Samson was in prison. They sent someone to the prison to get Samson; they wanted to mock him at their party.

A small boy brought him into the temple. His hair had grown back, but he didn't have eyes anymore and needed help with everything. The boy brought him to two of the pillars that held up the temple while the people mocked and made fun of him. Samson prayed to God after he rested his hands on the pillars. He asked, "Lord, that Thy power might return to me once more…." The Lord heard his prayer. Samson took a strong hold of the pillars, pushed with all his might, and the whole temple came crashing down. All the people that were in the temple died, together with Samson. This time, Samson killed more Philistines than all the Philistines he killed in his entire life. By laying down his life, Samson delivered his people and is a type of the Lord Jesus.

The Lord was also mocked and also died, but He was perfect and conquered evil. His death saves many people, children and adults alike. The Lord's sacrifice is amazing grace. Do you love Him?

What does the life of Samson teach you?

Ruth — Ruth 1:1–5

Moving

And they came into the country of Moab.
— Ruth 1:2

There was a famine in Canaan. The God-fearing people knew very well why the famine had come; Israel had not listened to the Lord their God. The famine was a punishment for their sins. Elimelech and his wife, Naomi, left their hometown, Bethlehem; they would travel to Moab. They had two sons, Mahlon and Chilion, who came with them.

Their move to Moab, a heathen country, didn't end very well. Elimelech became ill and died. Naomi and her two sons were very sad when he died. Later, Mahlon married Ruth and Chilion married Orpah. Both women were Moabites and they did not know the Lord. Sadly, Mahlon and Chilion also died. Now Naomi was left with her two daughters-in-law. When she received the news that the famine in Israel was over, she decided to move back home. She would return to Bethlehem.

Moving to another town can be both difficult and exciting. But moving to another country is even harder. You have to learn another language and they usually have different customs to get used to. You wonder who serves the Lord, and what church you could go to. There are many uncertainties involved in such a big move. Naomi's family experienced all of these, too.

When you have plans to move somewhere else, what should be your first priority in deciding where to go?

Ruth — Ruth 1:6–18

Decisions

Thy people shall be my people, and thy God my God.
— Ruth 1:16

In our lives there are many decisions to make. Who should I ask over to my house for a birthday party? Who will I sit beside on the school bus when we go on our class trip? Do I want to play hockey or soccer? You face many more decisions in the future.

Today we read of the two women, Orpah and Ruth, who had to make a decision. Naomi had decided to go back to Canaan. Her two daughters-in-law went part of the way with her. Then Naomi told them to go back to their homes. Orpah listened, said goodbye, and returned to Moab and to her own family. What about Ruth? Did she go back, too? No, Ruth didn't leave Naomi. She wanted to go with her mother-in-law to Canaan. She told Naomi, "Thy people shall be my people, and thy God my God."

Somehow Ruth had discovered that there was something joyful in serving the Lord. She would like to know more of this God. She was convinced that she wanted to belong to His people.

What about you? Maybe you think you are far too young to decide to follow the Lord. You want to discover many other things in life first. It is true that you still have a lot of learning to do in life, but you can never be too young to serve the Lord. The Bible tells us that those who seek Him when they are young will find Him. How amazing this is! There is no better life than living your life for the Lord. You will never regret it.

Why is it so important to serve the Lord in your youth?

Ruth — Ruth 1:19–22

Mara

Call me not Naomi, call me Mara. — Ruth 1:20

Naomi and Ruth arrived in Bethlehem. Naomi had lots to think about. She had memories of how happy she had been when she still lived there, but happiness was far from her mind now. Everything she had when she still lived in Bethlehem was gone. The people in the town recognized her. They talked to each other and said, "Isn't that Naomi? She looks very old. Where are her husband and her two sons? Who is the woman walking up with her?"

Naomi knew the people were talking about her so she explained her return. She said, "Don't call me Naomi anymore; call me Mara. Mara means bitterness. The Lord has given me much sorrow and grief. My husband and my two sons have died." Naomi was rebelling against her God and was full of bitterness. Why did all of this have to happen to her?

Maybe you sometimes struggle with the same feelings. You wonder why there is suffering in your life, or in the life of your loved ones. "Why did grief have to come into our family?" "Why doesn't my dad have a job?" "Why did my grandpa have to die? I loved my grandpa so very much. I don't understand it."

Go to the Lord with all your grief. Tell Him everything that burdens you. The Lord will not always take the burden away immediately; you may not always get an answer to all your questions. But one thing is sure: the Lord will give you strength to carry on. He is our Comforter. Stay close to Him in all your grief.

What should you do when you experience sad things in your life?

Ruth — Ruth 2:1–13

Protection

Let me find favour in thy sight.
— Ruth 2:13

It was harvest time. The barley on the fields was ready. Ruth went to the fields to reap some of the grain. She happened to reap grain on fields that belonged to Boaz, a man who was related to Elimelech. That was no coincidence; the Lord guided Ruth to these fields of Boaz. The Lord guided the life of Ruth just as He guides your and my life. Sometimes surprising things happen!

Boaz said to Ruth, "Don't go to any of the other fields. You can stay here and reap with the other reapers. Nobody will do you any harm. When you get thirsty, you can go and drink from the water that my young men put in the vessels."

Ruth bowed down deeply before Boaz. She asked him why he was being so friendly to her when she was only a stranger to him. Boaz answered, "I have heard how you have taken good care of your mother-in-law. The Lord will bless you for it." Ruth was touched by his kindness. She knew that the Lord was very good and merciful to her. He was with her in everything, protecting her in this strange country.

The Lord is still the same today. He takes care of those who put their trust in Him. Never forget He will never leave you alone if you put your trust in Him!

Do things ever happen to us by accident?

Ruth — Ruth 2:18–23; 3:8–13

The Redeemer

The man is near of kin unto us, one of our next kinsmen.
— Ruth 2:20

Do you know what a kinsman is? Sometimes they call it a redeemer. When the people of Israel arrived in Canaan, every family received a piece of land. They owned that piece of land from then on. But occasionally, the family was forced to sell their property. Maybe there was a bad harvest, or they didn't have any money left. A rich relative then had to step forward to buy the property from them. This relative would then give it back to the family it belonged to. If the husband of that family had already passed away, the redeemer had to marry the widow as well. These were the responsibilities of a redeemer.

Naomi was quite surprised to hear that Ruth had worked in Boaz's field. She told Ruth that Boaz was their relative and that he was even one of their kinsmen.

One evening, Ruth went to the threshing floor where Boaz was and hid herself. Boaz was having a party there. In the middle of the night, Ruth asked Boaz if he would be her redeemer. This would mean that Boaz also had to marry her. Boaz was very thankful that she came to him for protection. He had to ask another of the kinsmen first for permission, and he promised her to look into the matter the next morning. Ruth happily returned to her home. Of course she was happy! What was better than knowing that the Lord would bring deliverance and send her a husband to care for her and Naomi?

Have you ever felt very happy because you could see how the Lord was taking care of you?

Ruth — Ruth 4:1–12

An Unexpected Development

Moreover Ruth the Moabitess…have I purchased to be my wife.
— Ruth 4:10

Boaz took immediate action. He went to the gates of Bethlehem the next morning. A city's gates were where you went for justice. Important matters were taken care of there. Boaz spoke with another relative who was closer to Naomi and had more rights to redeem them. But this man did not want to redeem Elimelech's family; he already had a wife. So Boaz declared all those present to be witnesses that he would redeem Naomi, Ruth, and their piece of land. He would also marry Ruth.

Unexpected things were happening in Bethlehem! Naomi was getting her land back and becoming part of the community once again. Ruth was getting married, and she and her husband could serve the Lord together.

Sometimes God's ways are hard to understand. Difficult and confusing things may happen in your life, but the Lord can make all events turn out well. When you look back on your life you can say, "The Lord guided my life in unexpected ways, but, in the end, it was the best way possible." No matter what happens in your life, if the Lord is your God, you are safe and protected.

Trace how the Lord took care of Ruth one step at a time.

Ruth — Ruth 4:13–22

Obed

And they called his name Obed.
                    — Ruth 4:17

Boaz and Ruth were married, and after a while a son was born to them. The neighbor women went to tell Naomi. They said to her, "Blessed be the Lord which hath not left thee this day without a kinsman! May his name be famous in Israel." Naomi was very excited to hold this little boy in her arms. This son would take the place of her husband and her two sons. The name of her husband Elimelech was restored!

The women called the name of the boy Obed. Obed means "servant." The Lord had been very merciful to Naomi and Ruth. After so much grief, He gave them great joy.

Obed would later become the grandfather of King David and, even further in the future, the Lord Jesus would be born from this family.

The Lord Jesus came to this world to carry the punishment of sin for all His people. He wants to be our Redeemer. You can go to Him with all your sinful thoughts, actions, and words. When the Lord redeems you, you will sing His praises. Just like Naomi's neighbors, you will say, "Blessed be the Lord. He sent a Redeemer for me!"

Examine your life for how the Lord cares for you.

Samuel — 1 Samuel 1:1–18

A Special Child

Then Eli answered and said, Go in peace: and the God of Israel grant thee thy petition that thou hast asked of him.
— 1 Samuel 1:17

Have you ever read a book where the main character was described as a special, unique person? The Bible portion you read today is about such a special, unique person. It is a true story, and it is about Samuel. He was special because his mother was unable to have children. This was a great sorrow for her, and many times she was teased about it.

Do you get teased at school? Are you teased about your grades or something else that you are not good at? That hurts, and you might get angry or get into a fight. But look at what Hannah did. She cried to the Lord when she could not take the teasing anymore. Her husband, Elkanah, could not help her, but the Lord could. Hannah received an immediate answer through Eli, the High Priest. He told her that she would soon receive a son—a special son.

Does God answer all of our prayers?

Samuel — 1 Samuel 1:19–28

A Promise is a Promise

"For this child I prayed; and the LORD hath given me my petition which I asked of him."
— 1 Samuel 1:27

Hannah's prayers were answered and her sorrow had been taken away. She had received a son! She named him Samuel, which means "asked of God." Hannah had promised the Lord that she would give her son to the Lord's service, so when Samuel was three years old, Hannah gave him back to the Lord. A promise is a promise, and we should always keep our promises.

Elkanah, the father of Samuel, also had to let go of his son. It was as if he said, "I am not his father anymore; I have given him to another father, the heavenly Father." This Father also gave His Son away, His only Son, the Lord Jesus. This Father saw His Son hanging on the cross and did not intervene because He had promised to send a Savior. That is how the Lord Jesus took our sins upon Himself. A promise is a promise!

What would you promise to the Lord?

Samuel — 1 Samuel 2:12–26

A Child Girded with an Ephod

But Samuel ministered before the LORD, being a child, girded with a linen ephod.
— 1 Samuel 2:18

A parsonage is often built right beside the church. It is helpful for the minister to be close to his work. The High Priest Eli also lived beside the house of God. Eli's family had grown when Samuel joined them; Samuel worked with the sons of Eli in the tabernacle. It says in the Bible that "Samuel ministered before the Lord." Samuel did his best because he loved the Lord. If you liked your teacher a great deal, you also would try your best, wouldn't you?

When Samuel did his work, he wore work clothes. In the Bible it says that he was "girded with a linen ephod." You could recognize a priest by this type of clothing. When his mother visited him once a year, she brought a new set of clothing. Even though she missed having him at her home, she was glad her son lived close to the Lord. She knew that Samuel was a child of God.

What kind of work can children do for the church of God today?

Samuel — 1 Samuel 3:1–10

The Voice of God

And the LORD came, and stood, and called as at other times, Samuel, Samuel. Then Samuel answered, Speak; for thy servant heareth.

— 1 Samuel 3:10

Have you ever seen a flock of sheep in a pasture? Hundreds of sheep follow a shepherd and his dog. And all those sheep know their shepherd's voice and follow him.

Samuel was in bed one night when he heard a voice in the middle of the night. He did not recognize the voice, for it was the first time God had spoken to him. This was very special because God had not spoken to His people for many years. In verse 1, we read, "And the word of the Lord was precious in those days."

Samuel thought it was Eli who had called him, but Eli did not need him. Eli told him to go back to bed and, when the voice came again, to answer the Lord and say, "Here I am." The Lord needed Samuel and had a message for him. It was a message for Eli and his children. Why didn't the Lord speak directly to Eli? He did not do so because Samuel would become God's prophet and mouthpiece, telling others what God had revealed to him.

How does the Lord speak to you today?

Samuel — 1 *Samuel* 3:11–21

God's Interpreter

And Samuel grew, and the LORD was with him, and did let none of his words fall to the ground.
— 1 Samuel 3:19

Do you know what an interpreter is? An interpreter is someone who changes one language into another language. When government officials from China come for important talks with your prime minister or president, an interpreter will be present to translate what was said.

Without an interpreter, things could go badly. This is what happened in Israel. The people did not understand what God commanded in His law. The priests did what was right in their own eyes. They stole meat meant for sacrifices to God. They loved strange women. Things were going from bad to worse.

But the Lord intervened for Israel. He used Samuel as His interpreter so that His message would become clear. The family of Eli was addressed first. Eli's sons would perish forever, and Eli's family was forbidden to work in the tabernacle. The nation of Israel would also be punished, for they would be defeated by the Philistines. This was terrible news.

The first message that Samuel delivered to the people was not a happy message; it was very dreadful. But the Lord was with Samuel and gave him wisdom and strength. As an interpreter of God, Samuel needed God's help.

What do you need from the Lord?

117

Samuel — I Samuel 8:1–22

One King Too Many

And said unto him, Behold, thou art old, and thy sons walk not in thy ways: now make us a king to judge us like all the nations.
— 1 Samuel 8:5

You have probably heard of Princess Diana of England. She was still quite young when she was killed in a car accident. She was well known for her fashionable way of dressing. What she wore became instant fashion, and many women wanted to dress like her.

A similar thing happened here in Israel. The Israelites looked around them and saw that other nations had a king. They wanted a king, too, so they went to Samuel. He was too old to become their king, and his sons were too dishonest to rule as kings. They needed someone from their own people, a strong and powerful person. But Samuel became angry when he heard their request. Was not the Lord in heaven their king? But the Israelites wanted a visible king, one that could be seen in a beautiful palace. It did not matter to them that a new king would cost them a lot of money. Israel wanted an earthly king and, in doing so, they rejected their God.

A thousand years later, a king came to Israel—the Lord Jesus. But Israel hung the Lord Jesus on a cross; they did not want Him as their King. Yet, by giving His life on the cross, Jesus showed that He was the King, for He destroyed the prince of darkness.

The Lord Jesus is still King, even in heaven. How does He rule from heaven?

Saul — 1 Samuel 9:1–27

Who Will Be Our King?

And when Samuel saw Saul, the LORD said unto him, Behold the man whom I spake to thee of! this same shall reign over my people.
— 1 Samuel 9:17

When your mother is expecting a new baby, you wonder what your new brother or sister will look like. You can hardly wait until the baby is born!

Israel had received a new king, for they were not satisfied to have God as their king. They wanted a king who could lead them into battle and would defeat their enemies. It was not up to them to choose a king, for the Lord would give them one.

The Israelites were curious and wondered who it would be. Even Samuel did not know. One day, a young man named Saul and his servant visited Samuel. They wanted to know if the prophet knew what had happened to their runaway donkeys. At that moment, the Lord revealed to Samuel who would be the future king of Israel—this man, Saul. He was a tall, handsome man, just what the Israelites had been waiting for. He was from the tribe of Benjamin in Gibeah.

Samuel invited Saul for supper and placed him in a prominent seat. Saul also received the best piece of meat. Saul, however, did not understand what was going on. The words of Samuel were puzzling to him; Samuel had told him that he, Saul, was to become the ruler of Israel. Saul was confused because he did not understand what Samuel and God wanted of him.

What does the Lord want from you?

119

Saul — 1 Samuel 10:1–16

A Kiss for Saul

Then Samuel took a vial of oil, and poured it upon his head, and kissed him, and said, Is it not because the LORD hath anointed thee?
— 1 Samuel 10:1

We often kiss people whom we love: our family, our grandparents, or close friends. It means that we love them. We read in this passage that Samuel kissed someone he had known for only one day. But why did he kiss Saul? He did not do it to show his love for him or out of thankfulness to him.

When Saul left for home, Samuel went with him and asked Saul's servant to go on ahead. Saul and Samuel stopped for a moment as Samuel took his jug of oil. He poured it over Saul's head; Saul was now anointed as king over Israel. The oil signified God's approval.

Samuel kissed Saul and this kiss was also meant as a sign. Samuel, the most powerful man in Israel, handed over his power to Saul with this kiss.

Can you think of another kiss mentioned in the Bible? Judas gave Jesus a kiss in the garden of Gethsemane. That kiss was a sign for the soldiers to capture the Lord Jesus. He was betrayed so that He could become your Savior.

Do you want the Lord Jesus as your Savior?

Saul — 1 Samuel 10:17–27

The Book of the King

Then Samuel told the people the manner of the kingdom, and wrote it in a book, and laid it up before the LORD. And Samuel sent all the people away, every man to his house.
— 1 Samuel 10:25

Most countries are ruled by politicians. They make rules and regulations that they think are necessary. These rules become laws and are recorded in books. Every citizen of a country has to obey these laws.

Everyone in Israel knew that the Lord had appointed Saul to become their king. But the new king hid himself between some luggage! He did not want to stand up in front of all the people. When Saul finally showed up, he was presented to the people. Samuel also took an empty book and wrote down all the directions how to rule and what was expected of the Israelites toward their new king.

Saul had to listen to God whatever the circumstances would be; this would be the most important rule for him. Saul was ready to rule, but everyone went home, including Saul. He did not go home alone, however, for some strong soldiers were with him. Now Saul had a small army that would protect him. The Lord was with Saul, too, and that, of course, is the best protection. God's presence is better protection than an army can give.

Who protects you? What does the Lord protect us from?

121

Saul — 1 Samuel 11:1–15

Driven by the Holy Spirit

And the spirit of God came upon Saul when he heard those tidings, and his anger was kindled greatly.
— 1 Samuel 11:6

Once there was a pastor who went on a mission trip to Russia. He had to preach at every stop he made. One day, he had traveled all day long in an airplane and then all night long in a car. When he arrived in the morning, he was exhausted. He had not slept and was expected to preach three times that day.

He prayed the Lord for His help, and the Lord answered his prayer and gave him strength and energy to preach. The people later commented that he looked so well rested! This was the work of the Holy Spirit.

The Holy Spirit worked in Saul's life, too. The city of Jabesh was surrounded by enemies. King Nahash announced that he would only spare the city if the right eye of every Israelite soldier were removed. This was called an "eye for peace." Without their right eyes, the men could not use their bow and arrows and so they would be useless in the army. When Saul heard this, he became very angry. He called all the men of Israel to fight the enemy. With 300,000 soldiers, Saul defeated the enemy and the city of Jabesh was delivered.

After the battle, Saul was proclaimed king again at Gilgal. The Holy Spirit had guided Saul in the fight and the people were very pleased with him.

Have you seen the Holy Spirit's work in your life?

Saul — 1 Samuel 13:1–14

Saul Becomes Impatient

*And Samuel said to Saul, Thou hast done foolishly: thou
hast not kept the commandment of the LORD thy God,
which he commanded thee.*
— 1 Samuel 13:13

Mother had made a delicious pan of soup. As she put the pan
on the table, she warned her daughter Jenny not to touch
the pan—it was very hot! But Jenny ignored her mom and
touched the pan anyway. She did not want to wait. That was
a bad idea. With a sharp cry of pain, she looked at her fingers;
red burns appeared on her skin.

Saul had been waiting for six days. On the seventh day,
Samuel still had not arrived to make an offering for the Lord
before battle. Two armies were facing each other. On one side
was the Philistine army. They could hardly wait to get into a
good fight. On the other side was the army of Saul. But Saul's
men were not ready for battle. They were scared and some
were deserting; soon there would be no soldiers left to fight!
On the seventh day, Saul did not wait any longer. Samuel was
not coming; he would make an offering himself.

When Samuel arrived later, he became angry with Saul
when he saw what he had done. Saul had been impatient and
disobedient; he should have trusted the Lord. With the Lord's
help, he could have conquered the whole world! Because he
had been disobedient, the Lord would look for another king.
That was the price he had to pay for being disobedient.

*Can you remember any bad consequences of sin you have
had to face?*

123

Saul — 1 Samuel 15:1–23

Saul is Rejected

Because thou hast rejected the word of the LORD, he hath also rejected thee from being king.
— 1 Samuel 15:23b

Maybe you have heard of Napoleon, the great general. He was an unimportant corporal when he entered the French army. But he quickly climbed the ranks and became an important general. When he was king, he crowned himself emperor, placing the crown on his own head. What a proud man he was! He thought too highly of himself; he thought no one was as important as he.

The same thing happened to Saul. Saul was told by the Lord to fight the Amalekites. They had attacked Israel in their wandering through the wilderness, and now they would be punished for it. Saul was commanded to kill both man and beast, but he disobeyed. He took the best animals home. King Agag was captured and taken back in chains. Saul hoped to impress the people so that they could see how mighty he was! At a place called Carmel he built a pillar in honor of himself. Saul forgot the Lord and thought only of his own honor. Samuel went to Saul again, this time with the message that God would not help him any longer. Without the Lord, there was no future for Saul.

Why is it wrong to think that we are more important than others? Did Jesus act that way?

Saul — 1 Samuel 26:17–25

Regret or Repentance

Then said Saul, I have sinned: return, my son David: for I will no more do thee harm, because my soul was precious in thine eyes this day.　　— 1 Samuel 26:21

Things were not going well with Saul. An evil spirit possessed him and he lost his temper over and over. He was especially angry with David. He did not want him to become the next king; Saul even tried to find David so that he could kill him. But David found Saul first, while he was sleeping. David could have killed Saul, but he took Saul's spear and water jug instead and then left. When Saul realized that David had spared his life, he showed remorse. "I have sinned," he said to David. Yet Saul was not really sorry; he only felt regret. He was fearful of God's punishment. But when the next opportunity came, he tried to kill David again.

I know a boy who loves teasing other children—not in a mean way, yet they get very annoyed with him. They tell him to stop it. He apologizes and promises to stop because he does not want to get punished. But the next time they are together, he teases them again.

Sometimes when we sin, we regret that it brings us into trouble, but we do not really repent—just like the boy who teased and just like Saul. But when we are truly sorry for the wrong we did, we will confess it to the Lord. Then He will forgive us for Jesus' sake.

Are you sorry that you sin against the Lord or only sorry that it gets you into trouble?

125

Saul — 1 Samuel 28:3–19

The Lord is Silent

And when Saul inquired of the LORD, the LORD answered him not, neither by dreams, nor by Urim, nor by prophets.
— 1 Samuel 28:6

Saul is afraid. The Philistines had come with a great army and Saul thought that they would be defeated. He had asked God for an answer, but the Lord was silent. So Saul went to a witch who lived in Endor, for he wanted an answer, one way or another.

Saul told the witch to let him talk to Samuel, even though Samuel had died. But he really was talking to Satan. Satan took the form of Samuel and told Saul that he would die and David would become the next king.

Because Saul disobeyed God, God had forsaken Saul, and that was the worst thing of all. Saul had started off so well, but everything ended terribly for him. The Lord wants us to listen to Him; He deserves for us to listen to Him and obey Him. He sent His Son to this earth for us, and He overcame the devil at the cross.

What did you learn from Saul's life?

David — 1 Samuel 16:1–13

A Young Man After God's Own Heart

For the LORD seeth not as man seeth; for man looketh on the outward appearance.
— 1 Samuel 16:7

Samuel was in Bethlehem. The Lord had sent him with a secret mission. Samuel was to anoint one of the sons of Jesse as king, but Samuel did not know which one. Samuel and the elders got the sacrifice ready first. Then Jesse called in his sons. Samuel saw the oldest son first. "This will be the new king," he thought, "for what a strong, large man he is!" But Samuel was wrong; the Lord does not look at the outward appearance—He looks at the heart!

The next sons were not chosen either. Jesse told Samuel that there was only one more son, the youngest and eighth in the family. He was seventeen years old and his name was David. When David kneeled before Samuel, the Lord told Samuel: "This is the one!" While the older brothers looked on, David was anointed by Samuel, for David loved the Lord.

What does the Lord think is most important in a person?

David — 1 Samuel 16:14–23

Immanuel

Behold, I have seen a son of Jesse the Bethlehemite, that is cunning in playing, and a mighty valiant man, and a man of war, and prudent in matters, and a comely person, and the LORD is with him.
                                                    — 1 Samuel 16:18

The name "Emmanuel" is often used around Christmas time when we celebrate Christ's birth. It means "God with us," and refers to the Lord Jesus.

In our text, it says about David that "the Lord is with him." It also mentions that David was handsome in appearance and he was also a strong, sensible, courageous hero. But what mattered most was that God was with him.

David could play very peaceful music—that is how Saul had David serve him. Saul was troubled with an evil spirit and it made him restless. Saul's companions felt sorry for him and asked David to come and play on his harp. By the power of the Holy Spirit who lived in David's heart, the evil spirit left Saul whenever David played.

This same Holy Spirit can give you rest through faith in the Lord Jesus. Then God will be with you, too.

How do you know if the Holy Spirit lives in your heart?

David — 1 Samuel 17:1–16, 32–58

In the Name of God

But I come to thee in the name of the LORD of hosts, the God of the armies of Israel, whom thou hast defied.
— 1 Samuel 17:45

I used to play soccer on the street and we picked teams before starting a game. Everyone wanted to be on the team with the best players. Then you would have a much greater chance of winning the game. The best players were usually the biggest boys.

In this portion of Scripture, two camps are mentioned: the army of Saul against the army of the Philistines. The Philistines had a giant in their midst who had won many battles in the past. This giant soldier was about three yards tall and had been fighting since his childhood. None of the Israelites dared to fight him; even King Saul was scared! The Philistines were expecting a great victory.

One day, David arrived at the camp and became angry when he heard the giant mocking God. Nobody stopped David when he approached the giant. He was not going alone, however, for the Holy Spirit was with him and, in the name of God, he would kill this Philistine. The stone from his slingshot hit its mark, and the giant fell down dead. All along, the Israelites had been stronger than the Philistines, for the Lord God was with them, and He was victorious!

How do you talk about God and the people who serve Him?

David — 1 Samuel 19:1–11

Just in Time

And Saul hearkened unto the voice of Jonathan, and Saul sware, as the LORD liveth, he shall not be slain.
— 1 Samuel 19: 6

Imagine someone robbing a bank. He gets caught and has to appear before a judge. With tears in his eyes, the robber swears an oath that he will never steal again. But the first thing he does when he is released is rob a store! Your trust in that man would be shattered.

After David slew Goliath, he became commander of the army. He won many victories against the Philistines. He was so victorious that Saul became very jealous of David and wanted to kill him. He announced it to everyone who could hear him. His son Jonathan also heard Saul's threat and became very worried. David was his best friend and he did not want any harm to come to him.

Jonathan went to his father to discuss his terrible plan to kill David. Saul swore in God's name that he would not kill David. But Saul did not keep his word. When David played his harp for the king, Saul took hold of a spear and threw it at David! Frightened, David ran away, never to return again.

Just like the robber who broke his promise, Saul could not be trusted. How different the Lord is, who always keeps His promises. We can trust everything that we read in His Word.

Do you always keep the promises you make?

David — 1 Samuel 20:1–43

Two Friends

So Jonathan made a covenant with the house of David, saying, let the LORD even require it at the hand of David's enemies.
— 1 Samuel 20:16

Jonathan and David were good friends, sharing the same faith. Jonathan was the crown prince, but he knew that David would become king rather than he. This did not make him angry, though, for he knew it was the Lord's will. David and Jonathan were very sad when Saul tried to kill Jonathan. They knew that they could not be seen together, lest Saul attack Jonathan again. David and Jonathan made a covenant together, and David promised he would spare the lives of Jonathan's children.

I can think of another Prince; His name is Jesus. He left his royal throne to become poor and live on earth. He also made a covenant; whoever believes in Him will be saved. What a wonderful covenant!

Has the Lord made a covenant with you?

David — 1 Samuel 21:1–10

In the Lion's Den

And David arose, and fled that day for fear of Saul, and went to Achish the king of Gath.
                                        — 1 Samuel 21:10

Is a lion's den a safe place to be in? Probably not. You'd be risking your life; if the lion is hungry, you are finished!

David risked his life in the "den" of the Philistines. Danger threatened him and he narrowly escaped; he had to become a refugee with Saul's spies on the lookout for him. He fled to Nob and got some food. Afterwards, he ran to the land of the Philistines with the sword of Goliath in his hands. He was recognized because of the sword he carried and they captured him and brought him to the king. David was afraid they would not spare his life because he had killed so many Philistines. What should he do?

David acted as if he was not in his right mind. He scratched at the door and let drool fall down on his beard. When he appeared in this condition before King Achish, he was sent away and thrown out of the city. David was free! But he was not free because he had been so clever. David wrote in Psalm 34: "This poor man cried, and the Lord heard him and saved him out of all his troubles."

Why did David call himself "a poor man" in Psalm 34?

David — 1 Samuel 24:1–23

David Spares Saul's Life

The LORD judge between me and thee, and the LORD
avenge me of thee: but mine hand shall not be upon thee.
— 1 Samuel 24:12

We can read in the Heidelberg Catechism that "we are prone by nature to hate God and our neighbor." You read it in the headlines of your newspaper—cheating, murder, and disagreements happen every day. By nature, we love ourselves. But the Holy Spirit can change this as is seen in David's actions. Guided by the Spirit, he spared Saul's life.

We read in chapter 23 that David was surrounded by Saul and his soldiers. They were ready to capture him when news reached them that the Philistine army had invaded Israel. Saul rapidly pursued the enemy and David was delivered out of his hands. However, Saul came back to the wilderness to search for David again. Saul was confident that he would catch him this time, but things turned around.

As Saul was resting in the cave where David was hiding, David had a chance to kill Saul. His troubles would have been over and he would no longer have to flee. But David waited on the Lord and spared Saul's life, for Saul had been anointed by the Lord. The Lord Himself would support David and punish Saul. How faithful and merciful David was! He spared Saul's life while Saul wanted to kill him. The Lord is also gracious to you in giving His Word, so that you can be saved.

Do you love the Lord? Why or why not?

David — 2 Samuel 2:1–7

Still No Rest

And the men of Judah came, and there they anointed David king over the house of Judah.
— 2 Samuel 2:4a

Saul was defeated and killed when battling the Philistines. An end had come to David's wandering and he could finally live in the land of Israel. After asking the Lord where he should live, the Lord told him to live in Hebron.

The men of Judah came and anointed David as their king. We would think that now David could rest, but this was not to be. David was only king over Judah, and the other tribes were ruled by Ishbosheth, the son of Saul. Ishbosheth wanted to add Judah to his territory. This meant that more battles had to be fought. In verse 1 of the next chapter, we read, "Now there was long war between the house of Saul and the house of David."

David would have to fight for seven more years, but the Lord resided with him. He would become king over the whole nation of Israel, for God's promise will not fail.

David had to be patient until the Lord gave him all of Israel. Are you patient?

David — 2 Samuel 6:1–11

David's Plan

And they brought it out of the house of Abinadab which was at Gibeah, accompanying the ark of God: and Ahio went before the ark.

— 2 Samuel 6:4

David has finally become king over Israel. Roads were made and gardens were planted. His palace was built in Jerusalem and a wall was built around the city. A big plot of land was left empty which would be the future site of God's house. A big feast was planned in Jerusalem to celebrate the return of the ark, for the ark was still at Kirjath-Jearim.

The onlookers saw how the ark was placed on a wagon. Then, on the way to Jerusalem, the oxen pulling the wagon stumbled, causing the ark to fall. Uzzah reached out to keep the ark from falling and he immediately died. David became frightened when he heard the news and left the ark at the house of Obed-edom. He was sad over Uzzah's death and knew it was his own fault. The ark should have been covered, and carried by the Levites as God had commanded. David had not followed the laws. The Lord is a holy God and His ark had to be handled in a special manner.

Do you keep God's commandments? Which commandment is the hardest to keep?

David — 2 Samuel 6:12–23

David is Glad

And David danced before the LORD with all his might, and David was girded with a linen ephod.
— 2 Samuel 6:14

Would you recognize a doctor working in your local hospital if you met him shopping with his family? Probably not. But if you saw him in his white lab coat, you would recognize him. The white coat belongs to his profession.

While the ark was at Obed-edom's house, that house was being blessed. David knew this was a good sign; now he could bring the ark to Jerusalem. This time it would be done in the proper way, the Lord's way. The ark was to be carried on staves, and many people followed the ark with David in their midst. He had changed his royal clothing for priestly clothing and was hard to recognize. He was dancing and leaping for joy and did not behave like a king.

David's wife, Michal, was not happy when she saw David dancing. She thought that he was making a fool of himself. But David told her that, in God's eyes, he was unimportant so it didn't matter what he wore. It only mattered that he loved the Lord his God.

Centuries later, the Lord Jesus would also take off His royal clothes. He would be wrapped in swaddling clothes in the stable of Bethlehem. The Savior would become poor for you and me.

Do you feel small before the Lord? Why is it a good thing when we do?

David — 2 Samuel 7:1–17

A Palace for the Lord?

He shall build an house for my name, and I will stablish the throne of his kingdom for ever.
— 2 Samuel 7:13

Have you ever been inside a palace? The rooms and halls are beautiful and so richly decorated that you can hardly believe your eyes! The palace where King David lived was also very beautiful. He had conquered all his enemies and peace reigned in Israel. He could now retire from all his warring. As he looked around his palace, he saw how splendid and beautiful it was. He enjoyed the riches God had given him.

But when David went to sacrifice, he saw the difference between his palace and the tabernacle where the ark was placed. This ought not to be, for the Lord was much greater and more glorious than David was. So David made plans to build a palace for the Lord. The Lord approved of the plan, but David was not allowed to carry it out. He started the building, but the Lord's house was finished by Solomon, David's son.

Another son of David, born centuries later, was David's greatest descendant: the Lord Jesus. He is building His church with all those who believe in Him. That church will last forever on earth and in heaven.

Do you belong to the Lord Jesus' church?

David — 2 Samuel 12:1–13

A Black Page

Thou hast killed Uriah the Hittite with the sword, and hast taken his wife to be thy wife.
— 2 Samuel 12:9

Some say that our life is like a book. Each day is a page and what happened on that day is recorded there. When something terrible happens or we make a very bad mistake, we call the day a black page.

David had a black page in his book. We have one of the pages before us: David sinned against God. David had one of his soldiers, Uriah, purposely killed in battle so that he could marry that soldier's wife, whose name was Bathsheba. Nobody would find out that he had sinned.

But, one day, Nathan the prophet came to David. He told David the story of a rich man who arrogantly took his neighbor's only sheep to make a feast for himself. When David heard this he became very angry at that mean rich man and ordered him to be killed. But Nathan pointed at David and told him: "You are that rich man!" Then David understood that God had seen what he had done and that he deserved to be killed for killing Uriah. This did not happen; the Lord punished David a different way.

David repented and begged the Lord for forgiveness. The Lord heard his prayer, and on this black page of his book was written in red letters: "forgiven." It was written in blood, Jesus' blood.

Which commandment did David sin against?

138

David — 2 Samuel 15:1–13

Revolt against David

And there came a messenger to David saying, The hearts of the men of Israel are after Absalom.
— 2 Samuel 15:13

Long ago, the Roman empire was ruled by Constantine. He had a nephew whose name was Julian. This young man seemed very pious because he went to church and read his Bible. But he really worshipped the sun. He later rebelled against his uncle and became emperor. He was a hypocrite who mocked God and worshipped idols.

What we read in the Bible today is a very similar story, but Absalom rebelled against his father. He acted very devout and asked his father if he could bring a sacrifice to the Lord in Hebron. His real plan was to proclaim himself king. He had made many preparations and made sure that he was in favor with the Israelites. Many influential friends helped him. When the trumpet sounded in Hebron, the Israelites cheered and applauded for Absalom.

So David was driven away by his own son; he had to flee. David knew this was the punishment for his sin with Bathsheba. He was troubled when he had to leave Jerusalem, but did not become angry. The Lord was still with him, no matter what Absalom did to him.

Do you love your parents? How do you show it?

David — 2 Samuel 18:1–53

Substitute

O my son Absalom, my son, my son Absalom! would God
I had died for thee, O Absalom, my son, my son!
— 2 Samuel 18:33b

In a concentration camp in Russia stood a row of prisoners. A guard counted them, and every tenth prisoner was to be killed by the firing squad. It was a young man's turn, but an older man took his place and was killed instead.

In our Bible passage today, Absalom sat on David's throne, but he still had to defeat his father. David did not join the battle, though. He had instructed his generals to spare his son's life. David knew that Absalom was not ready to die because he was living without God. David waited in anxious suspense to see how the battle would end. His soldiers were winning the battle, but then he heard the terrible news: Absalom had been killed! David fell down on his knees and cried out: "Had I but died in thy place!" David loved the Lord and would have gone to heaven.

David loved his disobedient son so much! David died at an old age. It was not important that David became old; it only mattered that his sins were forgiven him through the Lord Jesus' work. Jesus died as the substitute on the cross of Calvary. Did He die for you?

What did you learn from David's life?

Jonathan — 1 Samuel 14:6–10

God Fights for Jonathan

For there is no restraint to the LORD to save by many or by few.
— 1 Samuel 14:6

Jonathan was on his way to a camp of the Philistines with a young man who was carrying his armor. His father, Saul, was sitting under the trees, for he had given up the fight against the Philistines. But someone needed to do something to free the Israelites from the dominion of the Philistines. A courageous deed was needed. The Lord's help was needed. So Jonathan told the young man going with him that the Lord could save by many or by few. He had faith in the Lord and knew that nothing could stop the work of the Lord.

The road they walked on went between two rock formations. The only weapon that Jonathan carried was a sword. He went first and his armor bearer followed. It would be a matter of victory or death.

The Philistines saw them coming, and mocked them, saying, "Look, the Hebrews are coming out of the holes where they have hidden." They waited for the two men at the top of the rock. They taunted them, telling them to keep coming up so they could show them a thing or two. For Jonathan, this was the sign from God for which he was waiting. Jonathan climbed to the top and his armor-bearer kept following. The Philistines did not even stand a chance. After a short battle, twenty of the soldiers were dead and the watch post was defeated. Saul and his men could get through now, for there was no obstacle anymore. The remaining Philistines became so afraid that they fled as quickly as possible. They realized just how brave the two soldiers were. If all the Israelite soldiers were this brave, they must be a very strong army. But Jonathan knew something that they didn't know—the Lord had given them the victory.

Do you trust the Lord like Jonathan did?

Jonathan — 1 Samuel 14:24–30

God Rescues Jonathan by His People

So the LORD saved Israel that day.
— 1 Samuel 14:23

The coast was clear for Jonathan's father, Saul. Israel's soldiers went up towards the Philistines. It was a heavy battle. The Philistines were very confused and surprised. They even began killing each other. Some of the Israelites who had deserted their own people, fighting instead for the Philistines, returned to their own army. But more importantly, the Lord fought for Israel. The Philistines fled in total panic.

Then Saul did something very foolish. He didn't want his soldiers to quit the fight too early, so he did not let them eat anything before the evening. He even swore an oath that anyone who didn't obey orders would be killed. That very oath became a threat to his son's life. It was getting darker and the soldiers were very hungry after fighting for so long. Saul was told that Jonathan had eaten some honey he had found in the forest. Jonathan hadn't heard what his father Saul had commanded. He went to Saul. "Here I am. Do I have to die?" asked Jonathan. Saul was going to follow through with his oath; Jonathan would have to die. But the people began protesting because Jonathan was their hero. He had fought in the battle with them. Wasn't the Lord with Jonathan? "So the people rescued Jonathan that he died not."

Who is looking out for your life, taking care of you every day?

143

Jonathan — 1 Samuel 17:55–18:4

The Friendship of Two Heroes

Then Jonathan and David made a covenant.
                                                    — 1 Samuel 18:3

There is a saying that goes like this: "Tell me who your friends are, and I will tell you who you are." This saying means that close friends are often alike. They like doing the same things, they think the same way. Do you have a true friend? A friend who listens to you carefully and who plays with you? Real friendship often lasts for a long time. Sometimes friendships even last a lifetime. But friendships end when one of you dies.

Jonathan had a good friend. His friend was David; he loved David as much as he loved himself. The friendship between David and Jonathan was from God. You can read in your Bible that the souls of these two friends were united. Jonathan had seen how David killed Goliath. When David told Saul who he was, Jonathan was already beginning to like him. They became such good friends that they made a covenant: they would stay friends forever. Their friendship would not end with death. Nothing could break their friendship.

Jonathan and David both loved the Lord and served Him. Both of them were heroes in Israel, too. They belonged together. As a sign of their friendship, Jonathan gave David his clothes and his weapons. It was a token of his love for David.

Who is the best friend anyone could have?

144

Jonathan — 1 Samuel 19:4

Jonathan Protects David

And Jonathan spake good of David.
— 1 Samuel 19:4

Sometimes your parents might ask you to tell them your side of a story to figure out what actually happened. Maybe your brother or sister helps you by telling how you were actually doing the right thing. You are relieved when you avoid being punished.

Jonathan was doing the same thing. He told his father, Saul, good things about David. Jonathan needed to do so because Saul said that he wanted to kill David. Saul didn't want David to become the king. He wanted Jonathan to be king. Saul was jealous of David, but Jonathan loved David. He tried to help his friend.

David had never done anything wrong to Saul. Why did Saul want to kill him? In fact, David had done very good things for Saul. He even risked his life on Saul's behalf several times. "Why would you sin against innocent blood?" Jonathan asked. Finally, Saul swore by God that he would let David live. David was allowed to return to the palace to play the harp for Saul. Jonathan submitted to God's will that David would become king instead of him. He had peace in his heart about it all, for who can be wiser and mightier than God Himself?

Can you think of situations where you can stand up for what is right?

Jonathan — 1 Samuel 23:14–18

Strong in the Lord

…and strengthened his hand in God.
— 1 Samuel 23:16

David was running for his life. Saul was after him, but there weren't many places to hide. He decided to flee into the desert. There were lots of mountains and rocks there. Maybe Saul would not come there to look for him. David was overwhelmed with grief and saw no escape route.

But then he saw someone walking toward him. It was Jonathan, who had come to David to show he was a true friend. He wasn't jealous that David would become the future king. He knew that the Lord's ways were best. Jonathan tried to comfort David by saying, "Do not fear, for the hand of Saul my father will not find you. You shall be king, and I shall be next to you."

Jonathan proved to be a true friend. He stayed with David even when it was dangerous to do so. He encouraged David by pointing out that his life was in the Lord's hands. They made another covenant before the Lord. Jonathan then returned and David stayed where he was. He was strengthened and encouraged, for God had given him strength to carry on. Whatever the future would bring, he was ready. He would need this renewed strength for what would soon take place.

Where do you get your strength from? Do you see how the Lord used Jonathan to encourage David?

Jonathan — 1 Samuel 31:1–6

Faithful until death

And the Philistines slew Jonathan.
— 1 Samuel 31:2

Saul was not pursuing David as much anymore. The Philistines were becoming bolder and Saul was too busy trying to defeat them. Saul was very afraid, so he went to a lady who predicted the future. He was desperate. She predicted that he would lose the battle and that he would die. What a terrible thing to hear!

When Saul returned to the battle he could already see that things were turning against him. Thousands of his soldiers were killed and, in desperation, the army fled. Only a few of them kept fighting. Among those were Saul and his sons. Saul's sons were killed in front of his eyes, and Jonathan was killed also. He helped his father until the end.

But, for Jonathan, his death wasn't a miserable end. He loved the Lord and his soul met his Savior in heaven. He was forever with his Lord. There was eternal peace and rest waiting for him. What a contrast between Jonathan and his father! Saul killed himself. He died in his sin and carried the consequences in eternity. He was without the Lord forever. How terrible if our lives end like Saul's!

What will your future be like? Why do you think so?

Jonathan — 2 Samuel 9:6–8

David Takes Care of Mephibosheth

What is thy servant….
— 2 Samuel 9:8

Are you athletic? Do you walk, run, and play with other kids? Is your schoolwork pretty easy for you? If so, sometimes it is good to remember that not everyone is blessed like you are.

A man named Mephibosheth lived in a town called Lodebar. Mephibosheth couldn't walk and was therefore disabled. He was a son of Jonathan, who had died years ago when Mephibosheth was only five years old. A nanny had been taking care of Jonathan when she heard that Jonathan had died. She took Mephibosheth in her arms and fled. Suddenly, she tripped on a rock and fell. Mephibosheth tumbled out of her arms onto the ground; ever since that day, he had been a cripple.

David had promised Jonathan to take care of his children, so he asked for Mephibosheth. Mephibosheth came to David, bowed down before him, and greeted him by saying, "Here is your servant." Mephibosheth was very nervous, but he didn't have to be nervous! He was about to hear such wonderful news! David would take care of him from now on. Mephibosheth could come to the royal palace every day to eat his meals. He would receive all the land that belonged to Saul. David did this because he had loved Jonathan so very much.

Mephibosheth was surprised and very happy. What did he ever do to deserve this? He felt very small and unimportant

148

in front of David. He knew that he had not done anything to deserve David's kindness.

The Lord Jesus takes care of sinners the same way. Because He gave His own life, He can be merciful to you. You do not deserve it in any way, but He is willing to be merciful.

Have you experienced the Lord's mercy in your life? How?

Solomon — 1 Kings 3:5–10

A Wise Heart

Give therefore thy servant an understanding heart.
                                                          — 1 Kings 3:9

Going to school can be very enjoyable, especially when you have no trouble understanding what the teacher explains. Is schoolwork easy for you? Or are you having a difficult time at school? Maybe you need extra help in language or math.

This week you will learn more about the life of Solomon. He was famous for his extraordinary wisdom. How did he become such a wise person? Was he simply born a very smart man? No; his wisdom wasn't from himself. God made him that wise.

The Lord spoke to Solomon in a dream one night. Solomon had to decide what he would like to have, for God promised to give him anything he asked for. He wanted to reign over his people with understanding, so he asked the Lord for wisdom. He knew that wisdom would help him to discern good from bad and right from wrong. The Lord gave him this wisdom, for Solomon made a good choice. He didn't have to go to school to become so wise, for the Lord put this wisdom in his heart in a special way. There never was and never will be anyone on earth who would be wiser than Solomon. The Lord also taught Salomon to listen to His voice, for then he would be truly wise.

What is wisdom? If someone offered to give you anything you asked for, what would you request?

Solomon — 1 Kings 3:23–28

A Wise Judgment

...the wisdom of God was in him.
— 1 Kings 3:28

Two brothers were fighting. The parents separated them and asked what happened and who started it. Both boys blamed each other. Mom and Dad didn't know who was lying or who was speaking the truth. Which one was right? Whom should they believe?

Solomon faced a similar dilemma. Two women told him what had happened the night before. But their stories of what happened were opposite. Solomon listened intently so that he could judge who was right.

This is what happened. Two mothers were sleeping in one house, and each had a baby with her. One of the women rolled onto her baby in her sleep and the baby died. When the mother woke up and saw that her baby was dead, she quietly went over to the other woman. She switched the babies and went back to bed. The next morning, the other woman found the baby dead beside her. But she looked at the baby, took a second look, and realized this dead baby was not her child. She figured out that the other woman had taken her baby. But the woman denied that she had switched the babies and, after a vicious exchange of angry words, they decided to go to the king.

There they stood in front of Solomon. Who was telling the truth? Solomon commanded his servants to get him a sword. Solomon decided that a soldier would cut the living child in two pieces; that way, both mothers would take home half of the child. Cut her baby in two? Oh no, the real mother didn't want that to happen! She would rather give her own child away than have it killed. She told Solomon to give the baby to the other woman. That was exactly what Solomon had been waiting for; a true mother would never want her child to be killed. He decided that she would get her child back, alive and well. The people were amazed at Solomon's wisdom. It was obvious that the wisdom of the Lord was with him.

Have you been honest today?

Solomon — 1 Kings 6:7–14

The Building of the Temple

Then will I perform my word with thee.
— 1 Kings 6:12

Have you ever watched construction workers build a house? Maybe you saw them build your own house. What was it like? It was probably quite dirty and noisy at the construction site. Framers sawed and hammered the wood and machines were running. Many things were happening.

A building project was also taking place in Jerusalem. They were building the temple, the house of God, under Solomon's command. But something was different. It didn't look at all like a construction site. There weren't any noisy construction workers hammering or sawing. It was very peaceful and quiet at the site. It would be inappropriate to have so much noise at the house of the Lord, for it was a holy place. And miraculously enough, they didn't have to make any noise at the building site. So how was that possible?

Outside Jerusalem, a large crew of busy workmen were making preparations. They did all the work there so that, at the actual building site in Jerusalem, they only had to put the pieces in place. So all the sawing, measuring, and actual work happened in a totally different spot than where the temple was being built. They must have put a lot of time and planning into making and fitting all the separate pieces precisely. They had to figure out all the sizes and measurements ahead of time. God gave Solomon the wisdom needed for this project.

Why don't we need a temple today?

Solomon — 1 Kings 8:27–30

Solomon's Prayer

That thine eyes may be open toward this house night and day.
— 1 Kings 8:29

Solomon stood in front of all the people in the temple of the Lord. He stood in front of the altar as he spread out his hands to pray. The people were filled with holy reverence and a cloud filled the temple, signifying the presence of the Lord. Solomon prayed and the people prayed with him.

You just read part of this prayer. You can find the complete prayer in 1 Kings 8:23–54. You should read it sometime. It was a very solemn prayer; Solomon prayed for the Lord to live in the temple and he pleaded with the Lord to hear their prayers.

Many times in his prayer, Solomon asked the Lord to "hear and forgive." Solomon knew the people, how easily they departed from the Lord again and again, and how they needed continual forgiveness. If they departed from the Lord, He would punish them for their sins as He had done in the past. Enemies would fight and plunder the land. The Israelites' harvest would be ruined and sickness would be among the people, all because of sin. But the history of God's people also showed that, when the Lord punished them like this and they repented and returned to Him, He forgave them. They had to pray to their God for mercy. That is why Solomon humbly prayed, "Then hear thou in heaven, and forgive thy people Israel."

Do you have a humble and reverent attitude when you pray? The Lord is a holy God. He will hear your prayers and forgive your sins for Jesus' sake.

What attitude do you have when you pray?

Solomon — 1 Kings 10:7

The Queen of Sheba

And, behold, the half was not told me.
                                    — 1 Kings 10:7

The Queen of Sheba came from far away to visit King Solomon in his palace. She had heard of Solomon's great wisdom and riches. She could hardly imagine these rumors to be true. Who on earth could be that wise and rich? It seemed impossible! Deep down, the real reason she came was to hear more about the God of Solomon, the God who gave him this wisdom. She didn't want to rely on reports; but she wanted to find out for herself.

She was greeted by Solomon himself and invited into his palace. She came into the throne room. Solomon was sitting majestically on his throne and answered all of her questions. She didn't ask easy questions, but very difficult riddles and mysteries. No matter how difficult the questions were, Solomon's wisdom was so great that he knew the answers to all of them! The queen was very impressed, but her amazement didn't stop there. She was led into the dining room where she noticed that everything was very orderly. Everything was taken care of in a peaceful and respectable manner. It was unimaginable to her that this king and his servants had such a lifestyle in the palace. Travelers who had reported these things to her back home had not even told her half of the beauty and peace she witnessed during her visit. It was all so beautiful! The scene made her speechless.

Many centuries later, the Pharisees demanded a sign of Jesus. They did not believe Him and challenged Him to show them something to make them believe. Jesus mentioned two signs: He told them the story of the people of Nineveh and about the Queen of Sheba. These Pharisees had Wisdom Himself with them but they didn't believe in Him.

To whom should we take all of the questions that live in our hearts?

GOD!

Solomon — 1 Kings 11:1–6

Solomon is Seduced Into Idolatry

Solomon clave unto these in love.
— 1 Kings 11:2

Being rich and wealthy is not always such a great thing. You have to be a strong person to stay humble and close to the LORD if you are very rich. Riches will tempt you to forget the God who gave them. Did that happen to Solomon or was he strong enough to stay humble? Sadly, no; Solomon could not carry the burden of wealth. He began to forget the LORD and he took many wives. Most of them were heathens who served idols, and Solomon built high places for them so they could each serve their own idol.

Then we find Solomon bending his knees before these idols. He worshipped heathen gods in the city of Jerusalem, the city of the Lord Himself. Did he think the Lord would not punish him? Well, Solomon quieted his conscience by also going to the temple of the Lord. He didn't forget the covenant God altogether, but he didn't serve the Lord with all his heart. He served the Lord and idols at the same time, giving some of his attention to each. But the Lord asked Solomon to give his whole heart. Because of these great sins of Solomon, terrible things would happen to him and his people. The Israelites followed his example and began serving idols as well, and soon the kingdom was under destruction. The people went through so much misery because they forsook their own God.

Who has your heart, God or the world?

Solomon — 1 Kings 11:28–32

The Division of the Kingdom

Behold, I will rend the kingdom out of the hand of Solomon.
                                                    — 1 Kings 11:31

Jeroboam was a young man who lived in Solomon's kingdom. He was a hard worker and had a lot of construction experience. He was very useful to King Solomon, and the king made him overseer over the other men of his tribe.

This same Jeroboam walked along the road leaving the city Jerusalem. While travelling, an old man walked towards him and it quickly became clear that the old man was the prophet Ahijah. The prophet took off his brand new coat and ripped it in twelve pieces. Jeroboam watched in surprise as Ahijah handed him ten pieces of the torn garment. Ahijah was delivering a message from the Lord to Jeroboam. Israel would be torn to pieces like his coat. He would become the king of ten tribes, while the son of Solomon, Rehoboam, would lead the remaining two tribes. The two remaining tribes would continue to belong to the house of David.

The dividing of Israel was a punishment because of Solomon's sins. It would take place after Solomon's death. Solomon had ruled Israel for forty years at the time of his death. His sins caused terrible things to happen to his people, but the LORD still cared for him. When he died, he entered eternal life in peace by God's amazing grace and mercy.

How have you experienced God's existence in your life?

Elijah — 1 Kings 16:29 – 17:1

The Idol Worship of Ahab

And Ahab...did evil in the sight of the LORD.
— 1 Kings 16:30

In the next two weeks, we will discuss different aspects of the prophet Elijah. Elijah had many encounters with Ahab, the king of Israel. Ahab was king over the ten tribes, but not the first. Jeroboam was the first king of the ten tribes.

Ahab ruled for twenty-two long years. Sadly, he was a wicked king who had married the ungodly Jezebel. Jezebel was the daughter of the heathen Ethbaal, highpriest of Astarte, a heathen idol. Ethbaal became king of the Zidonians through terror and murder. This was the kind of family Ahab had married into. Jezebel was a clever woman and tried to introduce her religion to the Israelites. She was successful, thanks to her husband's weakness. He gave her free reign to do whatever she wanted, even murder the prophets. By letting her, Ahab became guilty of that sin, too. He was the first king to allow Baal worship to flourish. A temple was built for Baal complete with an altar and a statue. An image of Astarte, the wife of Baal, was also made and worshipped by Ahab. How dreadful!

Because of all these things, God sent Elijah to Ahab. The name Elijah means "the Lord is my God." Baal is not God, but the Lord is God. As a result, Ahab was punished by God with three years of drought.

Whom do you worship? How do you show it?

Elijah — 1 Kings 17:2–7

God Takes Care of Elijah

And I have commanded the ravens….
— 1 Kings 17:4

We don't know what Ahab thought after Elijah brought him the message that there would be no rain. Baal was the god of rain after all. But, if it was true, it would mean there would be hunger and thirst in the land, and eventually, death.

Elijah left Ahab to go to the Jordan River where the brook Cherith met the larger river. The Lord sent Elijah there and He would take care of him. There was enough to drink, for the brook had plenty of water. But how was Elijah to get his food? Where could he go? The Lord provided because He is ready to help in times of need. Every day, in the morning and at night, ravens brought food for Elijah. They carried meat and bread in their beaks and dropped it in front of Elijah for him to eat. What a miracle this was, especially when you consider that ravens don't take good care of their own young. They were unclean birds that ate meat for their meals. But now, instead of eating the meat themselves, they brought it to Elijah. Elijah walked closely with the Lord during his time at the brook. He was safe there from Ahab's warriors, and the Lord took care of everything he needed. Elijah was a servant of the Lord; he was His child.

The Lord takes care of this whole world, but especially of His own people. That is why God's people are so happy. This happiness could become yours as well.

Did you see God's caring hands in your life today?

Elijah — 1 Kings 17:8–16

Elijah's Stay in Zarephath

Fear not; go and do as thou hast said. — 1 Kings 17:13

After Elijah had been at the brook for a while, it dried up, so the Lord commanded him to go to a widow who was living in Zarephath. This widow would provide Elijah with food and drink and he would live in her house. The widow was faced with a dilemma. She had only a little bit of flour left in her barrel and her oil was almost finished. She had only enough to feed herself and her son, and after that they would die of hunger. But Elijah asked her to make a cake for him first, although he knew that this was the last food left in the house. The Lord worked a great miracle for the woman, giving her faith to believe that this was what she must do. She made the cake for Elijah, but her supply of flour and oil didn't disappear. For three long years, they lived from that little bit of food that was left in the house. She never ran out! She obeyed the Lord and was rewarded for it.

But this didn't protect the widow from grief entering her home. Her son died, and she questioned Elijah's presence in the house, suspecting he had something to do with it. She asked him, "What have I to do with thee, O thou man of God?" Elijah took the boy to his room and fell on his knees and prayed. He pleaded with the Lord to show another miracle in this house. He stretched himself out on the boy and prayed again, asking the Lord to give the boy life. He put all his trust in the Lord, and the Lord heard his prayers.

We can never trust the Lord enough! We must always have faith.

Do you find it harder to trust the Lord when times are tough? What can we learn from this story?

161

Elijah — 1 Kings 18:7–16

Elijah and King Ahab Meet

Go, tell thy lord, Behold, Elijah is here.
— 1 Kings 18:11

Imagine you just came home from school and put your empty lunch bag on the counter. You told your mom, "I'm hungry!" What you meant was that you would love to have something to eat, not that you were actually starving. Many children on this earth are truly hungry and tell their moms so, but their moms don't have anything to give them.

That is what it was like in Samaria. The drought was severe and it had been three and a half years since they had any rain. In search for grass for the animals, Ahab and his servant Obadiah went in two different directions. Hopefully, they would find food for the animals. Suddenly Obadiah fell to his knees; he saw Elijah standing in front of him. "Art thou that my lord Elijah?" Elijah told him he was. Obadiah had to call Ahab, but he was afraid that Elijah would be gone when he returned. He knew that Ahab might punish him if they came back here and no one was to be seen. He wondered if Elijah knew that he served the Lord. Obadiah had hid a hundred prophets to protect them from being killed by Queen Jezebel. He was very frightened he would be killed himself if he obeyed Elijah. But Obadiah had no reason to worry, for Elijah stayed there until he returned with Ahab. Elijah spoke with Ahab and told him that there would be rain in the land again and that the famine would be over.

Why did you pray before your meals today?

Elijah — 1 Kings 18:21–24

The Lord or Baal

How long halt ye between two opinions?
— 1 Kings 18:21

We all make decisions every day. You often need to decide between one thing or another. Do I do my chores first or do I finish that chapter in my book? Who should I invite to my birthday party? What present will I buy for my friend? Which game are we going to play?

Elijah gave the Israelites a decision to make. There they stood around the prophet on Mount Carmel. But the priests of Baal were also there. Even Ahab was present. Elijah was the only prophet of the Lord, but he was not afraid to ask the people the question: "How long will you refuse to decide whom to serve?" His fiery eyes pierced the Israelites as he gave them the choice in the name of the Lord. He told them they couldn't serve two masters. They either served the Lord or they served Baal. But there was silence after his question. No one answered him. Then Elijah asked for two young bulls to be brought to him. He kept one for himself and the other one was given to the priests of Baal. The priests had to cut their bull in pieces and put it on their own altar. Elijah would do the same to his bull and put it on his altar. They were not allowed to put the fire on the altar yet. The priests would call upon their god and Elijah would call upon the Lord. Whoever would answer the prayers through fire would be the true God.

The people all thought that this was a good solution. They waited to see what would happen.

Have you already made up your mind about whom you will serve? Do you serve the Lord with all your heart?

163

Elijah — 1 Kings 18:31–39

The Lord is God

Hear me, O LORD....
— 1 Kings 18:37

Elijah took charge of the situation by giving the priests of Baal the first opportunity. For hours on end, they called to Baal, dancing and jumping around and on top of the altar. Elijah watched as no answer came from Baal. Nothing happened. Elijah confronted them and their false religion. He said, "You should call louder. Maybe your god is talking or busy with something else. Or maybe he is on a trip and cannot hear you. Or could he possibly be sleeping?" So the priests began shouting even louder. They cut themselves until blood trickled down their bodies. Still there was no answer from Baal.

Elijah's patience was running out; he decided it was his turn now. He dug a trench around his altar and had twelve big barrels of water poured out on the altar. There was so much water on his altar that even the trenches were full of water. Everything was ready now and Elijah prayed to the Lord, asking Him to answer. Suddenly, flames of fire came down from heaven and burnt up everything! Nothing was left of the altar—neither the bull nor even the water. Shaken by this powerful answer, thousands of Israelites shouted that the Lord is God! God answered Elijah's prayer because He was with Elijah.

Why did nothing happen to the sacrifice that Baal's priests put on the altar?

164

Elijah — 1 Kings 18:40–46

God is Merciful

Behold, there ariseth a little cloud out of the sea….
— 1 Kings 18:44

Elijah's work was not finished yet. Baal's priests were captured and killed, according to God's commandment (you can read about this in Deuteronomy 13:9–10). Ahab was speechless as he watched what was unfolding in front of his eyes. He could easily have killed Elijah but the Lord protected His servant. Elijah sent Ahab back to his palace to eat and drink and celebrate the end of the drought. Rain was certainly coming.

As Ahab prepared to leave, Elijah knelt down to thank the Lord and pleaded for rain to come. While Elijah prayed, his servant went to the top of the mountain to check seven times. The seventh time, the servant saw a cloud as big as the hand of a man, a sign that stormy weather and abundant rain was coming. As Ahab traveled back to Jezreel, the clouds above his head darkened and soon a fierce rainstorm surrounded him. God was merciful towards the Israelites. Elijah honored Ahab by accompanying his chariot into the city, another sign for Ahab to serve the Lord God of Israel. But Ahab did not regard the sign, but hardened his heart.

Every time we read or hear God's Word, we are warned, just as Ahab was. Do you listen to the warnings you hear?

How do you serve Israel's God?

Elijah — James 5:16–20

The Lord Hears Our Prayers

And he prayed earnestly. — James 5:17

Does it make sense to pray? Does the Lord even hear your prayers? Maybe you've asked yourself at some point why someone you love is still struggling with disease when you've prayed for the person many times. Or maybe you see people who never pray but have a much better life than you have. Does this confuse you?

Today you read the passage in James about Elijah's prayer. He prayed twice and his requests were granted both times. You might think that your prayers and his prayers are not comparable because he was a servant of the Lord. But, in God's eyes, no one is more or less important. Everyone is equal. The good work that Elijah did serving God did not earn him anything. Even though Elijah was a prophet, he was still dependent upon God's mercy and grace.

The reason that James wrote about the prayers of Elijah is not to show us what a good person Elijah was, but to show us the power of prayer. It is a strong example to encourage us to pray because the Lord is willing to hear, for Jesus' sake! The Bible gives us many promises about our prayers. "Ask, and it shall be given you." These promises have power because of Jesus' sacrifice on the cross. We do not deserve to be heard by God, but He is merciful and kind. Whatever your needs are, you can find satisfaction with the Lord who gives abundantly. "Open thy mouth wide, and I will fill it."

What needs do you have? Can you find other Bible verses that encourage us to pray about our needs?

Elijah — 1 Kings 19:1–8

Elijah Flees from Jezebel

He arose, and went for his life.
— 1 Kings 19:3

Elijah was a very brave man. He wasn't afraid of Jezebel and he did not fear Baal's priests either. But now, it seems like Elijah has changed into a different person. He was afraid because Jezebel was so angry with him that she had sent a message to him saying he would be killed tomorrow. Elijah fled from her at once, going south. He knew that Jezebel's father lived in the north, so it wouldn't be wise to go in that direction.

Elijah was so tired of it all and thought that all his hard work was useless. He even asked the Lord to end his life. Exhausted, he fell asleep until an angel of the Lord woke him up. He ate and drank and again fell asleep. After he ate a second time, he stayed awake and traveled further into the wilderness. The Holy Spirit blessed the food he had eaten so that it gave him strength to travel for forty days. He reached Mount Horeb after a journey of over three hundred miles. There Elijah recovered and received new courage for his work.

The Lord cares for us, even for our health and strength.
Be sure to thank Him for His loving care today.

Elijah — 1 Kings 19:9–14

The Sound of Silence

What doest thou here, Elijah?
— 1 Kings 19:9

Elijah hid himself in a cave of Mount Horeb, thinking he was the last person left who still served the Lord. But then he heard the Lord speaking to him, asking him what he was doing there. At this point, Elijah opened his whole heart and told the Lord everything. He told how he had labored for God's cause, but the people were too stubborn to listen, and how he was left all alone working on a hopeless case. Elijah thought there were no children of God left. But the Lord took Elijah outside to show him something.

The Lord used His creation to teach Elijah. First there was an extremely strong wind raging, followed by an earthquake. Finally rocks were set on fire. Then peace and silence returned and Elijah recognized the Lord coming towards him in a still small voice. Elijah covered his face with his coat, for he knew the Lord was holy and majestic. He was so small and insignificant that he hardly dared look up. Elijah understood the Lord's lesson. Just like the still small voice, he had to be patient and gentle. God's coming judgment would be carried out by Hazael, Jehu, and Elisha. In peace and quietness, the Lord Himself would carry out His work in the hearts of seven thousand chosen ones, using His Word and Spirit. The Lord's work brings a peaceful quietness to our hearts.

Have you experienced the Lord's peace in your heart?

Elijah — 1 Kings 19:19–21

Elisha Takes Elijah's Place

And cast his mantle upon him.
— 1 Kings 19:19

Elijah was to anoint three people. These three men—Hazael, Jehu, and Elisha—would bring the judgment of God to the people. Elijah saw a man working the fields with his plow, close to Ahab's palace. Elijah knew this man was Elisha, so he threw his mantle on top of Elisha's shoulders. This sign showed that Elisha was taking over Elijah's work, and God was appointing him to do so. Elisha knew this meant he wouldn't continue his work as a farmer. To show that he understood the sign, he slaughtered his oxen. From the wood of his plow he made a fire, and gave the cooked oxen meat to the people. From now on, Elisha would go with Elijah wherever he went, first as a servant and, after Elijah's death, as a prophet. They worked together for ten years before Elijah died.

The Lord Jesus used this story as an example in Luke 9:61–62 to show that you must be able to leave everything to serve Him. If you want to serve the Lord, you have to leave the past behind and look to the future. The only goal in your life should be to work for the kingdom of God and deny yourself for His cause.

Who or what do you follow in your life?

169

Elijah — 2 Kings 2:1–6

Elijah's Last Journey

Tarry, I pray thee, here…
— 2 Kings 2:6

Elijah and Elisha were walking side by side, not talking to each other at all. Both of them knew that this was the last walk for Elijah on this earth. But neither one knew that the other also knew this fact. Elijah asked Elisha to remain while he continued the journey, for he didn't know if Elisha was allowed to see the end. But the Lord guided Elisha to refuse Elijah's request and he went along with Elijah. He was allowed to see the glorious departure of Elijah from this life.

The sons of the prophets in Bethel came walking towards them and asked Elisha if he knew that Elijah would die today. He told them he was aware of that and asked them to say nothing more about it. Again Elijah asked him to stay behind, and again Elisha refused. The sons of the prophets of Jericho asked the same question as the ones of Bethel, but Elisha told them to be quiet about it. Elijah knew that it was the Lord's will that Elisha stay with him after Elisha refused the third time to depart from him. Elijah knew that God's ways are always best, so they went to the Jordan River together.

Elijah was not nervous about death because he knew he would be going into heaven, just like all God's children know they will be in heaven when they die. The only hope of God's people in life and death is to have a sure trust in God.

Do you know where you will go when you die?

Elijah — 2 Kings 2:7–13

Elijah is Taken up into Heaven

And Elijah went up by a whirlwind into heaven.
— 2 Kings 2:11

Saying goodbye to someone can be really difficult when you don't know for sure if you will see each other again.

Elijah and Elisha stood at the side of the Jordan River, and Elisha knew the moment for the final good-byes had come. It was difficult to part with his master and friend, and he wanted to stay with him as long as possible. When Elijah hit the water with his mantle, the water parted and a dry path allowed them to safely cross the river. When they reached the other shore, Elijah asked if there were any requests he could grant Elisha before they separated. Elisha didn't think twice and asked if he could have a double portion of Elijah's spirit, more than the other sons of the prophets would receive. Elijah answered him that his request would be granted if Elisha saw his departure into heaven.

As they were still talking, a fiery chariot with horses separated Elijah from Elisha. Elijah was taken up into heaven by a whirlwind and Elisha saw everything. Elijah didn't die, but was taken up to meet his Lord while he was still alive! The mantle that once belonged to Elijah fell on the ground before his feet, and a double portion of Elijah's spirit came upon Elisha.

Does this event in Elijah's life remind you of the ascension of the Lord Jesus? How?

171

Elijah — 2 Kings 2:14–18

Not Elijah but Jesus Christ

Send. — 2 Kings 2:17

Elisha held Elijah's mantle in his hands while he stood on the shore of the Jordan River. Just like Elijah, he hit the water and called upon the name of the Lord, saying, "Where is the Lord God of Elijah?" This action convinced the sons of the prophets that Elijah's spirit was with Elisha and they bowed down before him. They told Elisha they wanted to search for the body of Elijah. Elisha answered them not to do so, but they continued to ask and eventually Elisha gave them permission. For three long days, fifty men searched for Elijah's body but they could not find it.

The Lord does not want us to worship anyone other than God alone, so in His wisdom He kept these sons of the prophets from finding Elijah. They might have been tempted to honor Elijah's body too much. Elijah was in heaven with body and soul. There he would worship God forever.

On one other occasion, Elijah appeared with Moses on earth. You can read about it in Mark 9:2–9. Elijah and Moses came down to talk to Jesus when the Lord Jesus needed some encouragement before making the journey to Jerusalem where He would suffer and die. His death on the cross paid for Elijah's sins and for all of God's children's sins. The blood of Jesus Christ, the Son of God, cleanses us from all our sins.

Do you need Christ's forgiveness in your life?

Elisha — 2 Kings 3:1–17

No Rain, yet Water

Yet that valley shall be filled with water.
— 2 Kings 3:17

When King Ahab died, his son Jehoram became king in his place. Like his father Ahab, King Jehoram would not listen to God. He did destroy the image of Baal, but he brought sacrifices to the golden calves.

King Mesha of Moab refused to pay his taxes. This meant a hundred thousand lambs and a hundred thousand rams less for King Jehoram. Jehoram wanted to teach king Mesha a lesson. He gathered his army and, together with the god-fearing King Jehoshaphat, went out to battle. They traveled through the wilderness for seven days, but then they ran out of water. The soldiers had nothing to drink. "Is there not a prophet of the Lord who can help us?" King Jehoshaphat asked. One of the soldiers called out: "Elisha is with us." Elisha received a wonderful message from God: "For thus saith the Lord, ye shall not see wind, neither shall ye see rain, yet this valley shall be filled with water." And what this servant of God predicted happened the next day! Enough water came to provide for everyone.

When the need is the greatest, deliverance is near. How mighty is our God!

Why did God help the ungodly King Jehoram?

Elisha — 2 Kings 4:1–17

A Poor Widow Richly Blest

Borrow not a few....
—2 Kings 4:3

This story is about a mother with two children. Her husband had attended the school of the prophets, but then he had died a few weeks ago. Now a man, a creditor, had come and demanded the money she owed him. "I don't have it right now," she told him, "but I will pay you back as soon as I can." The creditor was not happy with this answer. "I want it now," he threatened her. "Otherwise I will take your two sons as slaves."

The mother was beside herself with fear and went to Elisha to tell him her troubles. The prophet asked her: "What do you have in your house?" The mother told him that she had nothing besides a little oil in a jug. Elisha commanded her: "Borrow as many vessels from your neighbors as you are able to. Then go home with your sons and shut the door. Fill all those vessels with the oil from your jug." Acting in faith, the widow did what Elisha told her to do. A great miracle took place, for all the vessels were filled with the small amount oil from her jug. When she told Elisha what had happened, he said to her, "Go, and sell your oil and pay your creditor. There will also be enough money left over for you and your sons to live."

Nothing is impossible with the Lord!

You may always pray for help. But when God answers your prayer, what should you not forget?

Elisha — 2 Kings 4:38–44

Watch Out: Poison!

Give unto the people, that they may eat.
                                        — 2 Kings 4:42

There was famine in the land. Elisha was at the school of the prophets when one of the young prophets went into the field to gather some herbs. The only thing he found were some wild gourds, a sort of bitter melon. He chopped the gourds and threw them into a pot of boiling water. It looked appetizing, but when they ate of it, they cried out: "Oh no! Don't eat any more! It's poison; death is in the pot!" "Bring me some flour," Elisha ordered. He added some to the pot and told everyone to eat it. Now it tasted delicious!

A few days later, God performed another great miracle. A man from a neighboring village, Baalshalisha, brought Elisha twenty loaves of barley and a bag of fresh corn. "It is for the prophets," he said. Elisha gave it to Gehazi to make it ready for mealtime. "But this is not enough," protested Gehazi. "We have a hundred prophets." Elisha told him, "Go ahead, for the Lord has said, they will eat and have some left over." What the Lord promised happened, too. He is a God you can rely on.

Do you know any other stories in the Bible where the Lord provided plenty of food?

Elisha — 2 Kings 5:1–19

Washed Clean in a Dirty River

And his flesh came again like unto the flesh of a little child, and he was clean.

— 2 Kings 5:14b

What was an old Syrian general doing in the Jordan? Naaman didn't really know himself. When Elisha had told him to wash himself seven times in the Jordan, he had angrily turned around to go home. But one of his servants had pleaded with him, "My father, if that prophet had asked you to do something very difficult, you would have done it. But he asked you to do a very easy thing, and now you refuse! Therefore, please just do it; the prophet said that was how you can be healed." Naaman listened to his servant and obeyed Elisha's direction.

Suddenly, at the end of the seventh washing, a great miracle happened! His whole body was healed, and his skin looked like that of a little child. Naaman was very thankful and wanted to give Elisha many gifts. When Elisha refused, he asked if he could take some bags of soil with him. He wanted to build an altar in his own country and only sacrifice to the God of Elisha, the God who had healed him.

God deserves our obedience in easy things and in difficult things. What are some ways you find obedience hard to do? Pray about these and ask the Lord to help you.

Elisha — 2 Kings 5:20–27

If You do not Listen...

A leper as white as snow.
— 2 Kings 5:27

Gehazi overheard the conversation between Naaman and Elisha and could not understand why Elisha had refused the gifts that Naaman offered. All that gold and silver! This was a chance of a lifetime, he thought. When Naaman drove away, Gehazi ran after him. When Naaman saw him, he sprang off his wagon and asked if everything was alright. "Yes, it is," answered Gehazi, "but my master has sent me to tell you that two young prophets have come. Could you give them some silver and two coats?" "Take this silver and two coats," answered Naaman. Two servants walked home with Gehazi, and carried the bags of money. When they arrived at the house of Elisha, Gehazi took the bags of money and sent the servants back. Then he sneaked back into the house and found Elisha standing there.

"Where did you come from, Gehazi?" asked Elisha. "I have been nowhere," Gehazi answered. "But I know what you did, Gehazi," said Elisha. "This was not the time to take silver and clothing as gifts. Because you did this, the leprosy of Naaman will come upon you and your descendants." Immediately, white spots and boils appeared on Gehazi's body. He became a leper. Ashamed, he turned and left.

Why did the Lord give Gehazi such a heavy punishment?

Elisha — 2 Kings 6:8–33

A King who was Unthankful

Fear not: for they that be with us are more than they that be with them.
— 2 Kings 6:16

How shameful when we see the miracles that were done, and hear about other miracles, and still refuse to bow our knees before the Lord! Remember when Jehoram was in the desert and had no drinking water for his soldiers? God took care that the valley was filled with water. And what about the woman's jug of oil that kept pouring and never ran out? Poisonous herbs had turned into a delicious meal, and a Syrian general was cured of his leprosy. King Joram had probably heard about all of these.

This portion of Scripture speaks about the Syrian king Benhadad, who tried to attack the Israelites secretly over and over again. Elisha the prophet knew about these sneaky plans and immediately warned King Jehoram. Perhaps the king would put his trust in the Lord. But no; we read that, when the Syrian army besieged the city of Samaria and famine broke out, he wanted to kill Elisha. He did not want to have anything to do with the Lord, even though he knew the miracles that Elisha's God could do.

Elisha's life was safe in God's hand. Tomorrow we will read how the Lord gave deliverance even when King Joram was unthankful!

How would you react when someone was unthankful or even angry at you when you did something good?

Elisha — 2 Kings 7:1–20

Take God at His Word!

And it came to pass as the man of God had spoken.
— 2 Kings 7:18a

An angry King Jehoram stood before Elisha: "The Lord is to blame for the famine; why should I expect help from Him now?" But Elisha answered him, "Hear the Word of the Lord; tomorrow eight pounds of flour and sixteen pounds of barley will be sold for only eleven grams of silver." The chief officer of the king mocked and said, "Then the Lord has to make windows in heaven." Elisha rebuked him, and told him that tomorrow he would see it with his own eyes, but not eat of it.

That night, four lepers living outside of the city were going to raid the Syrians. To their surprise, they found no soldiers in their tents. What they did find was a lot of food! The Lord had worked another miracle. That night, the Syrian soldiers had heard the noise of a mighty army approaching them. They had all fled in haste, leaving everything out for the lepers to find. When the lepers had eaten their fill, they told the news to the watchmen on the wall. The news spread like wildfire through the city, and the people could not be stopped. The gates were opened when it seemed safe to do so. The unbelieving officer tried to keep order, but the people trampled him underfoot and he died. How terrible this was for this officer; he died after mocking the Lord and not repenting of it!

Why was it so terrible for the officer to die in the state he was in?

179

Jehu — 2 Kings 9:1–10

A Message from Heaven

For the whole house of Ahab shall perish.
                                        — 2 Kings 9:8a

The officers of the army of Israel were together in Ramoth to discuss their tactics to defeat the army of Syria. Suddenly, the door swung open and a young prophet ran in and told the captain, Jehu, that he needed to talk to him privately. He had a message from heaven for the captain. Listening to the young man, Jehu jumped up and walked the messenger into another room to listen to him. Instead of talking to Jehu, the young prophet took out the oil from underneath his garment and poured it over Jehu's head to anoint him as king. Jehu received the message from God that he had to kill all of the house of Ahab. Jezebel had killed many servants and prophets of the Lord and there would be a special punishment for Jezebel: she would be eaten by dogs.

Jezebel lived in a beautiful palace where everyone thought she was an important and rich person. But don't be jealous of her riches and fame, for it was not what it appeared to be. The Lord knew exactly who she was and how she had mocked and blasphemed the Lord. She deceived the people of Israel to serve Baal. The Lord had been patient with her for a long time, but now her punishment would come. This rich woman was nothing but poor and wicked in God's sight.

Would it be better to be rich but without the Lord, or poor and have His forgiveness?

Jehu — 2 Kings 9:11–15

Watch What You Say

Wherefore came this mad fellow to thee?
— 2 Kings 9:11b

The other officers asked Jehu what this crazy fellow told him. "He made me king over Israel." Suddenly they were very quiet, wondering if he was joking, but they could tell he wasn't joking at all. Realizing this was a serious message, they grabbed their coats and draped them over the top of the stairs and put Jehu right on top of them! The trumpets sounded and they shouted, "Jehu is king, Jehu is king!" They did not waste a moment and Jehu began his work as king. The gates of the city were closed so that no one could escape to tell Joram, King Ahab's son, that Jehu had been anointed. A little later, Jehu's chariot was on its way to Jezreel. The time had come for God's judgment to be fulfilled.

When the officers that were in the room with Jehu saw the prophet come, they thought at first he was a little strange and overly religious. But when they heard his message and really understood what he had said, they realized that this man did not speak his own words, but words of God. That is why it is wise to be careful what you say about God's servants, for they serve the highest King.

How can you show respect for ministers?

Jehu — 2 Kings 9:16–29

A Terrible Death

And Jehu drew a bow with his full strength.
— 2 Kings 9:24a

A watchman on one of the towers of the city of Jezreel spotted a group of horsemen in the distance, coming toward the city. He wondered if they were friends or enemies. The city quickly sent two men right after each other to check out who these men were and why they were coming. They were to ask the group if there was trouble. However, neither of them returned; they both stayed with the group of horsemen as they approached the city.

Finally the group came close enough for the watchman to see it had to be Jehu and his men, for he was driving so furiously. Joram couldn't wait any longer and decided to go out to meet them himself. His servants quickly prepared two chariots, one for himself and one for King Ahaziah, who was visiting. They drove towards Jehu and called out to him, "Is it peace, Jehu?" Jehu's answer made it very clear why he had come. He said, "What peace, so long as Jezebel's sins are so many?" Joram didn't need to hear any more; he quickly turned his chariot and called out to Ahaziah that they had been deceived. But Jehu was faster than Joram. He grabbed his bow and shot an arrow into Joram's heart. Joram died in his chariot, and they threw him on the earth of Naboth's property. Jezebel had once stolen this property from Naboth very wickedly (see 1 Kings 21). Ahab's grandson, Ahaziah, was pursued and killed as well. God's wrath proved to be terrible!

Why was God so angry at Joram?

182

Jehu — 2 Kings 9:30–37

The LORD is God!

And he said, Throw her down.
— 2 Kings 9:33a

The news of Joram's death had already reached the palace. His mother, Jezebel, feared that she would not be spared either. She put on some make-up to try to appease Jehu, but it was all of no use. Jehu entered the palace grounds and looked up to the open window where Jezebel was looking down at him. She called out to him that he should remember what happened to Zimri (1 Kings 16:9–13) when Zimri rebelled against his master and killed him. But Jehu didn't listen to her at all. He noticed three of Jezebel's officials standing behind her at the window. He called out to them that, if they were on his side, they should throw Jezebel out of the window. They obeyed, and Jezebel fell to the ground in front of Jehu's chariot and was trampled by his horses. Jehu entered the palace and they gave him a meal to eat. When he sent out some servants to bury the body of Jezebel, they couldn't do so for the dogs had already eaten her body.

Many warnings had been given to Jezebel by the Lord, but she decided to follow her own wicked desires. How terrible it must have been for her to appear before the living God and to acknowledge that the Lord is God, not Baal! By then, it was too late for Jezebel to be saved, and she perished forever.

It is important to stand up for the Lord and for what is right. How can you do that today?

Jehu — 2 Kings 10:1–6

Scared "Friends"

We are thy servants, and will do all that thou shalt bid us.
— 2 Kings 10:5b

King Jehu sent a letter to the men of Samaria who took care of seventy of King Ahab's sons and grandsons. He asked these men to show that they still supported the cause of Ahab as they had in the past. He commanded them to pick the strongest and best suitable man out of these seventy males, and make him their king. Then Jehu would fight the Samaritans as they protected their own king.

The men did not dare do what Jehu commanded them to do. They were so afraid of King Jehu; he already killed two other kings! They decided they would rather be on his side. Their choice was fine with Jehu, but to prove they were really willing to serve and fight for him, they had to kill Ahab's seventy sons and grandsons and deliver their heads to Jezreel the next day. They did as they were told, and they killed these seventy men. These friends of Ahab proved to be false friends. They only served their king for their own personal gain. It didn't matter if the king's name was Ahab or Jehu.

What kind of friend are you?

Jehu — 2 Kings 10:12–17

God's Honor or Your Own Honor?

And he said, Come with me, and see my zeal for the LORD.
— 2 Kings 10:16a

The punishment on the house of Ahab continued. Many people had already died because of Ahab and Jezebel's sins —even many of Ahab's cousins were killed by Jehu's soldiers. On his way to Samaria, Jehu met a man who was known to be humble and God-fearing. His name was Jehonadab. God sent this man to Jehu and Jehu invited him to climb into his chariot. Jehu told Jehonadab that he killed all these people for the honor of God, and not for his own honor. He didn't want anyone to think he killed them for his own honor.

What do you think? Did Jehu fight this battle to honor God's name or do you think he did it so people would think he was an excellent warrior? Today, too, people say one thing but do another. It would be good to think about this today, and see if you agree.

What do you think is more important, God's honor or your own?

Jehu — 2 Kings 10:18–31

God Requires Your Whole Heart!

But Jehu took no heed to walk in the law of the LORD God of Israel with all his heart.
                                          — 2 Kings 10:31a

One day all the priests of Baal were together in the temple of Baal to have a party. They all dressed up in their white official clothes and came to worship Baal. Jehu had invited them to come, but he had other plans. When all the priests arrived, he gave the command to kill all these Baal priests. Soon the party changed into a massacre, for not one of the priests survived. When they were all killed, Jehu's servants continued to take out all the idols and images of Baal for burning. The temple was broken down and they made toilets with the scrap pieces. What a humiliation that must have been for these Baal worshippers!

The Lord encouraged Jehu after he did away with Baal worship and rewarded him by telling him his sons and four generations of his family would sit on the throne. What a privilege! But, despite the Lord's goodness to him, Jehu didn't serve the Lord with his whole heart, for he allowed the idol worship of Jeroboam to continue. What a blemish on Jehu's life!

Remember every day that the Lord asks us to give Him our whole heart, and not just part of it. Have you committed yourselves with your whole heart to the service of the Lord? That means that you want to live totally for Him.

Hezekiah — 2 Kings 18:1–8

The King Who Trusted in God

He trusted in the LORD.
— 2 Kings 18:5

The kingdom of Judah finally received a God-fearing King! Many of the former kings did not serve God. Joram, Ahaziah, Athaliah, Joash, Amaziah, Uzziah, Jotham, and Ahaz were ungodly kings; it went from bad to worse until Hezekiah became king. This is what we read about Hezekiah in the Bible: "And he did that which was right in the sight of the Lord." The future looked promising for the nation of Israel; a God-fearing king is like rain on a dry land.

Hezekiah commanded that all the idols be destroyed. He broke down the heathen alters and destroyed the brazen serpent which was still honored by the Israelites. The Lord gave them prosperity and peace, for Hezekiah trusted in Him and God honored that. No more taxes would be paid to the mighty king of Assyria. Hezekiah had many victories against the Philistines. He persevered, and the Lord never puts to shame those who trust in Him.

When you trust in the Lord, does that mean that everything will go well with you?

Hezekiah — 2 Kings 18:9–36

Dark Clouds

We trust in the LORD our God.
— 2 Kings 18:22

Hezekiah's kingdom was prospering. The citizens were wealthier than ever before and happier under their new king's reign. Then threatening news from the neighboring countries reached their ears.

The army of King Sennacherib of Assyria had arrived at their borders. The ten tribes had already been carried off—over a hundred thousand inhabitants were taken to Assyria. Do you know why? It was because they did not listen to the Lord, but did their own thing. With a God-fearing king, the nation of Judah should not have to fear the enemy. Their king said that he trusted in the Lord. But did he trust Him now, in the face of King Sennacherib?

The Assyrian king demanded huge amounts of gold and silver from Hezekiah. So King Hezekiah collected all the gold and silver from the temple and the palace. But Sennacherib was not satisfied. He sent his general back to Judah. The general, Rabshakeh, was screaming insults in front of the city gates. He mocked Hezekiah and his God. How would this all end?

When danger surrounds you, rely on the Lord! What does Psalm 25:2 say?

Hezekiah — 2 Kings 18:37–19:5

A Prayer in Great Distress

He rent his clothes.
    — 2 Kings 19:1

What was Rabshakeh boasting about in front of the gates of Jerusalem? It seemed that this malicious man was not afraid of anyone, not even the Lord.

Eliakim, Shebna, and Joah, three servants of the king, heard the words of the proud general and told King Hezekiah what Rabshakeh had said. When the king heard it, he tore his clothes and covered himself with sackcloth, as a sign of mourning. He went to the temple to pray, and sent Eliakim, Shebna, and some other priests to Isaiah, urging him to pray for deliverance out of this great trial. Would the Lord hear his prayer and send help?

What does Psalm 86:7 mean?

Hezekiah — 2 Kings 19:6–19

The Only Way to Be Saved

Be not afraid of the words which thou hast heard.
                                            — 2 Kings 19:6

Isaiah the prophet had a wonderful message for Hezekiah from the Lord: "Thus saith the Lord, Fear not the words of your proud enemy, for I will help you. I will make sure his life is taken in his own country."

Soon Sennacherib, the king of Assyria, received a message that a great army was on its way to attack them. Before he left the region, he had a long letter delivered to Hezekiah with the following message: "Do not trust your God. He said I will not be able to conquer Jerusalem, but I have defeated other nations, and their gods could not help them either."

Hezekiah took the letter to the temple and laid it before the Lord, beseeching: "O Lord, bow down Thy ear and hear the words of Sennacherib. Deliver us from our enemies, for then all the nations of the earth shall know that Thou art God alone."

Why could the gods of other nations not help?

Hezekiah — 2 Kings 19:20–37

Pride Comes Before the Fall

For I will defend this city.
                                        — 2 Kings 19:34

The help Hezekiah had received from God was amazing, and the punishment proud King Sennacherib had received was crushing. Isaiah, the servant of the Lord, had a twofold message for Hezekiah: "So says the Lord, the God of Israel; I have heard your prayer." Because Sennacherib had behaved himself so foolishly and proudly mocked the God of Israel, God would turn Sennacherib around like a bull is turned by a hook through its nose. Sennacherib would not enter Jerusalem; he would not even shoot one arrow at the city.

Hezekiah also received the message that there will be plenty of food from the Lord. There will be sowing and harvesting to their hearts' content.

That same night, the angel of the Lord killed one hundred and eighty-five thousand soldiers of the Assyrian army. The proud King Sennacherib had to flee to his own capital, Nineveh. Shortly thereafter, he was killed by his own two sons. This was the tragic end of a king who had insulted God.

Pride comes before the fall, but God will exalt the humble. What does this mean?

Hezekiah — 2 Kings 20:1–11

A Gift of Fifteen Years

And I will add unto thy days fifteen years.
— 2 Kings 20:6

I am sure you have been sick at one time or another. When you recovered, it felt so good to be healthy again, didn't it?

During the time that the Assyrians made the country unsafe, Hezekiah became ill. The prophet Isaiah came to him with the message the he was going to die soon. This was terrible news for Hezekiah, for he had so many plans! Moreover, he did not have a son yet, from whom the Messiah could be born.

Sick in his bed, Hezekiah turned his face to the wall and begged the Lord: "O Lord, I have always served Thee with an upright heart, I did what was good in Thy sight, so please let me live." And the Lord heard his prayer. Before Isaiah had left the palace, the Lord spoke to the prophet again: "Go back to Hezekiah, and tell him I have answered his prayer and have seen his tears. I will heal him. In three days, he will visit the temple and I will add fifteen years to his life." Isaiah advised the king to put some figs on his boil. The Lord also gave a sign to Isaiah that Hezekiah would certainly be healed. The sun was slowly moving forward when suddenly it moved backward. This sign was given for all the people to see. How mighty our God is!

Do you think that Hezekiah was afraid to die?

Hezekiah — 2 Kings 20:12–21

Important Visitors

They are come from a far country, even from Babylon.
— 2 Kings 20:14

When the king of Babylon heard about Hezekiah's healing, he sent distinguished guests. They brought lavish gifts with them to give to King Hezekiah. They congratulated him with the good health he had received again, and they wanted to know exactly what miracle had taken place. Hezekiah felt pleased that this mighty king paid so much attention to him. Instead of talking about the miracle God had done, he showed them his earthly treasures. "See, this is how rich I am!" he said.

But God would show Hezekiah that he could not live without Him. Shortly after, the prophet Isaiah came with a message from God: "There will come a time when all your treasures will be sent to Babylon." Hezekiah humbly bowed his head. He confessed his sins and asked for forgiveness.

How important it was that the Lord did not forget Hezekiah when Hezekiah forgot Him. He still remained a child of God, and, when he died, he would be forever with his Father in heaven.

When you sin against the Lord, immediately ask Him to forgive your sins, just like Hezekiah did. Do not wait until the evening; by then you might have forgotten.

Josiah — 2 Chronicles 34:1–13

Spring Cleaning

And he did that which was right in the sight of the LORD.
— 2 Chronicles 34:2

Josiah was the last God-fearing king of Judah. He was a great-grandson of Hezekiah. Josiah was only eight years old when his father died. This was really too young to be a king. When you read verse two again—"and he did that which was right in the sight of the Lord"—you know this is a beautiful statement about him. The nation would prosper with such a king and all would be well.

When Josiah turned twenty, some major work was done in his nation. The holy hills, the woods for the idols, and wooden and iron images were all taken away. The bones of the idol priests were burned and the altars of Baal destroyed. A few years later, the temple was renovated. Hilkiah, the high priest, gave the temple money to the builders. The Levites worked very diligently to make the temple a house of the Lord again. It all went well under the leadership of Josiah. Long live the king!

Do you do "what is right in the sight of the Lord"?

Josiah — 2 Chronicles 34:14–21

An Important Discovery

...found a book of the law.
— 2 Chronicles 34:14

When the priests and the Levites were diligently cleaning the temple, Hilkiah, the high priest, found the book of the law. The laws of the Lord were written in this book by Moses, as they were traveling through the wilderness to the Promised Land. Shaphan, the scribe, brought the important roll to the king. He also told the king that the restoration of the temple was going well.

The king listened with rapt attention when a servant read from the book of the law. When he heard the solemn words, he became alarmed, rent his clothes, and was very worried. Hilkiah and the other Levites were to come to him immediately. As they were standing before the agitated king, he told them: "Go to the temple, and ask the Lord if He will not punish us according to our sins. It says in the book of the law that the anger of the Lord will be poured out on us because our forefathers were not obedient to the Lord God."

Would Josiah find favor in the eyes of the Lord?

Think about Josiah's attitude toward the law that had been read to him. What kind of attitude do you have to God's law?

Josiah — 2 Chronicles 34:22–28

Punishment and Reward

Behold, I will bring evil upon this place.
                                        — 2 Chronicles 34:24

In great haste, the high priest, the secretary of the state, and the minister went to Huldah, the prophetess. She was a God-fearing woman who lived in the new part of Jerusalem.

When they told her how fearful the king was, she told them: "The Lord, the God of Israel, says that He will bring destruction on this city. All the curses that are written in the book of the law will be fulfilled. Because the people have forsaken God and have served other gods, God will pour out His anger upon them." "But," continued the prophetess, "tell the king that none of these calamities will happen during his reign. The city will be destroyed after his death, and Josiah himself shall die in peace."

Why was the punishment held back until after Josiah's death?

Josiah — 2 Chronicles 34:29–33

With Heart and Soul

…to perform the words of the covenant.
— 2 Chronicles 34:31

King Josiah wanted to serve the Lord, for he was a man after God's own heart. The king called the leaders of Judah and Jerusalem to his palace, and, with the priests, Levites, and the people, they went to the temple. There the book of the law was read to them again. While Josiah stood before them, he made a covenant with the Lord. He solemnly promised his willingness to obey God's commandments, with heart and soul, as they were written in the book of the law.

Josiah commanded all the people who gathered together with him to promise to be faithful to this covenant as well, so they did. Everyone sought to keep God's covenant. With fresh courage, Josiah began to work. Some images and idols could still be found in some parts of the country. The king privately traveled throughout the land and had them destroyed; they even demolished some beyond the borders of Israel.

How wonderful that the whole nation promised to be faithful to the Lord! God would bless such love and obedience.

Have you ever promised the Lord that you would faithfully follow Him? This is a good promise to make every day. God always blesses such obedience.

Josiah — 2 Chronicles 35:1–6

A Celebration in Honor of God

Moreover Josiah kept a passover unto the LORD.
— 2 Chronicles 35:1

It is a great blessing when a nation has a king who serves the Lord. King Josiah announced that the Passover would be celebrated in Jerusalem. He told the priests to do their work in the temple joyfully. Because the ark was now placed in the temple, new orders were given to the Levites: they should spend more time in the service of the Lord and His people, since the ark did not have to be carried around anymore. Thus, Josiah also charged the Levites to "keep yourself to the guidelines that were given by King David and King Solomon and were instituted by them. Slaughter the lambs, sanctify yourselves, and have everything ready for the people when they come."

These were the directives given by King Josiah so that the Passover could once again be celebrated as the Lord had commanded. Do you remember what was celebrated at Passover?

We can do every job we have for the honor of God, even if we do not work for a church. How does that change the way we work?

198

Josiah — 2 Chronicles 35:7–19

This is the Right Way!

And the children of Israel that were present kept the passover.
— 2 Chronicles 35:17

Thousands of Israelites were gathered in the city of Jerusalem. If you were to ask an Israelite what was going on, the answer would be: "The king has called us to celebrate the Passover." King Josiah had given many of his own animals for the sacrifices: thirty thousand lambs and young goats, and three thousand young bulls. Josiah's princes also contributed willingly on behalf of the people: 2,600 sheep and goats and three hundred oxen. Thousands more animals were offered. The Levites were very busy sacrificing animals. They also killed the Passover lambs and gave the blood to the priests to be sprinkled on the altar. Then the meat for the offerings of each family was gathered so that each family could have their own burnt offering to present to the Lord. The same was done with the meat of the oxen. Then the Passover lambs were roasted, and the leftover meat was boiled in pots and kettles and handed out among the poor.

The king enjoyed the singers who were singing songs to the glory of God. The Passover was celebrated to the honor of his God. Never before in Israel's history had God received such rich gifts!

Why don't we have to offer sacrifices anymore?

Josiah — 2 Chronicles 35:20–27

The End of a God-Fearing King

Have me away: for I am sore wounded.
— 2 Chronicles 35:23

A large army marched through Judah, the country of King Josiah. It was the mighty army of the Egyptian king, Necho. He was on his way to Assyria and therefore did not want any fight with the Israelites. He warned Josiah: "I do not want to fight you. I am on my way to Assyria. Just leave me alone!"

But Josiah would not listen to King Necho and gathered his army. Fierce fighting broke out between the Egyptians and the Israelites in the valley of Meggido. King Josiah received a deadly wound from an Egyptian archer and died from his wound on the way back to Jerusalem. He was buried in the royal burial grounds of the kings. All the people of Jerusalem and Judah mourned for him; he had been a good king, faithful to the Lord and his country. Josiah had not feared dying; death meant that he would be forever in God the Father's house of many mansions, singing at the throne of the great King!

Every Israelite knew that Josiah loved the Lord. Do you love the Lord, and do others see that?

Ezra — Ezra 1:1–11

Finally Free!

And he hath charged me to build him an house.
— Ezra 1:2

So many things happened after Josiah's death. The Israelites were taken away by King Nebuchadnezzar to Babylon. But then Babylon was taken over by the Persians, who were ruled by King Cyrus. Something wonderful happened during Cyrus's reign. He made a law that the Jews could return to their own country. The law also allowed them to rebuild their temple which had been destroyed by Nebuchadnezzar. After years of captivity, things were turning out so much better than the Jews could have hoped for. Do you know why? Read the answer in verse two. The Lord had given this command to King Cyrus. The Lord had remembered them.

All the Jews had to return and help with the rebuilding of the temple. The Jews who remained behind were also to help by giving gold and silver or cattle. Moreover, King Cyrus also gave back a number of precious vessels which had been taken away from the temple by Nebuchadnezzar.

Forty-two-thousand Jews, including women and children, got ready for the journey, a journey the Lord had already promised long before.

Can you find where the Lord had promised that they would eventually return to Jerusalem?

Ezra — Ezra 3:8–13

A Smile and a Tear

And all the people shouted with a great shout.
— Ezra 3:11

Laughing and crying seldom go together, yet, in this Bible passage, both of these happened.

Under the leadership of Zerubbabel and Joshua, the Jews began to rebuild the temple. When the builders had completed the foundation, the priests put on their robes and blew the trumpets as the Levites played their cymbals. All the people praised the Lord and sang to the Lord: "The Lord is good, His mercy endureth forever toward Israel." They were so happy because the foundation of the new temple could be seen by all.

The people shouted for joy and out of thankfulness. But, among the shouting, the elderly were weeping. Why? Because they remembered the temple of Solomon and all its glory and beauty. The older people cried while the younger people shouted for joy. The crowd made such a loud noise to the Lord that no one could tell who was crying and who was shouting with joy. The noise could be heard for miles around.

Why were the people so happy about the temple's foundations?

Ezra — Ezra 4:1–24

Opposition

...and troubled them in building.
— Ezra 4:4

The people were happily working on the temple when, one day, a group of people approached Zerubbabel and Joshua. They lived nearby. They wanted to help with building the temple, but Zerubbabel and Joshua shook their heads. "No, we do not need your help, and King Cyrus would not approve of it." The men became furious and began to spread lies about the Jews. They tried to hinder the work being done at the temple in many ways.

After King Cyrus died and a new king had begun to rule, these heathen men sent a letter to the new Persian king that said, "King, do you know that the Jews want to rebuild Jerusalem? You should stop them, for when the city has been rebuilt, they will rebel against you. They have done this in the past."

While this letter was just a lie, it frightened the Persian king. He wrote the Jews a letter that told them they had to stop building. Would the lie win against the truth?

Do you know of another example from the Bible where people tried to spoil God's work?

Ezra — Ezra 7:1–10

God's Work Continues

...to seek the law of the LORD, and to do it.
— Ezra 7:10

The building on the temple continued, for God's work can never be stopped, even when the devil tries to destroy it.

After the Jews wrote back to the Persian king, he allowed them to continue building the temple. Under the direction of Ezra, and led by a priest who was a descendent of Aaron, a second group of Jews was going back to Jerusalem. Among them were ordinary, common people, but also priests, Levites, singers, gatekeepers, and slaves.

The Lord kept them safe as they traveled back. Ezra was determined to return to Jerusalem to study the law of the Lord and to obey it. He wanted to be able to explain the law to the Jews.

God's work will not be turned aside,
because He watches over it.
And the Spirit breaks through all barriers
that are set up by mankind.

Can you say in your own words what these last four lines mean?

Ezra — Ezra 7:11–18

A Very Special Letter

Blessed be the LORD God of our fathers.
— Ezra 7:27

Before Ezra left Persia for Jerusalem, he received a wonderful letter from King Artaxerxes. Had you been Ezra, you would hardly have been able to believe your eyes when you read the contents of this letter, it was so wonderful. The king made the following rulings:

1. Any Israelite who desires to go back to Canaan is free to do so.
2. Take a book of the law of God with you.
3. Find out if the people are keeping God's commandments.
4. Take the gold and silver that is given you to the temple.
5. Buy sacrificial animals from the money that is given you and offer them to the Lord.
6. If you are short of money, the king will provide you with more.
7. Give Ezra everything he needs.
8. Give the God of heaven everything He commands.
9. People that work in the service of the Lord do not have to pay taxes.
10. Teach the nation the laws of the Lord.

All these rules were written and commanded by a heathen king. God used this mighty Persian king to fulfill His plan.

Do you know of another heathen king who was used by God as well?

Ezra — Ezra 9:1–15

This is Wrong!

O my God, I am ashamed and blush.
— Ezra 9:6

Under Ezra's guidance, a second group arrived in Jerusalem. It had been a long, dangerous journey. For three months, they had traveled through the desert where many gangs of robbers hid, but the Lord had watched over them.

When Ezra arrived, he was alarmed at what was happening there. Many Jews had married heathen women who were living in Canaan at that time. Even some priests were married to heathen women! Ezra tore his clothes and pulled the hairs out of his head and beard due to his grief and distress. For hours, he just sat by the temple while a big crowd began to gather around him. They stood there quietly, fearful and afraid of the punishment of God.

Ezra interceded and begged God for mercy. From out of the depths of his heart, he prayed to his almighty God: "O Lord God of Israel, Thou art righteous; yet look on us for we are guilty and are not worthy to live in Thy sight." Was this the thanks God received from His people for bringing them back to their own land? Why had they disobeyed God?

What are some ways you can fight against sin in your life?

Ezra — Nehemiah 8:6

Praise the LORD, for He is Good

And Ezra opened the book.
— Nehemiah 8:5

After Israel had confessed their guilt before the Lord, and the men had sent the heathen women away, Ezra was going to read from the book of the law. The road was filled with people all the way to the Water Gate, so Ezra stood on a high, wooden chair. When he opened the book of the law, everyone reverently stood up. Before he started to read, Ezra gave praise to God, and all the people responded with "Amen, Amen." Then they knelt down and worshipped God with their faces to the ground.

During the reading, some priests and Levites walked alongside the people to explain what was being read by Ezra. When they understood the meaning of the words, they burst into tears, for they realized that they had sinned. But Ezra, Nehemiah, and the Levites told them, "Do not cry, because this is a holy day of the Lord your God. It is a feast day; prepare a festive meal. Give some of your food to the poor, for the joy of the Lord will be your strength." The people left to celebrate, for they had heard and understood God's Word. "O give thanks unto the Lord; for he is good: for his mercy endureth for ever" (Psalm 136:1).

What were the people celebrating?

Nehemiah — Nehemiah 1:1–11

Nehemiah's Prayer

O LORD, I beseech thee, let now thine ear be attentive to the prayer.
— Nehemiah 1:11

Hanani arrived in Babylon after a long journey all the way from Jerusalem. He went straight to Nehemiah's house because Nehemiah was his brother. Nehemiah was a servant of the king. Hanani was bringing a message to Nehemiah, and it was not a nice message. This was what he told him: "The restoration of the temple is completed, and the people have started to rebuild the walls, but the king has forbidden this work. He is afraid that the inhabitants of the land will start protesting again. So instead of being safe and secure, the people of Jerusalem are unprotected and vulnerable. Any of their enemies can come to them and attack, like some of them have already done. They broke down all the pieces of the wall that had just been rebuilt. They also burned all the gates."

When Nehemiah heard this message, he sat down, and folded his hands, and prayed, "O Lord, please hear my prayer and the prayers of all those who call upon Thy name. Remember the covenant made with Thy people, I pray, and help me when I go to the king to ask for help for the Israelites."

Notice how the first thing Nehemiah did when he heard the bad news was to pray. Why do you think he did this before going to the king? Does the Lord always hear our prayers?

Nehemiah — Nehemiah 2:1–10

God's Answer

So I prayed to the God of heaven. — Nehemiah 2:4

Nehemiah dreaded bringing his request to the king. Four whole months passed before the Lord heard Nehemiah's prayer. Nehemiah was asked to come to the king. While he was doing his job, pouring wine into the king's cup, King Artaxerxes asked him, "Why are you looking so sad, Nehemiah? Is something bothering you?" Nehemiah was very afraid, for he knew the time had come to ask for the king's permission, but he didn't want to ask. So he answered the king, "I am so sad when I think of the city of Jerusalem. All the walls are broken and the gates are burned." The king wondered what could be done about the problem. Before Nehemiah suggested to the king that he would like to go to Jerusalem to help, he prayed to God for courage. Amazingly, the king allowed Nehemiah to go. Even more amazingly, the king sent letters along with Nehemiah to show to the keeper of the king's forest; they gave Nehemiah permission to take as much wood as he would need to build the wall.

Have you ever dreaded doing something? Nehemiah's attitude shows that the Lord can direct our ways and answer our prayers, even though the answer is sometimes different from what we expected. When we're dreading something, we should take it right away to the Lord in prayer and ask for His help and intervention.

Does the Lord always grant us our requests when we ask Him? Why or why not?

Nehemiah — Nehemiah 2:11–20

Jerusalem's Walls

The God of heaven, he will prosper us.
                                    — Nehemiah 2:20

When Nehemiah arrived in Jerusalem, he rested for three days. He secretly went around the city at night to investigate. He wasn't very happy with what he saw, but he didn't lose heart either. He knew that the Lord had given him this task, so he was convinced that the Lord would also help him to accomplish it. The next day, he immediately called together all the people of Jerusalem and this is what he told them: "I am here in the name of the Lord to help you restore and repair the walls. I have permission from the king to do this. Israel's enemies will surely come to laugh at us and mock us; they will tell us that it is impossible and unrealistic to rebuild the walls. And it will be difficult, but with God's help nothing is impossible. We will surely succeed!"

Your heart is like the walls of Jerusalem, broken and vulnerable because of sin. But the Lord Jesus came to earth to restore the broken walls of your heart. He came to offer you a new life.

Can you think of some signs in your life that show that the walls of your heart are broken because of sin?

Nehemiah — Nehemiah 4:1–23

God's Work Continues

Our God shall fight for us.
— Nehemiah 4:20

Israel's enemies were very mean. First, they laughed and mocked the Israelites, saying that they could never rebuild the walls. "And," they added, "if you will ever rebuild any of the walls, they will fall down as soon as a fox walks upon it." How differently they talked after seeing that the work was going very well! They stopped laughing but they made plans to destroy part of the restored wall. Nehemiah heard about their wicked plans and the first thing he did was pray to the Lord his God. Then he gave the people weapons to defend themselves. The people had a basket with building stones in one hand and a weapon in the other hand. Nehemiah told his people not to be afraid, for the Lord would fight for them.

As soon as the enemies saw the weapons that the Israelites carried with them, they quickly backed off. Their plans for attack fell through. The Israelites worked at the walls from early morning until late at night every day until the walls were finished.

We should do our work the same way. We should first pray to the Lord for help. Then, after He helps us complete our task, we must not forget to thank Him for it.

Is there something specific you should pray for tonight? What can you thank the Lord for?

Nehemiah — Nehemiah 5:14–19

Nehemiah's Gift

Think upon me, my God, for good.
— Nehemiah 5:19

During a church service, the deacons usually go through the church collecting the gifts from the congregation. Do you give of your own money to the collections on Sunday? The Lord Jesus taught us to do so when He said, "Give of your own riches to those who are less fortunate than you are. Whatever you give to others in My name, you are actually giving to Me." Through the money that we give, other people can be reached with the gospel.

Many people in Jerusalem were very poor; they couldn't even buy food or drink for themselves anymore. They sold everything they possessed in exchange for food. Nehemiah heard about it and called together all the rich people he knew in Jerusalem. He told them about the previous leaders and how those leaders took advantage of their position. Nehemiah never did that. He never tried to get richer because of his position. Nehemiah even paid the people with food instead of a salary. The rich people of Jerusalem understood that something had to change. They all agreed that the poor people wouldn't have to repay their debts and could use their money for food.

Nehemiah took care of these people to honor God, not to gain fame or honor.

What are some others ways you can help people besides giving money?

Nehemiah — Nehemiah 6:1–19

The Plans Failed

God had not sent him.
    — Nehemiah 6:12

At school during recess, a group of children were playing a game of soccer. They were playing nicely together, but one boy was watching the game from a distance. He looked grumpy, jealous of the children playing their game. Suddenly he decided to do something about it. He ran through the game and kicked the soccer ball far away. He ruined the whole game, and that is exactly what jealousy does—it ruins everything.

This happened to Nehemiah, too. The kings who mocked Nehemiah became very angry when they saw that the rebuilding of the walls was almost complete. They were so jealous of his success that they planned to kill him. Their plan failed, but they plotted again. They tried to get Nehemiah to disobey God by telling him to flee to the temple to hide from the Samaritans who wanted to kill him.

Nehemiah had only one answer to give them: "I trust in the Lord." In an unbelievably short time—only fifty-two days—the walls were completed and the work was done. The only thing left was to hang the doors on their hinges in the gates. Israel's enemies were getting nervous; they were surprised by how quickly the work was completed. There could only be one explanation: God had helped the Israelites.

Are you sometimes jealous? Why? What can you do to change jealous thoughts?

Nehemiah — Nehemiah 13:1–19

Obeying the Lord

Remember me, O my God, concerning this.
— Nehemiah 13:14

Do you love and respect your parents? Of course you do, and one way you show that is by obeying their rules. They don't give you these rules to bother you, but to protect you. When you disobey your parents, you hurt them. God gave us rules as well; He gave the ten commandments. The people of Israel received even more rules from the Lord, but many times they disobeyed them. Time after time, they were punished by the Lord in order to turn them back to Him in obedience.

When Nehemiah returned to Jerusalem after being away a long time, he was very disappointed to see that the people had departed from the Lord. To remind them again of what God required, he read the law of God to all the people. He restored the Sabbath as a day of rest, for the people were buying and selling on the Sabbath.

Do you see any similarities between Nehemiah's time and our time? It is important for us to repent and return to the Lord, just as it was for the people of Nehemiah's day.

What are some of those similarities?

Esther — Esther 1:1–22

A Great Feast

But the queen Vashti refused to come.
                              — Esther 1:12

If you have ever been to a museum, you may have seen beautiful gold or silver objects, treasures made with expensive stones, or maybe extraordinary clothing from long ago. Beautiful things like that were being used at the feast of King Ahasuerus. All the cups were custom-made of gold; none of them were the same as another. All the rooms in the palace were decorated with beautiful tapestries. It is hard to imagine how splendid the palace looked.

The king and his guests were done eating and drinking. The king decided to call Queen Vashti to come to him. He was eager to show to his guests how beautiful his wife was. But Queen Vashti refused to come. She thought the king was being foolish and she did not want to be shown off.

King Ahasuerus was furious. After consulting his wise men, he decided to send the queen away. He didn't want her in the palace anymore. Messengers went around the country to inform all the citizens of Ahasuerus's great empire. Everyone would hear what had happened to the queen.

Should Ahasuerus have sent Vashti away?

Esther — Esther 2:1–20

Esther Becomes the New Queen

And the king loved Esther above all the women.
— Esther 2:17

The king regretted sending away Queen Vashti because now he didn't have a wife. The king's servants had a plan that they presented to the king. "King, we will bring all the beautiful girls from the entire country to Sushan, your palace. You can look at all of them to see who is the fairest and decide who will become the new queen." The king thought this was a great idea, and the plan was put into action.

Imagine what that must have been like for the girls. If you were physically beautiful, you were taken away from your family; you would live far away from your loved ones. Among those girls was also a Jewish girl whose name was Esther. She was very beautiful and the king picked her to be the new queen.

For many of us, our looks are quite important. But who we are is not determined by what we look like, but by our actions and what is in our hearts.

What do you think is most important in a person? What would be most important to the Lord?

Esther — Esther 2:21–3:15

Haman's Plan

Neither keep they the king's laws.
— Esther 3:8

Did you ever consider how terrible it is to hate someone? When you hate someone, you are unwilling to forgive the other their sins against you. Hate makes you to enjoy someone else's grief. The opposite of hatred is love. Love belongs to the Lord, and hate belongs to Satan. The love of God must replace the hate that lives so naturally in our hearts.

Haman was the most important man in the kingdom, after the king. A Jew named Mordecai didn't want to bow before this Haman of Babylon. Mordecai refused because Haman was an Amalekite, and the Amalekites were enemies of the Israelites. When Haman found out that Mordecai didn't bow before him, he became very angry. He wanted to punish Mordecai—and not just him, but all the people of Israel. Haman set a date for the execution of all the Jews in the kingdom. All the Jews, whether young or old, would be killed. Haman promised that whoever would help him kill the Jews could take all the Jews' possessions. When the people heard that, many were willing to help. Even the king approved of Haman's plan.

What should you do if you find yourself disliking someone? How can you change hatred into love?

Esther — Esther 4:1–14

Showing Your True Colors

And who knoweth whether thou art come to the kingdom for such a time as this?
— Esther 4:14

Sometimes it is hard to show your true colors. For example, when nobody prays for their meal but you, or to tell others that you are a Christian and it hurts you when they take God's name in vain. Even though it can be hard, God wants us to show that we belong to Him. It should be easy for others to see that you are a Christian.

Esther heard that Mordecai was very sad. Mordecai was her cousin, so she was concerned. She sent one of her servants to see what was wrong with him. When she heard about Haman's plan, she was afraid. She wanted to go to the king, but to do so without an invitation from him could mean her death! Mordecai told Esther she had to make up her mind. He said, "Now is the time to show who you are: an Israelite. If you don't say anything the result for you and the people will be very different. Maybe the reason that you became the queen is to help your people."

The Lord wants the same thing from you: He wants you to follow Him no matter what the cost. Tell the Lord everything, even if you are afraid.

Why is it so hard to be a witness of the Lord?

Esther — Esther 4:15–5:14

In the Likeness of Jesus

And if I perish, I perish.
— Esther 4:16

Do you look like your mom or dad? If you look like one of them or a mixture of both, we say that you resemble them. Sometimes people can look at you and know immediately who your parents are without you even saying a word.

There was a kind of resemblance between Esther and the Lord Jesus. Esther was willing to give her life to help save her people. The Lord Jesus did that, too. But being like someone else doesn't mean you are exactly the same. The king allowed Esther to ask her question, and she didn't die. The Lord Jesus, on the other hand, did lose His life to save His people from their sins.

If we are to compare King Ahasuerus and the Lord Jesus, there is no resemblance at all. This king wasn't like the Lord Jesus. Do you know what the biggest difference was?

You are always welcome to come to the Lord Jesus; you never have to be afraid of Him. He will never punish you for coming before Him. He welcomes you! This is what the Lord Jesus once said: "Those who come to Me, I will in no wise cast out."

How could you be like the Lord Jesus today?

Esther — Esther 6:1–7:10

God is Mightier Than Man

So they hanged Haman on the gallows.
— Esther 7:10

Do you sometimes make plans for the weekend? You try to plan everything so that it works out smoothly. It is always important for you to ask for God's guidance and blessing for the plans you make, no matter how big or small, because He leads your life. Regardless of what we want or plan, the Lord ultimately decides the course of our lives.

What an impressive story you read today about the evil plan Haman brought to the king. The Lord made the king unable to sleep at night; that was how he discovered that Mordecai hadn't received a reward for saving the king's life. God turned the evil plan around, and instead of Mordecai being killed, he was honored.

Did you notice that the king had all these events written down in a book? The Lord also keeps track of our lives' events in a book. He knows everything we do, whether good or evil. The great miracle is that He is willing to take all our sins out of this book if we love Him. For Jesus' sake, He is willing to forgive. Isn't it wonderful to belong to Him?

Are you comforted, knowing that the Lord directs all events in this world? Can you explain your answer?

Esther — Esther 8:1–17

Sadness Turned Into Joy

The Jews had light, and gladness, and joy, and honor.
— Esther 8:16

Esther was not very happy yet; there was still something on her mind, bothering her. She knew she didn't have to be afraid of Haman anymore. She didn't need to keep it a secret anymore that Mordecai was her cousin because now the king knew about it. The king even made Mordecai the second most important man in the kingdom, what Haman used to be. It was the evil law that was bothering Esther, for this law was still in effect. Esther went to the king one more time and fell down before him. She was crying when she pleaded with him to make the law invalid. Although the king could not take back the law, he was willing to make another law. He gave Mordecai his ring, so Mordecai would be able to make a new law stating that the Jews were allowed to defend themselves. This was such good news for the Jews. There was hope!

That is exactly what happens when God gives new life to sinners. They become very happy and are filled with hope. The Lord is always willing to give a new life to whoever asks Him.

What changes do you think the Lord would want to see in your life?

Job — Job 1:1–5

Job Fears the Lord

There was a man in the land of Uz, whose name was Job; and that man was perfect and upright, and one that feared God, and eschewed evil.
— Job 1:1

If your friend asks you about someone you know, do you speak nice things about that person? Or do you say mean things? You know that people will talk about you, too, and that it would be wonderful if only good things were said of you. However, people can be fooled. What the Lord thinks of us is much more important.

The Lord said of Job that he was an upright man who feared Him and avoided evil. What a wonderful thing to have said about you! Do you wish that the Lord could say that about you? We know that Job's God still lives. He is willing to give you everything you need if you walk in His ways. Then you will avoid evil, like Job—not living for the world, but serving God. You cannot serve God and love the world a little at the same time. Your prayer should be that God would set your life apart for Himself and for His glory.

How do you think other people would describe you? How do you think the Lord would describe you?

Job — Job 1:6–22

Job Praised God

The LORD gave, and the LORD hath taken away: blessed be the name of the LORD.
— Job 1:21b

Have you heard this saying: "Where the Lord builds His church, Satan will build his chapel"? That means that Satan will always try to undo the good that the Lord does; he will always attack people who love the Lord. This becomes clear in the life of Job. Satan arrived at the scene because Job feared the Lord.

"It is obvious why Job serves Thee," Satan said to God. "He has everything his heart desires. Take it all away and he will curse Thee." So God gave Satan the freedom to do with Job's possessions as he saw fit.

In one day, Job went from being a very wealthy man to becoming as poor as a beggar. Satan had taken everything away, even Job's children, whom he loved so dearly. Job had only his wife and his health left. But He still had God, which meant everything to him in this life. Is God everything for you, or are you only attached to your daily things?

What Satan expected to happen did not happen. Instead of cursing God, Job praised Him. When you read today's text again, can you understand how Job was able to praise God despite what happened to him? It was possible because God's love is stronger than the hatred of Satan.

Does Satan trouble you at times? What does the Lord promise to do when Satan tempts us?

Job — Job 2:1–13

Job Looks Unto His God

What? Shall we receive good at the hand of God, and shall we not receive evil? In all this did not Job sin with his lips.

— Job 2:10b

Job continued to serve God, but Satan would not leave him alone. "When Job loses his health, he will curse Thee," he said to God. God had told Satan he could do whatever he wanted with Job's circumstances, but he couldn't touch Job's health or life. Immediately, Satan grabbed this opportunity to blame something else; this is what he likes best, destroying and spoiling everything. He also wants you to be lost forever!

The Lord gave Satan permission to afflict Job's health as long as he did not kill him. Big boils now covered Job's body and, as he sat on a pile of rubbish scratching his sores, Satan shot his last arrow from his devilish quiver. Now even Job's wife sided with Satan, and said to Job, "Are you still the pious Job? Curse God and end your life."

Satan thought he would find Job's weak spots by giving him painful boils and by turning his wife against him. Still Job did not curse God, but instead told his wife, "Shall we receive good from the Lord and not receive evil?" Job did not sin! This was a miracle of God's grace.

It is important to know the weak spots in our lives—the areas where we are most tempted to sin against God. Think about what yours are, and ask the Lord to give you the grace needed to fight against temptations in those areas.

Job — Job 6:1–10

Job Does Not Listen to His Friends

*The things that my soul refused to touch are as my
sorrowful meat.*
— Job 6:7

Have you ever tried to comfort a friend who was very sad?
This can be quite difficult. Sometimes we say the wrong words
and make things worse. That is what happened with Job's
friends. "God punishes sin," they said to Job. "It is your own
fault that you are suffering." The friends were not helping
Job feel better or helping him better understand the Lord's
work in his life.

Job did not understand why God punished him so
severely, for he served the Lord with his whole heart. He did
not find his friends' words comforting; in fact, he compared
their words to bland food. Egg whites are tasteless if no salt
has been sprinkled on them; you wouldn't want to eat them.
The words of Job's friends were as dull as egg whites to Job.

Job did not want to "eat" the words of his friends. He was
learning that it is better to trust in the Lord than to trust in
people.

*Are you trusting people instead of God in any part
of your life?*

Job — Job 6:22–30

Job Asks His Friends
for True Words

How forcible are right words!
— Job 6:25

Job was disappointed in his friends. You would expect your friends to help you. When you are upset, you want your friends to be understanding and speak comforting words!

This is why Job was complaining—his friends accused him without listening to him. If Job's friends had spoken the truth, their words would have been comforting and strengthening for Job. Sadly, they were not. Instead, they accused Job of sinning; they said that all of this trouble would not have happened if he had not sinned.

Do you quickly form an opinion about others? We usually are, but how often do we know enough about others to have a true opinion? Remember, God had said that no one was as pious as Job was; that was why Satan attacked him. If Job's friends had known this, their advice to Job would have been much different and much more helpful.

Job asked his friends to stop accusing him. We should not be quick to accuse someone who is in distress; we should be gentle, loving, and helpful. This is a wise lesson to learn.

Imagine how you feel when you are being falsely accused.
How do you react to such accusations?

Job — Job 42:1–6

Job Prays to God for Himself

Hear, I beseech thee, and I will speak.
— Job 42:4

At the beginning of his suffering, "Job did not sin with his lips," says the Bible. Sadly, Job did not stay free from sin. Later on, he said wrong things about the Lord. This was very wrong of him, but Job's faults are not recorded in the Bible. Why do you think God did not include them here? Perhaps it is so that we wouldn't look down on Job. Remember, when you point your finger at someone else, three fingers are pointing at yourself. You probably have not had to suffer as much Job did, but do you agree with what God is doing in your life, or are you quick to complain?

Job became very sorry about the harsh words he had spoken to God. He admitted that it was terrible that he had rebelled against God's dealings.

Job began talking in a different way. The work "speak" in the text of today's meditation really means "pray." Job prayed to God to teach him how to submit to God's will without complaining. The Lord can also teach you, through His Word and Spirit, to listen to Him. That is why we must read our Bibles and pray every day!

Why should we never complain?

Job — Job 42:7–17

Job Prays to God in Behalf of His Friends

And the LORD turned the captivity of Job, when he prayed for his friends: also the LORD gave Job twice as much as he had before.
— Job 42:10

A large part of the book of Job is about the conversation between Job and his friends. The conversations were not uplifting as you would expect from friends. Instead, Job and his friends tried to convince each other that they were right. But God had the last word, as He always does. God reprimanded Job's friends for their foolish words about Him. He commanded Job's friends to ask Job to offer a burnt offering for them and to pray in their behalf.

Thus, while Job was still suffering, he prayed for his unfaithful friends. Can you think of someone else in the Bible who did this? The Lord Jesus. He even prayed for His enemies who nailed Him to the cross! You and I are just like those enemies, and yet we are still invited by the Lord, if we honestly confess our sins and listen to His voice. He will give everything we need and all will be well. Just look at the life of Job! He became twice as wealthy as he was before his suffering. He had seven more sons and three more daughters. How good the Lord is!

Do you pray for people who are unkind to you?

Isaiah — Isaiah 6:1–13

God Calls

Go, and tell this people.
—Isaiah 6:9

"Come downstairs!" Have you heard that before? It's usually your mom or dad calling you. Do you respond immediately? When it's your birthday and they call you, you come quickly. But when they call you for supper and you are in the middle of a game, calling once is usually not enough.

Today, God is calling you. God does not always call us to the easiest tasks. Isaiah saw God in a vision, and what happened? Isaiah was afraid. He saw the angels covering their faces. They could not look God straight in the face, even though they were sinless creatures. Isaiah was a sinner; surely he would have to die now that He had seen the Lord! But instead, God called Isaiah and gave him instructions. He was told to tell the people that the Messiah was coming. This was a very special task but also difficult because Isaiah knew that many would not listen to him.

What is God calling you to do today?

Isaiah — Isaiah 7:1–14

Immanuel Is Coming

…and shall call his name Immanuel.
— Isaiah 7:14

Children often recite Bible verses. Did you ever have to say this Bible verse yourself? Even if you haven't, you may have heard other people recite these famous words.

The wicked King Ahaz turned his back on God, but now he was afraid. He knew that a big army was coming, and they were much stronger than his own army. He knew he would lose the battle. Just then, Isaiah came to him and said, "King, do not be afraid, for your enemies will not defeat you. Ask for a sign from God to show you that what I'm saying is true." But the king didn't want to ask the Lord anything; he didn't believe in God.

The Lord was very kind to this king. He didn't leave Ahaz alone and let him take care of himself since he didn't want to hear the Lord anyway. In fact, He did the opposite: He gave a sign and prophecy about a virgin who would become pregnant.

Hundreds of years later, this prophecy was fulfilled when Mary gave birth to a baby and called His name Jesus. Jesus was the Immanuel mentioned in this verse of Isaiah. Immanuel means "God with us," for the Lord Himself came to live among us. He came to carry your sins and give you a new life. When that happens, then He lives in your heart.

How do you know if the Lord is with you?

Isaiah — Isaiah 9:1–6

The Names of the Lord Jesus

The Prince of Peace.
— Isaiah 9:6

Isaiah had already heard from the Holy Spirit what the names of the Lord Jesus would be. Some of Jesus' names were known for a long time; every time the people of God heard those names, they were comforted by them. We can also be comforted by the names of the Lord Jesus. Some of those names mentioned here in Isaiah are Wonderful, Counsellor, the mighty God, the everlasting Father, and the Prince of Peace.

These names comfort us because they remind us that we should never be afraid when the Lord is with us. It doesn't matter what happens in your life; even in the worst experiences, the Lord is there. He is strong, He is God, and He gives peace. He wants to take care of you like a father does. He wants you to become His child. You can read about that throughout the Bible. That is why He came into this world.

Which name of the Lord Jesus do you think is most beautiful? Why?

Isaiah — Isaiah 11:1–9

The Kingdom Will Come

And the spirit of the LORD shall rest upon him.
— Isaiah 11:2

Have you ever been to the zoo? If you have, you probably felt quite small when you were looking at the lions in their cages, only separated from you by some bars. Or what about the snakes? When you look at them, they seem quiet and slow, but watch out! They are very dangerous. It is hard to imagine that one day we won't have to be afraid of these wild animals anymore.

Although it is hard to imagine, that was exactly what the Lord was showing Isaiah. Picture it: a little boy will walk alongside a lion, and a baby will play close to the hideout of a snake. How is that possible? It is possible only in the new heaven and the new earth, because God will make everything perfect again.

But this peaceful picture is not the most important element in the new heaven and the new earth. The most beautiful thing will be the presence of the Lord Jesus Christ. With Him, there will be peace forever. The Lord Jesus purchased this peace for everyone who belongs to Him, and everyone who loves and knows the Lord will be happy. Nobody there will ever be sad and no pain will exist. Do you wish that everything would be made new again? Pray to the Lord that He would work in your heart so that you can enjoy this heaven Isaiah talks about.

What are some more differences between our world and God's kingdom that will come?

Isaiah — Isaiah 32:1–8

Christ Will Reign

And a man shall be as an hiding place from the wind, and a covert from the tempest; as rivers of water in a dry place.
— Isaiah 32:2

Imagine going for a walk with your parents on a sunny afternoon. Your brothers and sisters are with you, too. You walk for a while. The walk ends up being much longer than you originally anticipated, and you get tired. You wish you were back home. Besides being tired, the weather is changing and raindrops are about to fall. The wind comes and the rain makes you cold and wet. Imagine how happy you would be when you see your house in the distance, knowing you will be in your own home soon, warm and dry.

That is how Isaiah looked forward to the day that God's heavenly kingdom would become a reality. There would be justice and peace; blind people would be able to see. During Isaiah's lifetime, most people had turned their backs on the Lord and injustice was everywhere. But to these people Isaiah prophesied about a King, Jesus Christ, who would reign justly in His new kingdom.

Our world today is much like Isaiah's; many people don't want to have anything to do with God. How wonderful it is for God's people to know we have a refuge with Christ, for His kingdom will surely come. What a wonderful future!

Do you look for refuge with the Lord? When do you long for refuge most?

Isaiah — Isaiah 40:1–11

The Prophecy of the Coming of John

The voice of him that crieth in the wilderness....
— Isaiah 40:3

If your parents promise to buy you new skates in six months, you trust them. You might even look in some catalogs to see which ones you would like. Even though it is going to be a long time before you get them, you know that your parents will eventually buy them. They promised you, so you trust them.

Compared to our promises, the Lord's promises are much surer. Look at what Isaiah tells us: "The Lord promises that one day someone will be born who will tell the people that the Messiah is coming. He will call himself 'the one crying in the wilderness.'" Isaiah is talking about John the Baptist.

"Make straight in the desert a highway for our God." Isaiah and John the Baptist both said this. What does this mean? For the Lord to be able to live in your heart, everything between you and the Lord has to be smooth and clean, just like a straight road. There cannot be potholes and the dirt of sin in your life. Your life has to be cleaned up. When you earnestly pray to the Lord, He will clean your heart and make the road of your heart straight and smooth.

What has to change in order for the Lord to live in your heart?

Isaiah — Isaiah 53:1–12

The Chastisement of Our Peace Was Upon Him

Yet he opened not his mouth.
— Isaiah 53:7

Imagine you are playing a game of soccer during recess. You know you aren't allowed to play soccer so close to the school building, but you do it anyway. You give that soccer ball a good kick and, to your surprise, the ball ends up hitting the school window. A huge crack is visible. The teacher on duty comes running over and tells you that you will have to pay for it. Pay for a window? How will you get that much money together? In the end, your dad pays for it, but he also punishes you for it. That is fair, since it was your fault.

Paying for a window may require a lot money, but paying for your life is impossible. Life is priceless. In this chapter, we read about God the Father, who made His Son pay for the sins of many other people. God has to punish sin, but we cannot pay for sin ourselves. So Jesus Christ pays for it, even though He Himself never sinned and is not guilty. Do you know the price Jesus paid? He paid with His own life, after a lot of suffering. He died in order to take our place and receive the punishment that was meant for us. Instead of punishment, God offers us His peace. What a miracle that is!

What do you think "the peace of God" means?

Jeremiah — Jeremiah 1:1–10

Don't Be Afraid!

Behold, I have put my words in thy mouth.
— Jeremiah 1:9

In many countries around the world, people are beaten and mocked simply because they belong to a certain group of people. You can imagine how these people are often afraid, especially if they live in a country where there is war.

The Lord called Jeremiah to tell the Israelites that war was coming. He had to call the people to repentance. Jeremiah dreaded bringing this message because he knew the people wouldn't like to hear it. He brought up all sorts of excuses to the Lord. "I cannot do it, Lord; I am far too young. Besides, I do not even dare to speak in front of so many people."

But the Lord, who knows everyone thoroughly, told Jeremiah, "Don't be afraid! I will help you and tell you what to say." When the Lord is with you, there is no reason at all to be afraid, no matter what you have to do or what happens. Even today, the Lord tells you, "Don't be afraid, for I am with you."

Why is it comforting to know that the Lord is with us?

Jeremiah — Jeremiah 1:11–19

God's Warning

For I will hasten my word to perform it.
                                        — Jeremiah 1:12

When you speak out of turn in the classroom, your teacher will warn you that, if you continue, there will be consequences. You know that if you ignore this warning, punishment will follow. Jeremiah brought a warning from God to the people just as a teacher to students. To make it clear to everyone what God's warning meant, Jeremiah gave two examples.

First, Jeremiah used the example of a flowering rod of an almond tree. Just like this rod shows that spring is beginning, so God's punishment will come if you don't repent and turn from your sins.

The second example showed the people how terrible the punishment would be and where this punishment would come from. It would be like a pan with boiling water falling on you. Boiling water would be terribly painful, wouldn't it? You would have awful burns on your body. Jeremiah explained to the people that God's punishment of sin would be like that.

The Lord is still hurt when you sin against Him, even today. God is warning you, too. Listen to Him, for the punishment will be terrible if you don't repent.

How do you know what sin is?

Jeremiah — Jeremiah 3:17–25

Losing a Friend

For thou art the LORD our God.
— Jeremiah 3:22

Having a best friend means you have someone you can trust. Imagine if your best friend ignored you and found someone else to be friends with. You would feel betrayed and sad, especially when you saw that your friend didn't even miss you.

That is the way the Lord looks at His people. It is as if the Lord had married His people, explains Jeremiah. You only marry someone you would like to share the rest of your life with. The Lord wanted His people to belong to Him forever, but they turned their backs to Him. They disobeyed the Lord by serving idols instead. Disobedience to God is not just something from the past, it still happens today. We do it every day! But, amazingly, the Lord invites us to come back to Him anytime. The Lord is waiting with open arms for you to return to Him, just like the father in the story of the prodigal son.

Do you see similarities between yourself and the prodigal son?

Jeremiah — Jeremiah 20:7–18

Jeremiah Prays

Thou art stronger than I.
— Jeremiah 20:7

Many boys like wrestling with their friends or with their dad. Maybe you are one of them. Of course, you want to be the strongest one. We are like that a lot of times—we like to be the strongest, the smartest, the best.

Today you read how Jeremiah prayed. He was confused, scared, and angry. Because he was prophesying the words of the Lord, he was captured by a priest. This is what he prayed: "Lord, Thou hast been too strong for me; I surrender. But the people are mocking me. They laugh in my face. But, what is worse, they mock Thee, too, O Lord."

Jeremiah's prayer suddenly changed when he realized what he was saying. He suddenly realized that, even though he was in prison, the Lord was with him! Jeremiah and the Lord Jesus both experienced the mockery of people around them; they were both attacked and scorned. But the Lord Jesus endured even more than Jeremiah; He died on the cross in order to pay for our sins and give us life.

Why is it so terrible to mock God?

Jeremiah — Jeremiah 36:27–32

Jeremiah's Book

And write in it all the former words that were in the first roll.
— Jeremiah 36:28

When you think of opposites, you might think of darkness and light. Love and hate are opposites, just like the Lord Jesus and the devil are. The Bible tells us about people who sin, and how the Lord Jesus shows them His love—these are opposites. The devil is always busy destroying the work of God, but the Lord is always there to make all things right again. The devil tries to spread as much darkness as possible in this world, but the Lord brings light again. The Lord uses His Word to bring light in the lives of His people again, for His Word endures forever.

Today you read how the Bible came into existence. Through His Holy Spirit, the Lord told people like Jeremiah what they had to write down. Jeremiah told God's exact words to Baruch, who in turn wrote it all down. They had to write it down to make sure they wouldn't forget any of the words of the Lord. Because of the work these men did long ago, we are able to read the Bible and be close to the Lord. The Lord comes to us to offer His light through His Word.

Why is it so important to read your Bible every day?

Jeremiah — Jeremiah 38:1–13

Rescued From the Dungeon

So they drew up Jeremiah with cords, and took him up out of the dungeon. — Jeremiah 38:13

Have you ever been locked up somewhere and you couldn't get out? Perhaps you were very scared. Jeremiah went through something far worse than that. He delivered another message from the Lord: "Surrender to your enemies, which is the only way you will live. The Lord has promised that you will survive if you listen, but you will die if you don't." The kings were so mad about Jeremiah's message, they wanted to kill him! They reasoned that all the people in the land would lose courage if they heard Jeremiah. The kings came up with a mean plan. They lowered Jeremiah into a deep, muddy dungeon. Would Jeremiah die there?

No, he did not die there. God helped him just like He had helped David, who wrote in Psalm 40: "He brought me up also out of an horrible pit, out of the miry clay." God used an Ethiopian man to rescue Jeremiah out of his dungeon.

Through this story, the Lord is telling you that He wants to save you just like He saved Jeremiah. He wants to take care of you.

How did the Lord take care of you today?

Jeremiah — Jeremiah 39:11–18

God's Word is Truth

But I will deliver thee in that day.
                                        — Jeremiah 39:17

Do you know of any of God's promises that haven't been fulfilled yet? The most important one is the promise of Jesus' return. He will come on the clouds of heaven, and it will be clear who belongs to Him and who does not. Do you believe this promise?

In today's story, you are reminded that the Lord's Word is always true. Jerusalem was taken by the enemies, just like Jeremiah had prophesied. The kings who had wanted to kill Jeremiah were dead, and King Zedekiah was captured. However, the entire chapter is not all sad; there is a message near the end for us. You can read that message in verse 18: "For I will surely deliver thee…because thou hast put thy trust in me, saith the Lord." To trust God is the most important lesson every person has to learn in this life. God's promise is that, if we trust Him, He will deliver us. This promise is true for everyone who trusts Him—we will go to heaven with Him when Jesus returns on the clouds. This prophecy will be fulfilled because the Lord has promised it.

Are you ready to meet the Lord Jesus when He returns?

Daniel — Daniel 1:1–21

Daniel Obeyed God

But Daniel purposed in his heart that he would not defile himself with the portion of the king's meat, nor with the wine which he drank.
— Daniel 1:8a

The nation of Judah had not obeyed God, and God was very angry with them. The Lord sent them away into captivity in a faraway, foreign land. Daniel was one of the first to be sent away, along with other young men. He lived in the court of Babylon. He and the other young men would be educated by the king of Babylon and therefore had to obey his law. That included the food they ate and the wine they drank. A wonderful future awaited these young men. All they had to do was eat, drink, and be merry.

That's what we all would like to do, too, wouldn't we? It would be so easy to just go along with the royal lifestyle. But that was not true of Daniel. He wanted to keep the laws of the Lord about what foods were allowed to be eaten. It was forbidden to eat certain foods. Wine was not completely forbidden, but Daniel knew that too much drinking was going on at the court, so he did not drink any. Daniel obeyed the Lord no matter what would happen.

The name Daniel means "God is my Judge" and that is exactly how Daniel wanted to live. God was his Judge, not the king or anyone else. God's will was the deciding factor in Daniel's life.

Do you dare to say no when asked to do something against God's will?

Daniel — Daniel 2:1–18

Daniel Trusts In God

That they would desire mercies of the God of heaven concerning this secret; that Daniel and his fellows should not perish with the rest of the wise men of Babylon.
— Daniel 2:18

The king of Babylon had a dream—a very unsettling dream. He could not even remember his dream anymore, but his magicians, astrologers, or sorcerers should be able to tell him his dream, right? But the king was mistaken, for they could not help him. They had not received their wisdom from God. Nebuchadnezzar was furious at his wise men and wanted to kill them all, including Daniel. What should Daniel do, hide or try to escape? Actually, he did the opposite. He went to the king and told him that he would interpret the dream, if he was given some time, because his God was almighty.

How could Daniel be so sure? He trusted in the great King of heaven and believed that He would help him. Daniel went to his friends and told them everything. And what did they do? They prayed together to God. Daniel knew that God alone could reveal the dream. How blessed we are when this God is our King!

Do you believe that the Lord will give you what you ask of Him?

Daniel — Daniel 2:19–49

The Kingdom of God

And in the days of these kings shall the God of heaven set up a kingdom, which shall never be destroyed.
— Daniel 2:44a

Daniel's prayer was heard by God; God revealed the king's dream to him. Daniel thanked and praised God for His answer. Do not forget to thank the Lord when He answers your prayers. Daniel knew that he was not wiser than the other wise men in the kingdom. When he told Nebuchadnezzar his dream, he also told him that the Lord had helped him.

The king had dreamed about a great statue made of gold, silver, brass, iron, and clay. This stood for the mighty kingdom of Nebuchadnezzar. After his kingdom, lesser kingdoms would rule. Then a big stone would fall on the statue and destroy it. This was the kingdom of Christ. All the kingdoms of this earth would pass away, but Christ's kingdom would remain forever. Jesus Christ is the almighty King who would come down to die for sinful people. How wonderful to be a citizen of this kingdom!

Is Jesus Christ your King or do you rule your own life?

Daniel — Daniel 3:1–30

Bow Before God Alone

These men, O king, have not regarded thee; they serve not thy gods, nor worship the golden image which thou hast set up.
— Daniel 3:12b

Nebuchadnezzar had made a large image and commanded everyone to bow down before it. If someone did not obey, they would be thrown into the fiery furnace. "When the music plays, you have to bow before the image," instructed the voice of the messenger throughout the valley of Dura. The music began and everyone bowed down—except for three men. They were Shadrach, Meshach, and Abednigo, the friends of Daniel. They would not bow down to this idol because they served the true God. They were taken before the king. Their God, they told Nebuchadnezzar, would deliver them from the fiery furnace.

They were then thrown into the fire, but it was not a terrible experience for them. The Lord made it so that the fire did not burn them or their clothes. They came out of it without any pain or scars.

Maybe your computer or toys are more important to you than serving God. If that is true, then they have become your idols. Worshipping idols is against God's commands, and people who do not repent are thrown into hell. However, the Lord wants to deliver you as He delivered the three friends of Daniel. He asks only that you bow before Him and trust in Him alone for salvation.

Can people see that you love the Lord? Are you willing to obey Him no matter what the cost may be?

Daniel — Daniel 4:29–37

God is Almighty

And all the inhabitants of the earth are reputed as nothing:
and he doeth according to his will in the army of heaven,
and among the inhabitants of the earth: and none can
stay his hand, or say unto him, What doest thou?
                                                    — Daniel 4:35

Today's text was spoken by Nebuchadnezzar, who still did
not serve God after everything that had happened to him.
Yet God worked again in his life and made him able to speak
those words and to confess that God was almighty.

Seven years ago, Nebuchadnezzar was walking on the roof
of his palace. As he looked around at his kingdom, he became
very proud. "Everyone should honor me," he thought. This
made the Lord very angry; we must not be proud and think
we have done anything good without His aid. God punished
the king so that he had to live like an animal. He had to live
in the fields and eat grass like the cows. His hair became like
the feathers of an eagle and his nails looked like the claws of
a bird of prey.

After seven years, the Lord restored his mind. Nebuchadnezzar had to admit that only God ruled; he could not
deny it. The Lord has His own way and always has the final
word. Do you think you are important? The Lord hates proud
and high-minded people.

Do you feel pride after receiving good grades in school?
What is the best attitude to have when something good
like that happens to us?

247

Daniel — Daniel 5:1–30

God Speaks at the Banquet

*And the God in whose hand thy breath is, and whose are
all thy ways, hast thou not glorified.*
— Daniel 5:23b

Nebuchadnezzar had died and now his grandson, Belshazzar,
sat on the throne. He knew what had happened to his
grandfather, but he did not take it to heart. On the contrary,
he ridiculed the Lord.

Belshazzar was having a banquet and serving wine in the
holy vessels that were stolen from God's temple. His wives
and prominent servants worshipped the idols made of metal,
wood, and stone. It was a wild party—until God made it
known to Belshazzar that an end had come.

A hand suddenly appeared on the wall, writing something. Nobody could explain to the king what the words
meant. Daniel was summoned to explain the words to the
king. Daniel was honest with the king and first reprimanded
him for his ungodly lifestyle. Belshazzar did not love the
Lord God and had only lived for his own pleasures. Daniel
proclaimed the Word of God at this heathen banquet. Do not
be afraid to side with God's Word wherever you are. That is
always the right side to be on.

Do you warn others when they ridicule the Lord?

248

Daniel — Daniel 6:1–29

Daniel Prays to God

Then these men assembled, and found Daniel praying and making supplication before his God.
— Daniel 6:11

Daniel prayed to the Lord his God every day. Even when the king commanded that only he should be honored for thirty days, Daniel prayed on. He could not obey that law; praying was as important to him as breathing, which we know we need to do in order to live. So Daniel knelt down three times a day before an open window.

The princes and governors watched Daniel with glee. They had gone to his house to catch him in the act of disobedience, and they had seen him kneeling and praying as he had always done. Daniel had not obeyed the king's command, but rather he obeyed his Lord.

Was Daniel devoured by the lions? No, for the Lord is victorious and protected him all night long in the lions' den. God wants to protect you today from the lion called Satan. Satan goes around roaring, seeking to devour you. Seek God's help every day to fight against Satan and his tricks.

How did Satan tempt you today? Pray to the Lord about it before you sleep tonight.

Amos — Amos 1:1

The Shepherd Amos Keeps His Sheep

The words of Amos, who was among the herdmen of Tekoa.
— Amos 1:1a

Have you ever heard of Amos the shepherd? In the coming days we hope to study the words he spoke long ago. The Bible doesn't tell us much about Amos. We only know that he was a shepherd and that he was from Tekoa. The city of Tekoa was in Judah, not far from Jerusalem and Bethlehem.

The Lord didn't want us to know any other details of Amos's life, except for the message he had to deliver from God to the Israelites. Maybe it seems strange to you that the Lord chose this simple shepherd. You might think that other candidates were more suitable for this task. But the Lord chose Amos. The more you know about the Bible, the more you realize that God is not looking for important people to serve Him, but for people who love God and for whom He is the most important thing in their lives. These types of people do not depend on their own abilities, but ask God for strength. They know they are helpless without God.

Are you fine by yourself in life, or do you need God?

Amos — Amos 1:2–8

The Lord Roars

And he said, The LORD will roar from Zion, and utter his voice from Jerusalem.
                                                    — Amos 1:2a

Today's verse may surprise you a little. Maybe you wonder why it says that the Lord will roar. Amos must have thought of the roaring of a lion. When you hear the roar of a lion in the wilderness, it's frightening. But just as lions roar a warning, so the Lord warns us.

Do you know why the Lord warns us? We depart from the ways of the Lord so often, and His warning is meant to keep us from sin. Sometimes it is necessary for God to roar; He does not roar to scare us, but because He loves us. That is how He tries to bring us to repentance. He doesn't want us to be lost without Him forever.

Do you know how the Lord roars today? Do you know how to recognize His warnings? Think about how someone you know becomes very sick, or how someone has a terrible car accident. The Lord warns us in many different ways. Accidents and sickness are just some of God's many warnings to us. The Lord also roars in the Bible, when He warns us that, if we do not turn to Him from our sins, we will not be allowed to live with Him in heaven.

Have you ever received a personal warning from the Lord?

Amos — Amos 3:1–8

Walking Together

Can two walk together, except they be agreed?
                                        — Amos 3:3

Sometimes it is nice to go for a walk when you want to have a good talk with someone. If you decide to go for a walk you don't do so with a stranger, but with someone you know quite well. That way you can talk and enjoy the outdoors together. If you don't have a good relationship with someone, you cannot go for a walk with him. Today's verse tells us about this.

This verse is a picture of the people of Israel and the Lord. The people of Israel left the Lord through their sins, so they were not walking together anymore. There was a separation between the Lord and His people. The Lord wanted them to return to Him and to walk with Him so He could show them the way. The only way these people would be able to return was to obey His commandments again.

Do you know what it is like to be at odds with the Lord? When you feel that way, what should you do?

Amos — Amos 5:4–6

To Seek the Lord

For thus saith the LORD unto the house of Israel, Seek ye me, and ye shall live.
— Amos 5:4

I'm sure all of you can remember looking for something. Maybe you were searching for something you lost. If it was something very valuable, you would look high and low and you wouldn't give up until you found it, would you?

Today you read about how Israel also lost something— the Lord. The Lord told them that they had lost Him. When we are born, we are already sinners who don't know where to find the Lord. The Lord says, "Seek ye me, and ye shall live." You cannot live without the Lord; you have to keep searching until you find Him. But maybe you wonder, "Where can I find Him, where do I search for Him?" You can find Him by reading in His Word. Search the Scriptures often and ask the Lord to show you Himself through what you read in the Bible.

Have you searched for the Lord and have you found Him?

Amos — Amos 5:14–17

Good or Evil?

Seek good, and not evil, that ye may live.
— Amos 5:14a

Yesterday you read that we are called to search for God. When you search for God, you will be encouraged to search for what is good and to leave behind what is evil.

Do you seek what is good? Maybe you wonder, "What is good? How do I search for it?" When you love the Lord, you start looking for opportunities to find what is good, instead of just looking for things that are appealing and attractive to you. You find yourself asking what the Lord wants you to do. The Bible tells that we must love the Lord above all and our neighbors as ourselves. So now we know what is good.

Not only will you search for what is good for yourself, but also for the people you know—your friends at school and also the boy or girl in your class you don't like very much. You will look for the best for those who have no friends simply because other people think they are a bit different.

You cannot do this in your own strength; it is not just difficult to do, but impossible without the help of the Holy Spirit. The Lord is willing to give us His Spirit when we ask Him, for we will only do good in His strength.

Do you ask for God's Spirit to guide you to do that which is good?

Amos — Amos 9:1–6

Hidden from God?

Though they dig into hell, thence shall mine hand take them; though they climb up to heaven, thence will I bring them down.
— Amos 9:2

Even after God did so much to bring the children of Israel back to Him, they continued in their disobedient and sinful ways. Punishment would come, for they refused to listen to His voice. The people of Israel would try to get away from getting punished, but the Lord said that, wherever they hid, He would find them.

There is no place in this world where the Lord cannot find us. The Lord used the example of digging into hell or climbing up into heaven, although this is not really possible, of course. This warning was not only meant for the Israelites but also for us, for if we do not listen to His voice and if we continue to go our own way, the Lord will punish us, too. When we die after living our life without serving the Lord, we will be terribly punished. We will be forever without the Lord.

Do you believe that God will punish you if you do not listen to Him?

Amos — Amos 9:11–15

The Promise of Christ's Birth

In that day will I raise up the tabernacle of David that is fallen, and close up the breaches thereof; and I will raise up his ruins, and I will build it as in the days of old.
— Amos 9:11

How incredibly good God is! Yesterday we read about the punishment Israel would receive. Today the Lord comes with a promise to restore the tabernacle of David. The Lord takes care that His promise will be fulfilled. He promised David that his house would stand forever and that his kingdom would be an eternal kingdom. One of David's descendants would be the eternal King.

You must have guessed by now that this king is the Lord Jesus Christ. From this part of Scripture, we are given hints about Christmas. Through the Lord Jesus Christ, salvation is possible for the nation of Israel and for us. The Lord is shining a bright light in the dark world of sin. Satan and sin will not triumph, but the child in the manger will. Glory be to God!

God is good to His people of every generation. Think about how good He was to you today and thank Him for it.

Jonah — Jonah 1:1–3

Jonah's Flight

*But Jonah rose up to flee unto Tarshish from the presence
of the LORD.*   — Jonah 1:3a

The Lord had called Jonah to go to the big city of Nineveh. He
had to tell the Ninevites that, if they continued in their sins,
the Lord would punish them. Jonah, however, fled because
he did not want to go to Nineveh! He disobeyed God. He
thought that this mission was too difficult for him. Do you
find it hard to obey what the Lord tells you to do?

Jonah was afraid that the Lord would spare the city if they
listened to him. He knew the Lord was merciful and would
gladly forgive the people's sins. The Ninevites would laugh
at God and Jonah when they realized that none of His threats
actually happened. Jonah did not trust the Lord and did not
want the heathens to mock God or himself. But Jonah should
have known that God would look after His own honor.

So Jonah fled in a ship to Tarshish and thought that his
encounter with God was over. But God knew Jonah's thoughts,
just as He knows everyone's thoughts, including yours!

*Would you like to tell people outside your church about
God or would you be afraid?*

Jonah — Jonah 1:4–10

Jonah is at Fault

And they said everyone to his fellow, Come, and let us cast lots, that we may know for whose cause this evil is upon us. So they cast lots, and the lot fell upon Jonah.
— Jonah 1:7

The Lord sees everything and everyone, no matter where they go. He saw how His disobedient servant Jonah tried to flee. But God called him back! The Lord sent a storm that tossed Jonah's ship on the waves, rolling it to and fro. The sailors screamed and were terribly frightened. They prayed to their gods and threw barrels of goods overboard to lighten the ship. Meanwhile, Jonah was fast asleep, unaware of the storm raging around them. The captain woke him up and asked if he would pray to his God. Lots were cast, and God directed the lot to fall on Jonah, showing that he was the cause of the storm.

You and I are also disobedient to God and turn away from Him. But He knows what you do and think and will show you that sin is why bad things happen in your life. Does this make you angry? Jonah not only told the sailors that he was fleeing from the Lord, but that he also feared the Lord. I hope that you will do the same thing.

Have you honestly confessed the sins you have committed today to the Lord?

258

Jonah — Jonah 1:11–17

Jonah's Punishment

Now the LORD had prepared a great fish to swallow up Jonah. And Jonah was in the belly of the fish three days and three nights.
— Jonah 1:17

The sea was tumultuous, thunder crashed, and lightning lit up the ship. The terror-stricken sailors shouted at Jonah and asked what they should do with him. Jonah told them to throw him overboard into the sea, but the sailors wanted to spare his life. They tried to row to shore, but without success. Finally, they gave in; they knew they had to throw Jonah overboard. As soon as they did, the sea became calm.

But what happened to Jonah? The Lord, who rules and reigns over everything, sent a great fish that swallowed Jonah. He was in the belly of the fish for three days and three nights. Wasn't this a great miracle? Jonah knew that it was his own fault and that God was punishing him for his sins.

Do you know who went into the "belly" of the earth for three days? The Lord Jesus, who had no sin; He was buried in the grave for disobedient and stubborn people like Jonah. Through Him alone there is hope for sinful people and for you, too!

Why was it merciful for God to send the big fish?

Jonah — Jonah 2:1–10

Jonah's Prayer

Then I said, I am cast out of thy sight; yet I will look again toward thy holy temple.
— Jonah 2:4

Jonah was afraid, for it was very dark in the belly of the fish that had swallowed him. You would think that Jonah would despair, but he knew who to turn to. He had hope in a hopeless situation. But what could you hope for after being swallowed by a great big fish? Jonah turned back to God, from whom he had run away. Deep in the sea, he prayed to God. He told the Lord how frightened he was, but also that he believed and trusted in Him.

Are you afraid sometimes? You might think that the Lord cannot see you or help you. But when you turn to the Lord, as Jonah did, He will help you. He rescued Jonah, for He spoke to the fish and the fish spit Jonah onto the dry ground.

He helps the needy when they cry;
He saves their souls when death draws nigh;
This God is our salvation.

What do you trust in when everything is going wrong?

Jonah — Jonah 3:1–5

Jonah's Sermon

So the people of Nineveh believed God, and proclaimed a fast, and put on sackcloth, from the greatest of them even to the least of them.
— Jonah 3:5

Jonah was commanded again by God to go to Nineveh. The Lord told Jonah what to tell the people of that great city. This time, Jonah obeyed. As he went through the city, he realized how large it was. It took him three days to walk through the city, preaching as he traveled. The message he preached was clear: "In forty days, Nineveh will be overthrown." The people of Nineveh listened and believed that God would do that very thing. Old and young fasted and put on sackcloth as a sign of mourning.

This one sermon brought about great change in the Ninevites. How many sermons have you heard in church? How many Bible stories have you been told by your teachers and parents? Have you repented? If you don't know the Lord, then turn to Him! He will give you strength to hate evil and to do good.

Do you listen closely to the Bible stories at school and the sermons in church? If you have a hard time understanding them, ask God to help you. He is ready to help.

Jonah — Jonah 3:6–4:2

Jonah's Anger

For I knew that thou art a gracious God, and merciful, slow to anger, and of great kindness, and repentest thee of the evil.
— Jonah 4:2b

God saw that the king of Nineveh and his subjects turned from their evil ways. The king commanded all the people and animals to fast and cover themselves in sackcloth. They were to repent and earnestly call to God. "Who knows? Maybe God will hear us and save our city," they said to each other.

The Lord did spare the city, for He is a God who does good. The people of Nineveh deserved punishment, but God showed mercy to them. The Lord also takes care of you, while you do not deserve it either. Count your blessings and you will observe God's goodness.

Jonah saw God's goodness, but he was angry about it. "I knew that Thou wouldst spare the city," he told the Lord. Jonah should have been glad, don't you think? When children or adults around you turn to the Lord and start serving Him, would it make you happy? Or does it make no difference to you? Jonah's anger was sinful. Pray that the Lord will bless you and the people around you.

What do you notice in God's people around you? How are they different from people who do not know the Lord?

Jonah — Jonah 4:3–11

A Lesson for Jonah

Then said the LORD, Thou hast had pity on the gourd, for the which thou hast not laboured...and should not I spare Nineveh, that great city?
— Jonah 4:10a and 11a

Jonah left the city and was waiting, under a roof of branches to see what would happen to the city. God miraculously made a tree grow in one night! You would think that this is impossible, but with God everything is possible. The next day, Jonah was glad to sit in the shade of this tree.

But on the following day, the tree withered, for God had sent a worm. Now there was no shade for Jonah to sit in. He felt miserable as the hot sun burned on his head. He was ready to collapse and die.

Then Jonah became angry. Why did the Lord allow this to happen? God told him that he was angry because a tree had died while the city with many people should have perished instead. Jonah only thought about himself and did not consider the precious souls of all those people. But God did! The story of Jonah is very comforting. It teaches us that God does not desire the death of sinners, but rather that they should repent and live.

Do you worry about the souls of your neighbors or do you only think of yourself?

Mary — Luke 1:26–38

Mary Receives a Heavenly Visitor

And Mary said, Behold the handmaid of the LORD; be it unto me according to thy word.
                                                    — Luke 1:38a

Mary lived in the little town of Nazareth. She was a descendant of David, as was Joseph, her fiancé. Mary was an ordinary woman with nothing special about her. But one day, something very unusual happened. Gabriel, the angel of God, told Mary that she would become the mother of Jesus. He would be called the Son of God and would reign forever on the throne of David. Mary was so surprised when she heard the news. She, a simple young woman, would be the mother of the promised Messiah!

Mary told the angel that she was willing to be in the service of God. She looked forward to the fulfilling of God's promises.

When you expect a big present on your birthday, you look forward to that day. Mary longed for the day when her promised Child would be born because she knew that this Child would also be her Savior.

Do you long for the second coming of the Lord Jesus? Why or why not?

Mary — Luke 1:39–56

Mary's Song

And Mary said, My soul doth magnify the Lord.
— Luke 1:46

Mary had been walking for almost five days. She was now entering the hill country of Judea, where her cousin Elizabeth lived. She wanted to visit Elizabeth because the angel had told her that Elizabeth was also expecting a child. Elizabeth was so happy to see Mary. She wasn't the only one happy, for the child in her belly leaped for joy when Mary's voice was heard. Do you know who this child would be? This child would be John, the forerunner of Jesus, who would later baptize the people in Jesus' Name. John was filled with joy for his Savior while still in the womb.

Mary also was glad because of the baby in her womb. She was filled with the Lord's presence and could not stop talking about Him. She praised the Lord and sang a song about the great deeds of God, known as "The Song of Mary." The Lord would love to hear you praise Him, too, for that is the purpose of your life. When you love Him, His mercies will surround you. Mary sang about them.

Are you ever so happy with the Lord that you cannot stop talking about Him?

Mary — Matthew 1:18–25

Joseph Considers Leaving Mary

Now all this was done, that it might be fulfilled which was spoken of the Lord by the prophet.
— Matthew 1:22

Joseph heard from Mary that she was expecting a child. He did not understand this at all. They were not married, so how could they be expecting a child? The best thing for him to do was to leave Mary. He would not marry her after all. Then an angel appeared to him in a dream. The angel told him that Isaiah had prophesied long ago that Mary would receive a Son who would be the Savior. The angel explained to Joseph that the Holy Spirit had created the child in Mary's womb and therefore Joseph should stay with Mary.

The angel wonderfully explained to Joseph what was said in the Bible. You are blessed to have a Bible; in God's Word, you can find everything you need, even though you might not understand all of it. Whatever the Lord promises, He will do. You can see this in our text today. He also promises you, "Whoever will seek Me early will find Me." Seek the Lord and live!

Do you know other promises of the Lord in the Bible?

Mary — Luke 2:1–7

Mary Receives a Kingly Child

And she brought forth her firstborn son, and wrapped him in swaddling clothes, and laid him in a manger; because there was no room for them in the inn.

— Luke 2:7

Caesar Augustus wanted to count everyone in his kingdom. He wanted to know exactly how many people lived in his empire, and what possessions they had. Joseph and Mary also had to be numbered, so they left for Bethlehem. It was the town where their forefather David had lived and been born. When they arrived, they looked for a place to sleep. The town was so busy that there was no room for them to lodge except in an empty stable. Jesus was not born in a palace that night, but in a place where animals slept! You were laid in a beautiful crib after you were born and a warm blanket covered you. Do you know where Mary had to lay Jesus? She laid Him in a manger, a feedbox for animals, and wrapped Him in swaddling bands of cloth.

The Lord Jesus became so poor to make poor sinners like you rich. We are poor because of our sins. We think and do many wrong things and our hearts are as dirty as a stable for animals. This does not look appealing. Isn't it amazing that the Lord Jesus is willing to live in such a heart?

What wrong desires live in your heart today? Have you brought your filthy heart to Jesus to be cleansed by Him?

Mary — Luke 2:8–20

Mary's Celebration of Christ's Birth

But Mary kept all these things, and pondered them in her heart. — Luke 2:19

Who was in such a hurry that dark night, going to Bethlehem? They were shepherds, thinking about the wonderful news the angel had just told them. The Savior had been born! They found their newborn King in Bethlehem in the stable, wrapped in swaddling rags. It was exactly like the heavenly messenger had told them.

After the shepherds saw Jesus, they told anyone who would listen to them about what they had seen and heard. The people thought that it was such a strange story, they didn't believe it; they continued on with their life as if nothing had happened.

How many times have you heard the story of Jesus' birth? Quite a few times, I imagine. Maybe you think it is just a nice story. But remember how Mary kept the shepherds' words in her heart and reflected on them, thinking about what those words meant? Christ's birth was a real celebration for her and I hope that you will celebrate Christ's birth the same way.

What do you think is the most important part of Christ's birth?

Mary — Luke 2:21–24

Mary Brings the Offering of Purification

And to offer a sacrifice according to that which is said in the law of the Lord, A pair of turtledoves, or two young pigeons.
— Luke 2:24

After Jesus' birth, Mary and Joseph took their child to Jerusalem. They had to bring an offering of purification. In those days, women who had given birth to a son were considered unclean for forty days. After the offering, they would be clean again. Mary and Joseph offered two doves, which was an offering of the poor. Maybe it seems strange to you that an offering for purification had to be brought after Jesus' birth, even though He was clean and sinless. It was necessary because Mary, His mother, was unclean.

Do you know that you are also unclean? This does not mean that you are dirty on the outside, but that you have a filthy and sinful heart. Your heart cannot be washed with water; only the blood of Jesus can cleanse it. He was born to offer Himself so that you could become clean.

Did your heart get dirty today because of the wrong things you did?

Mary — Luke 2:25–38

Simeon Talks to Mary

And Simeon blessed them, and said unto Mary his mother, Behold this child is set for the fall and rising again of many in Israel; and for a sign which shall be spoken against.
— Luke 2:34

Simeon was an old man who feared the Lord. One day, he felt that he should go to the temple. The Holy Spirit urged him to go and when he arrived there he saw Jesus! He was so glad that he could take the Savior in his arms. God had promised Simeon that he would see the Messiah before he died. Mary and Joseph listened to Simeon as he spoke wonderful things about Jesus. You should also listen attentively, as Mary and Joseph did, when you hear others saying good things about the Lord.

Simeon told Mary about two types of people: those who know Jesus as their Savior and those who do not believe in Him as Savior. The ones who would not believe would reject and crucify Him. To what group do you belong? Old Anna, who was also in the temple, gave a clear testimony, and we know which group she belonged to. She praised God and told the others who were looking forward to the Redeemer's coming that He had come. And now it has been told to you again.

Do you belong to the group of people that know the Lord as their Savior?

Mary — Matthew 2:1–12

Worship Christ?

*And when ye have found him, bring me word again, that
I may come and worship him also.* — Matthew 2:8b

King Herod and the people of Jerusalem were in an uproar
because wise men from the east had come to the city. They
were looking for a newborn king of the Jews and wanted to
worship him. A star in the east had shown them that He had
been born. Herod sent the wise men to Bethlehem and told
them to let him know where they found Him. It looked as if
Herod meant to worship the new king just like the wise men,
but his intentions were evil. He would not worship Christ,
but rather kill Him!

In church, it seems like everyone worships the Lord. But
sadly there are some people who do not truly serve Jesus.
Like Herod, they are afraid that Christ will rule over their
lives and bump them off their throne. They want to rule their
own lives, but that is very foolish. Thankfully, there are many
in church who serve the Lord and worship Him as their King,
as the wise men did. What about you? Do you belong to the
wise or foolish?

*At times do you act as if you are serving the Lord even
though you really do not want to in your heart? Confess
these times to the Lord and ask Him for a new heart that
will worship Him.*

271

Mary — Matthew 2:13–18

Called Out of Egypt

*That it might be fulfilled which was spoken of the Lord by
the prophet, saying, Out of Egypt have I called my son.*
— Matthew 2:15b

The wise men from the east had gone back to their country.
Herod did not find out where Jesus was; God did not allow it.
Herod was furious and commanded that all the little boys under
the age of two had to be killed. The mothers of the murdered
children wept and cried, but nobody could comfort them. Was
Mary also crying because her Child was killed? No, thankfully
not, for God knew that Herod wanted to kill His Son. He had
told Joseph in a dream that he should flee to Egypt with Mary
and Jesus. Egypt was a country where the enemy lived and
where the nation of Israel had been kept in bondage. Yet the
Lord directed it this way to fulfill Hosea's prophecy. His Son
would be called from the sinful nation of Egypt.

Do you know that our world is like Egypt? The devil wants
to keep you as his prey, bound to the sins of this world. But
the Lord calls you to leave them behind. Listen to His voice!

*Can you find the verse in Hosea that talks about Jesus
coming out of Egypt?*

Mary — Matthew 2:19–23

Jesus the Nazarene

And he came and dwelt in a city called Nazareth: that it might be fulfilled which was spoken by the prophets, He shall be called a Nazarene.
— Matthew 2:23

God told Joseph in a dream that Herod had died. He had to go back to Israel with Mary and baby Jesus. When Joseph arrived in Israel, he heard that Archelaus was now king of Judea. Archelaus was the son of Herod and was as cruel as his father. You can understand why Joseph and Mary were afraid to stay in Israel. At God's command, they went to Galilee and settled in Nazareth. It was a small and despised town. Besides His common name, Jesus also received the name, Nazarene. Jesus was called a Nazarene because he lived in a despised town, among sinful people. Wasn't this a miracle? Jesus became just like these people, but He never sinned. That is why He can change the name "sinner" to the name "Christian." Are you called by this new name?

Are you ever ashamed of the Lord?

Mary — Luke 2:39–52

Mary Looks for Jesus

*And he said unto them, How is it that ye sought me? wist
ye not that I must be about my Father's business?*
— Luke 2:49

The Passover was going to be celebrated soon. At God's
command, Joseph, Mary, and twelve-year-old Jesus went to
Jerusalem. After the celebration, Mary and Joseph traveled
back to Nazareth. When they were about halfway on their
journey, they realized that Jesus was not with the large
group of travelers with whom they were walking. They were
worried and immediately went back to find Jesus. Wouldn't
your father and mother be worried if they didn't know where
you were?

After a few days of searching, Joseph and Mary found
Jesus in the temple among the rabbis. Mary asked Him
why He had stayed behind. She and Joseph had been so
frightened! Jesus told them that they could have known. Was
Jesus disobedient to His parents? No, but Mary and Joseph
had to learn that Jesus was not, in the first place, their son. He
was the Son of God. He came to obey His Father in heaven
and do things for Him. Think about this, as Mary did. Seek
first the kingdom of God.

Do you love your father and mother more than God?

Mary — John 2:1–11

Jesus Reprimands Mary

Jesus saith unto her, Woman, what have I to do with thee?
mine hour is not yet come. — John 2:4

How good it is to invite Jesus to our celebrations. How could you enjoy your birthday without the Lord? He can be with you, even if you cannot see Him. You can ask Him to be with you wherever you go.

The Lord was invited to a wedding in Cana, and His mother, Mary, was also there. During the celebration, when Mary heard that there was no more wine, she went straight to Jesus and told Him. She believed He would help, for wasn't He the promised Messiah? But Jesus reprimanded her, calling her "woman" instead of "mother." Mary had to learn that Jesus needed to make His own decisions and that He was not her young, submissive Son anymore. This was a difficult lesson for Mary, but she bore His reproof and still believed that Jesus would help with the shortage of wine.

Perhaps you have found that the Lord has different ideas for you from the ones you have for yourself. Do you become discouraged? You shouldn't; hope in the Lord:

> *I will, if thou plead,*
> *Fill thine every need,*
> *All thy wants relieving.*

Does the Lord give you everything you want?

Mary — John 19:17–27

Mary and John

When Jesus therefore saw his mother, and the disciple standing by, whom he loved, he saith unto his mother, Woman, behold thy son!
— John 19:26

Many people were standing at the side of the road, watching a Man carrying a cross. This Man would be nailed to His cross and placed between two murderers. Who was this? It was the Lord Jesus, who had to suffer because of your and my sins. Later, a group of people were standing around the cross of Jesus, many mocking Him. Mary was among them, watching the suffering of her Son. Who knows how deep her sorrow was? Jesus spoke to Mary and His disciple, John, who stood beside her. Jesus told Mary that from now she should regard John as her son and that John should consider Mary as his mother.

How wonderful when people look after each other! You are also taken care of. There are meals for you every day and clean clothes to wear. Be thankful for this. And if your parents care for your soul, you are receiving the best care there is. They talk to you about the Lord and also talk to the Lord about you, asking Him to give you a new heart. You can ask for the same thing, and you can thank the Lord for loving parents.

Have you heard your father and mother praying for you to receive a new heart?

Mary — Acts 1:4–14

A Praying Mary

These all continued with one accord in prayer and supplication, with the women, and Mary the mother of Jesus, and with his brethren.

— Acts 1:14

The followers of Jesus were gathered in the upper room at Jerusalem. There were old and young people, men and women. At first glance, they looked very different from each other, yet there was a similarity among them. It was not outward; rather, the same desire lived in their hearts. The people you meet at home, school, and church are also very different from each other. It would be wonderful if they were all united in seeking the Lord!

The disciples in the upper room longed for the coming of the Holy Spirit. When Jesus ascended, He had promised He would send the Holy Spirit to the earth. Through His power, they would be able to spread the gospel all over the world.

Mary, the mother of Jesus, was also in the upper room. She might have been the mother of Jesus, but her needs were the same as the others'. That is why she prayed to God and pleaded with Him just like the others did. Pray along with Mary: "Send forth, O God, of my salvation, Thy light and truth to be my guide."

With whom can you pray?

John the Baptist — Luke 1:5–25

Speechless

And, behold, thou shalt be dumb, and not able to speak, until the day that these things shall be performed.
— Luke 1:20a

Elisabeth saw Zacharias coming home in the distance. He had been on duty as the priest in the temple in Jerusalem, and meanwhile Elisabeth stayed at home. Elisabeth and Zacharias loved the Lord and tried to live according to God's Word and commandments. They had prayed they would one day receive a child, but their prayer had never been fulfilled. They were so old now that they could not have children anymore.

Elisabeth was happy to see her husband coming home. Without children to liven things up, it had been very quiet at home. But even after his return, the house stayed just as quiet, because Zacharias could not speak a single word! He wrote on a tablet everything that happened to him while he was away. He wrote, "I went into the temple to burn incense on the altar when I saw the angel Gabriel beside the altar. I was very frightened! He told me that we will receive a son, and we have to name him John. John will be the last prophet announcing the coming of the Messiah, calling the people to repent and believe. I didn't believe what the angel told me. My punishment is that I cannot speak until this promise is fulfilled." And the miracle really took place! Elisabeth, who was already old, was expecting a baby!

Do you believe God's Word no matter how strange or difficult it may seem?

278

John the Baptist — Luke 1:57–80

A Covenant Child

His name is John.
— Luke 1:63b

The Lord's promises are always true. After nine months, Elisabeth and Zacharias's child was born. Everyone was happy. It was a son! On the eighth day, the boy was circumcised, as was the custom in Israel. Circumcision was the sign and seal of the covenant, and that day was also when the child was given his name. Family and friends decided that this small boy would be called Zacharias, just like his dad. They thought it strange when Elisabeth told them that the Lord wanted him to be named John. Nobody they knew had that name. They decided to ask Zacharias himself what his son's name would be. He wrote down that his name would be John. Then something amazing happened: after nine long and quiet months, Zacharias spoke! He praised God for the deliverance that would come through the Messiah. John would prepare the way for Him. All the people in the neighborhood were astonished at all that happened. This child would be special. Even his name preached a sermon because it means "the Lord is merciful." They were all witnesses of that truth.

What did the Lord promise when you were baptized?

John the Baptist — Luke 3:1–18

Repent!

Repent ye: for the kingdom of heaven is at hand.
— Matthew 3:2

People came from all directions to see what was happening at the banks of the Jordan River. It was crowded with all types of people. There were Pharisees, tax collectors, and soldiers among the large crowd. What was going on? A thirty-two-year-old man preached to the crowd, just like the prophet Elijah had done. He wore a coat made of camel's hair. It was John the Baptist. He told the people, "Repent of your sins and ask for forgiveness, for the Messiah is coming soon." One of the Pharisees challenged him, saying, "I am righteous; I have no sins to repent of. Besides that, Abraham is my father!" John the Baptist replied, "If Abraham is your father, than you should be doing what Abraham did."

One of the people whose conscience was affected by the preaching was a tax collector. John told him he may not collect any more than he was officially allowed to, and then the man was baptized. The soldiers who saw the baptism asked, "What about us? What should we do?" John told them to be satisfied with their salaries and not to plunder and steal anymore. The people wondered if John himself might be the Christ, but John put an end to their speculations. "I am not the Christ, for I baptize you with water, but Christ will baptize you with the Holy Spirit."

What happens if the Holy Spirit works in your heart?

John the Baptist — John 1:19–34

A Voice Calling

Behold the Lamb of God, which taketh away the sin of the world. — John 1:29b

The people continually asked, "Who are you really, John? You baptize just like we do, but we baptize heathen that want to become Jews, whereas you baptize Jews. Are you the Christ, or maybe Elijah who was prophesied to return?"

John told the priests and Levites to tell the people of Jerusalem that he was like a voice calling in the wilderness. He told them that he was only a voice calling them to prepare the way of the Lord, just like Isaiah prophesied. He also explained how he was only a forerunner of the Messiah. The Messiah was close; they just didn't know Him yet. John said he wasn't worthy to even loosen His shoelaces, like a servant would do.

The following day John met Jesus and said: "Behold the Lamb of God, which taketh away the sin of the world." This was who he had been talking about! God had said that a dove would descend on the Messiah, His beloved Son, who was well pleasing to Him. The Lord had also said that His Son would be baptizing with the Holy Spirit.

How does God call us to repentance today?

John the Baptist — John 3:22–36

The Bridegroom's Friend

He must increase, but I must decrease.
— John 3:30

John's disciples had a difficult time accepting what was happening. Many of them left John to follow Jesus instead. And now Jesus was even baptizing like John. They wondered out loud if John realized what was happening. But John reassured them that it was fine this way; he was only supposed to be the forerunner of Jesus. He told his followers he was like a bridegroom's friend who goes to the bride's house to pick her up and bring her to the bridegroom. The bride was a picture of the church, which was to be brought to Jesus, the Bridegroom, so He could speak to her. John explained that Jesus was sent from heaven, so it didn't matter if anyone left John's side and began following Him. Jesus had to increase; He had to become more important and John had to become less important.

John kept preaching and told all who would listen that they had to repent and turn to Jesus. They had to believe that He was sent to rescue them from their sins. God's wrath would rest on those who didn't listen, but those who believed in Him would inherit eternal life.

How can Jesus become more important in your life today?

John the Baptist — Matthew 11:1–19

Confusing Events

And blessed is he, whosoever shall not be offended in me. — Matthew 11:6

Jesus compared the Jews who were watching Him and John the Baptist to children playing. Jesus said, "You are like children pretending to get married. 'Yes, this is a fun game,' the children say, and one of them begins playing the flute. Someone else starts to dance, but... 'No, let's not play wedding after all. It's too hyper to jump around like that. You know what? Let's pretend we are having a funeral.' One child lies down and another starts singing sad songs, encouraging the others to cry. But no, they don't want to do that either because it is too sad."

Why did the Lord mention this example? The Jews said John was too negative and gloomy, but the Lord Jesus was too cheerful and optimistic. Their criticism was just an excuse not to repent of their sins and to remain in them. The Lord encouraged John's disciples with these words, "Blessed is he, whosoever shall not be offended in me." John's words to the people were not his own words but were given him by the Holy Spirit. He pointed out the people's sins. He also told King Herod about his sins, for Herod lived with his brother's wife as if she were his wife. Herod was angered and put John in prison. In prison, John started to doubt his mission and wondered why Jesus didn't get him out. What use was it to sit in prison and do nothing? Wasn't he a servant of the Lord? He even questioned if Jesus was the real Messiah. John sent his disciples to bring his doubts to Jesus. Jesus answered them, "Isaiah once said that when the Messiah comes, the blind will see again and the deaf will hear again. Tell John what you have seen here, and then he will know."

When disappointing things happen in your life, does that mean you are not a child of God anymore?

John the Baptist — Matthew 14:1–12

A Light Turned Off

He was a burning and a shining light.
                              — John 5:35

Your birthday is usually a happy day. Maybe your mom or dad thanks the Lord that you have been spared for another year. You probably get some presents and maybe you have some friends over for a party.

Today we read about Herod giving a birthday party. The room was filled with guests who had been drinking wine. Herod's daughter, Salome, danced for them. Salome was allowed to ask for a present for herself, up to half of Herod's kingdom, because he enjoyed her dancing very much. She asked her mom what her request should be and Herodias, her mother, came up with something evil. She hated John the Baptist for telling Herod and her that they lived in sin. She was married to Philip, Herod's brother, but she had left him and now lived with Herod. John told them that the Lord didn't approve of their actions. So Herodias told Salome to ask for the head of John the Baptist. Because Herod had sworn an oath, he had to grant her request, and the life of John the Baptist came to an end. But it wasn't really the end for him; now he would live forever with God.

What should you do when someone asks you to do something against God's commandments?

John — Matthew 4:12–22

The Calling of John

Follow me, and I will make you fishers of men.
— Matthew 4:19

Have you ever had this happen to you? Your mom calls you to come to her and you reply that you'll be there in a minute, but your mom insists that you come right away.

One day, when the Lord Jesus walked along the shores of the Sea of Galilee, He saw two brothers putting their nets into the water to catch fish. Jesus told them to follow Him and He would make them fishers of men. Peter and Andrew did not make the Lord wait for them, but followed Him right away. In another boat, Zebedee was mending nets with his two sons, John and James. Jesus called John and James and they also followed Him immediately, leaving their dad in the ship. Jesus spoke with power; His command would always be followed.

Why was Jesus there, walking along the shore? Didn't He live in Nazareth, which was far from this sea? He used to live there, yes, but He moved away and eventually ended up in Capernaum, where it was safer after the capture of John the Baptist. Capernaum was the last city in his search for a safe place to live, and this was called "by the way of the sea," just as Isaiah had prophesied. Jesus started to preach there so that those living in darkness would see a great light.

What would you have done if Jesus called you to follow Him?

286

John — Mark 5:21–43

Power Over Life and Death

Be not afraid, only believe.
— Mark 5:36b

Jairus was one of the leaders of the synagogue. When Jesus came to where he lived, he tried to push his way through the crowds. His face showed he was worried. He dropped on his knees before the Lord, saying, "My twelve-year-old daughter is sick and close to death. Please come to my house to put Thy hands on her, so she will live."

Jesus went with Jairus. Along the way, He also healed an exhausted woman who had been bleeding for twelve years. In the meantime, Jairus received the message that his daughter was dead. The Lord heard the message and said to Jairus, "Be not afraid, only believe."

Peter, John, and James followed Jesus and Jairus into the house. There were many people inside mourning, crying loudly, and playing sad songs. "What is all this noise? The child is not dead but asleep!" said Jesus. The people in the house were annoyed by Jesus' words. They said, "Don't say such ridiculous things, for we have seen with our own eyes that she is dead." The Lord sent them all away, then took the parents and the three disciples into the girl's room. He took her hand and said, *"Talitha kumi,"* which means "Girl, arise." And the girl sat up! The Lord told her to do so and made her hear His voice. "Give her something to eat," He said. What a miracle!

Do you think the Lord can make our dead heart alive again?

John — Matthew 17:1–13

The Transfiguration of Christ

Hear ye him.
— Matthew 17:5b

Going up the mountain with his brother and Peter must have been a special experience for John. The Lord Jesus didn't pick him to come along because he was better than the other disciples, but the Lord did love John very much. John had also been allowed to witness Jairus's daughter being raised from the dead, and now he was allowed to see the transfiguration of Christ.

"Transfiguration" is a difficult word which means that God the Father showed them how important and glorious His Son was. God showed that the Lord Jesus was the promised Messiah. On the mountain, the disciples saw Jesus' face as bright as the sun, and His clothes as white as light. Moses and Elijah talked with Jesus about His suffering, death, and resurrection while the disciples watched. They heard God's voice saying, "This is my beloved Son, in whom I am well pleased; hear ye him."

The Lord Jesus, being God Himself, was willing to become human just like us. How glorious! He was willing to carry the burden of God's wrath meant for us, so we would be able to receive forgiveness of sins.

When the disciples heard God's voice they fell on their faces to the ground in fear. Why were they afraid?

John — Luke 22:7–23

Christ Institutes the Lord's Supper

For even Christ our Passover is sacrificed for us.
— 1 Corinthians 5:7b

John and Peter prepared the Passover feast together. One of the things they had to do was buy ingredients for the bitter sauce. The sauce reminded them of the bitterness when the Israelites were the Egyptians' slaves. They also had to buy plenty of wine and bread. A lamb had to be slaughtered in the temple and then prepared in the room where they would celebrate the Passover meal.

To find a room for the Passover, Jesus told them to follow a man with a pitcher of water. He would lead them to an available room. The meal would begin when all the preparations were complete. The Lord Jesus looked forward to this Passover meal. This would be the last time they would celebrate the Passover, remembering the exodus from Egypt. After this celebration, the Passover would be replaced by the Lord's Supper.

Jesus broke the bread and gave a piece to each of His disciples. The cup of wine also went around the room. He explained that the bread and wine pointed to His death on the cross. Jesus would be the Lamb of God, taking away the sins of the world. "Do this in remembrance of me," said the Lord.

The Lord's Supper is still celebrated. There is always room for more people at the table. Who can go to the Lord's Supper?

289

John — Mark 14:32–42

Suffering in Solitude

I have trodden the winepress alone.
                                        — Isaiah 63:3a

Still deeply impressed by the supper they had with Jesus, the disciples made their way to the Mount of Olives. They went there with Jesus but without Judas. There was a garden at the foot of this mountain with walls all around it. It was called Gethsemane, which means "olive press." The Lord Jesus often went to this garden to pray. This time, He took Peter, James, and John with Him.

These disciples witnessed the suffering of their Lord. We cannot imagine what it must have been like for Jesus to know He had to appear before God's judgment throne to carry the sins of the whole world. What unimaginable suffering! Knowing He had to carry the wrath of God made Him afraid and sad. Even in these last moments, the devil was trying to keep the Lord Jesus from fulfilling the promise of saving sinners. The Lord confessed in the garden that He knew God's will had to be done. The disciples weren't much of an encouragement to Him, for they all fell asleep. An angel of God was sent to Jesus to sustain Him in the hardest moments, when giving up seemed so tempting. Love for His people made the Lord Jesus willing to do God's will.

Why did Jesus have to suffer and die?

John — John 20:1–10

The Day of the Resurrection

He is not here: for he is risen, as he said.
— Matthew 28:6a

Why do we go to church on Sunday? What is so special about Sunday? Do you know the answer?

Mary Magdalene stood in front of Peter and John on a Sunday, very early in the morning, and said, "The large stone is rolled away, and the sepulcher is empty! We don't know where they have laid Him." Peter and John didn't hesitate for a moment, but ran towards the sepulcher; John arrived there first. Both men saw that the stone had been rolled away. John stooped down to look into the cave and saw the linen clothes in which the body had been wrapped. The napkin that they used to put on the head was there. In the meantime, Peter also arrived and stepped into the sepulcher, where he saw the clothes neatly rolled up. When John saw all these things, he believed that the Lord had indeed risen from the dead!

This is why Sunday is such a special day for those who serve the Lord Jesus. Sunday was the day of His resurrection. From this point on, Christians gathered on Sundays to worship the Lord.

What makes Sunday special to you?

John — John 21:1–14

An Encouraging Catch

From henceforth thou shalt catch men. — Luke 5:10b

After being raised from the dead, the Lord told His disciples to go to Galilee so He could meet them there. The seven disciples waited for Jesus to come to them, but waiting made them impatient; when Peter said he was going fishing, they all joined him. They fished as hard as they could all night long. They threw out the nets, pulled the nets along the boat, and finally they hauled the nets into the boat. They did the same thing over and over again but with no results. Not one fish was caught!

When the early rays of sunlight shone over the water, they decided to call it quits and headed to shore. A Man waited on shore for them, asking them if they could give Him some fish to go with His bread. After telling the Man they had nothing, He advised them to throw out the nets on the other side of their boat. Because of His authoritative way of speaking, they obeyed instantly, and they were not disappointed. There were so many fish in their nets that seven strong men could not pull the net into the boat.

John was the first one to figure out who that Man on shore must have been. He said to Peter, "It is the Lord!" Peter didn't need to hear another word; he jumped overboard to be the first disciple with Jesus. The others came a little while later, dragging the net filled with fish behind them. Bread and fried fish were already prepared when they arrived.

When we obey the Lord and throw out our nets in obedience, miracles can happen!

What would have happened if they had not obeyed Jesus?

James — Mark 1:1–20

The Calling of James

And they shall be all taught of God.
                              — John 6:45a

When someone is called by the Lord, the Holy Spirit gives them the power to hear, listen, and obey. We often read in the Bible that large numbers of people followed Jesus. It probably was much like our churches on Sundays when many gather to hear the Word of God explained. Were all the people who followed Jesus converted? Are all the people who come to church converted?

The Lord told those who followed Him that they only did so to see more of His miracles. But not everyone who followed Him had wrong motives. God's Spirit worked in the hearts of many, drawing them to Himself.

When the Lord called the disciples, it was a special kind of calling. They witnessed all His works and listened to all His sermons. Some of them wrote it all down with the Holy Spirit's help.

The calling of James was that kind of special calling, even more so because his brother John was also called. Two humble fishermen, brothers in one family, were called to proclaim the gospel.

Did the Lord call any very smart people to be His disciples? Do you know an example?

James — Luke 5:1–11

A Special Pulpit

The blessing of the LORD, it maketh rich.
— Proverbs 10:22

James was a plain fisherman. He wasn't necessarily a poor man; he worked with John, his brother, on the boat of their father, Zebedee. His father owned the boat, and they even made enough money to pay some employees. One morning, they pulled their boats on shore after a night of not catching a single fish. On shore, they cleaned their nets. A great crowd started to form where Jesus was preaching. The Lord asked John and James if He could stand in their boat; the crowd pressed so close to Jesus that He was almost trampled underfoot. He asked them to push their boat a little ways from the shore, and they obeyed Him. The Lord Jesus used the boat as a pulpit and preached His sermon from it.

After the sermon, Jesus told the fishermen to bring the boat to deeper water and to throw out their nets. Even though Peter protested that they never went fishing during the day because it wasn't a good time for catching fish, he obeyed the command of the Lord. Surprisingly, their nets were filled to the point of bursting, and Peter was embarrassed about his earlier remarks. They returned to shore with two boats filled with fish.

Follow the Lord wherever He leads you, just like James did. That will always be the best place to be, even if you do not understand His ways.

Would you follow James's example? Or do you think you would have protested like Peter did?

James — Luke 9:46–62

Sons of Thunder

Be not overcome of evil, but overcome evil with good.
— Romans 12:21

Do you know who the Samaritans were? They were people from the city of Samaria. When Sargon defeated the Israelites in the year 722 B.C., he brought them to Assyria. Only a very small group of Israelites stayed behind. The heathen who used to live in Assyria moved to Israel and married the Jews who had stayed behind. The children born from those marriages were half Jewish; they were called Samaritans. Their religion mixed heathen and Jewish customs and they worshipped in their own temple on the mountain, Gerizim. Jews and Samaritans despised each other.

On His way to Jerusalem, the Lord Jesus took the shortest route, which was through Samaria. Jews never really traveled through Samaria; they would rather take the long way around. Seeing that Jesus was traveling to Jerusalem, the Samaritans didn't want Him to lodge overnight in their area. John and James were furious, showing their tempers as "sons of thunder." They proposed to have fire come down from heaven to destroy these Samaritans, but the Lord didn't allow it. Jesus told them that revenge and destruction are not a part of a Christian's life. He explained that He came to this world to save people, not injure them.

Do you sometimes have trouble controlling your temper? What should you do when you are angry?

James — Mark 3:7–19

Taught to Be an Apostle

And that he might send them forth to preach.
— Mark 3:14b

Your whole life will change dramatically when the Holy Spirit lives in you. You will want to live for the Lord, but you will also be eager to learn more and more about Him. When you receive the Holy Spirit, it doesn't mean that you know everything at once. On the contrary, you will quickly learn that you have much to learn.

The men Jesus chose to be His disciples were plain people. The Lord knew that, too. And He also knew that, when He left them, they would continue His teaching. Twelve of His disciples were chosen by Him to fulfill this special task of teaching. They had to become fishers of men, remember? They weren't chosen because they told the Lord Jesus they would be the right candidate to become an apostle. It was all in God's plan, and He chose them to be taught by Him. Every day He taught them, preparing them for preaching the gospel, performing miracles, and driving out evil spirits. This teaching was very important because Satan didn't spare any effort in opposing the Lord's work. Satan knew better than these men why Jesus had come to this world, and he would do anything to prevent the sacrifice of Jesus dying for His people. One of the twelve men the Lord had chosen was James.

Why is it so important to pay close attention in Sunday school or catechism classes?

296

James — Matthew 20:17–28

The Desire to Reign

For even the Son of man came not to be ministered unto, but to minister.   — Mark 10:45

While the group approached Jerusalem, which was located on a mountain, the Lord called together His twelve disciples. He wanted them to hear again, for the third time, that He was going to Jerusalem to suffer and die on the cross. But even after hearing it again from the Lord Jesus Himself, they couldn't—or maybe didn't want to—believe it. How many times had not the Lord told them that His kingdom was not of this world? The disciples still believed that Jesus would be crowned as king in Jerusalem, and John and James couldn't wait for it to happen. They would love to have an important position in the kingdom, reigning with Jesus, the one sitting on His right and the other on His left. Jesus told them that they didn't know what they were asking for, and that they were being driven by the desire for power and honor. "Learn from Me," He said, "for I came to serve." Jesus was their ultimate example—living the life of a servant.

The kingdom of God is in need of servants who are willing to serve others in love!

Deep down we all would love to be important. Does this ever bother you about yourself? How can you fight against it?

297

James — Matthew 26:31–46

No Compassion

And I looked, and there was none to help.
                              — Isaiah 63:5a

The Lord Jesus fought a lonely battle in the garden of Gethsemane. He took Peter, James, and John along with Him into the garden. John and James were convinced that they could drink the cup of suffering with Jesus. The Lord agreed that indeed they would suffer, but still, the disciples showed no compassion when the suffering of the Lord Jesus was most severe. The Lord asked the three disciples to pray for Him, but they fell asleep instead. Jesus asked for prayer from them three times, and three times their eyes were too heavy with sleep. In His final hours, the Lord Jesus experienced what it was like to suffer alone.

We don't naturally feel a great deal of sympathy for our neighbor. Oh yes, we ask how they are doing, but, five minutes later, our thoughts wander and we forget the other person's suffering. If we're ever in this situation, the Lord has compassion for us; He knows what it is like to suffer alone. He is able to give complete deliverance, even when we are close to death.

What are some ways you can show more compassion to the people around you?

James — Acts 12:1–2 and 20–25

James's Death

And he [Herod] killed James the brother of John with the sword. — Acts 12:2

Herod's grandson was a violent king like his grandfather who had killed all the babies in Bethlehem; he killed James with the sword. Peter was captured and thrown into prison but escaped from Herod in an amazing way. Herod was very frustrated when he couldn't find Peter. He decided to focus on fighting Tyre and Sidon's army instead, but Blastus, one of his servants, kept him from doing as he planned. Herod put his royal mantle on his shoulders before he spoke to his people. They chanted, "It is the voice of a god, and not of a man." Herod was very pleased with the shout, but the Lord was no longer patient with this king. An angel was sent to Herod and he made him terribly ill. While still alive, his body was eaten by worms, and eventually he died. God allowed James to be killed, but Peter to remain alive.

The Lord does not have to explain to us why one person suffers at the hands of the ungodly while another is spared from suffering. But you can be sure that the Lord will punish ungodly people. Maybe it happens in their lifetime, but certainly in the life to come.

Have you ever suffered for the gospel's sake? If you have, remember that you are not alone. So many people throughout history have suffered just as you have.

James — Matthew 13:54–58 and 1 Corinthians 15:7

Adopted Children

For whosoever shall do the will of my Father which is in heaven, the same is my brother, and sister, and mother.
— Matthew 12:50

God created many different kinds of birds: parrots with brightly colored feathers, nightingales that can sing amazingly beautiful songs. Sparrows were also created by Him. It would be ungrateful of the sparrow to say to its Creator that it is worthless because it is so plain and doesn't have beautiful colors or a nice voice! What we look like on the outside is not important to the Lord because He looks at our hearts. He knows if you want to follow His will. Those who do what God wants are adopted into His family. They become a member of His large family; they become His adoptive children.

James was a very ordinary person. He wasn't someone you would notice right away in a group of people. Even though James sometimes disagreed with Jesus, he didn't stop following Him. After Jesus' resurrection, Jesus visited James separately. This visit must have been necessary and very special for James. Finally James was convinced that God's will was best and he believed in Jesus. He became a true child of God.

Have you been adopted into God's large family?

James — Acts 15:1–21

The First Synod Meeting

But we believe that through the grace of the Lord Jesus Christ we shall be saved, even as they. — Acts 15:11

Do you know what a synod is? Sometimes ministers, elders, and deacons get together in a meeting called a Synod or Assembly. They discuss church life and talk about problems that may have come up in the churches.

There was a problem in the church of Antioch. Jewish Christians from Jerusalem had joined the church and were disturbed by the fact that Christians in Antioch did not keep all the laws of Moses. They kept the ten commandments, but the Jews from Jerusalem said they couldn't possibly be saved if they weren't circumcised. Paul and Barnabas disagreed on the issue, so Paul decided to go to Jerusalem with some members of the congregation. They asked the apostles Peter, James, and John what their opinion was. James explained that the prophet Amos had prophesied that Jews and Gentiles would be united in their faith in Christ. James suggested that they not insist that the Gentile Christians keep all of Moses' laws, as long as they did not serve idols. The men left in peace.

Synod literally means "to walk the road together." Isn't it amazing that Jews and Gentiles enjoyed peace among themselves while they all followed their God? What a special gift from the Lord!

Why was it so special for Jews and Gentiles to worship God together? Are you a peacemaker?

James — James 1:1–11

Patient in Adversity

Blessed are ye, when men shall revile you, and persecute you, and shall say all manner of evil against you falsely, for my sake. Rejoice and be exceeding glad: for great is your reward in heaven.
— Matthew 5:11, 12a

Stephen was the first martyr of the early church, which means that he was the first to be killed for his faith in Jesus. While a group of men stoned Stephen, Saul watched it all. Stephen's death was part of Saul's bigger scheme to persecute the Christians in Jerusalem. All the Christians fled for their lives. They left behind all their possessions; only the apostles stayed in the city.

These poor, tired Christians had to start their lives all over again far away from Jerusalem. Yet, as they traveled, they preached the gospel, which led to new churches forming all over. Despite their hardship and suffering, these people still spoke about how good their God was. James wrote a letter to these people, calling them "the twelve tribes which are scattered abroad." He wanted to comfort them after hearing of their suffering, for he knew that persecution was a blessing, too.

Being persecuted makes our hearts patient. James's letter is also written for you and me to read. Maybe you wonder why the Lord has given you such a heavy cross to bear—maybe it is a sickness or a hard situation at home. The Lord is more than willing to answer you, if you ask Him for wisdom.

What did David mean when he said that it was good to be afflicted, for then he could honor God's holy will?

302

James — James 1:12–18

The Test of Faithfulness

Be thou faithful unto death, and I will give thee a crown of life. — Revelation 2:10b

The devil works hard to tempt Christians to give up their faith and follow his evil ways.

The Lord Jesus was also tempted by the devil, but the devil did not succeed with Him. He promised to give the Lord riches, honor, and praise, but Jesus countered the attack by quoting Scripture. That is always your best weapon against the devil. When Adam and Eve were tempted by the snake, they disobeyed the Lord and didn't stand firm in what they knew was right. They fell for Satan's deceit; it all seemed so wonderful!

The devil is still at work, twenty-four hours a day, wanting us to fall just like Adam and Eve. He wants to deceive us. Why do we give in to these temptations so often? Our own heart is like an enemy inside us; it wants wicked things. It doesn't take much to make us fall into sin.

Do you think that we can blame God for our sins? No, it is our own hearts that pull us away from God. Ask for God's help when you are tempted and you know you cannot resist. But what should we do when we've already given in to these sinful temptations? We can always return to the Lord, for Jesus Himself made that possible. He is the Way, the Truth, and the Life.

How can the devil tempt you to sin?

James — James 2:14–26

Good Works

Show me thy faith without thy works, and I will show thee my faith by my works.
— James 2:18

Does this describe your life? You go to church two times every Sunday. If there is a gathering at church during the week, you are there. You give to charity using your own money. You believe that God exists, of course. You believe that the Bible is God's Word. You do not hang out with the wrong kids. You always wear decent clothing.

It sounds like you are living a good life. But does this make you a converted person? Look at Paul as an example. Before his conversion, he thought he was doing good works for God by persecuting the Christians. The only problem was, he didn't believe in the Lord Jesus Christ. That is why his good works were dead works and sinful before God.

Does that mean we should never do good works? No, of course not! Ask the Lord to give you saving faith. Saving faith will pour love for the Lord and His service into your heart —and also love for your neighbor. Your only desire will be to live to God's glory. It will give you compassion for those around you who don't know they have a soul that will perish if they aren't born again.

What exactly are good works?
What makes them truly good?

James — James 3:1–12

Keeping Our Tongue in Check

If any man among you seem to be religious, and bridleth not his tongue, but deceiveth his own heart, this man's religion is vain. — James 1:26

One major difference between humans and animals is that humans are able to speak. Some birds are capable of making sounds just like our words, but they are just imitating us. They cannot really talk because they do not understand each other.

When humans speak, they try to put their thoughts into words. Because the Lord created us after His own image, we have the ability to speak. In the garden of Eden, God spoke to Adam in such a way that Adam could understand Him. Adam must have been very pleased that he could speak with God. But when sin came into the world, our speaking was affected. In Paradise, the tongue was used only in ways that honored God. But now we use our tongues to sing a psalm one day and to gossip about someone the next. James tells us that it shouldn't be that way.

It may be very difficult to remain silent when someone says something mean to you. Our first reaction is to get even. But a sharp comment can start a war. If you know what your tongue is capable of doing, it is wise to ask the Lord every day to put a watch before your lips.

Could you think of a moment when it was hard to control your tongue? What does it mean to pray for God to "put a watch" before your lips?

305

James — James 4:13–17

D.V., or, "The Lord Willing"

If the Lord will, we shall live, and do this, or that.
                                                    — James 4:15

Imagine this conversation taking place after a boy named John showed his report card to his grandpa.

"You have a lot of good grades on your report card, John. I can see that you worked hard," said his grandpa.

"Yes, Grandpa; I worked hard to get ready for high school."

"That's good," replied his grandpa. "It pleases the Lord when you use your talents. But what about after high school?"

John thought for a minute. "I would love to go to college."

"Excellent!" said his grandpa. "The Lord wants you to work hard. But what about after college?"

"Well, I'll work in Dad's company as an accountant and makes lots of money."

John's grandpa nodded. "Well, that will give you a good opportunity to give liberally to charity to help those in need. But what comes after that?"

"I'll get married and maybe have some children," said John.

"Yes, John, it is good for a man to have a wife and children; these are blessings from the Lord. But after that?" he prodded.

"When I'm rich enough, I'll retire early and enjoy life."

John's grandpa asked another question. "You will

306

take some time to rest after all your hard work, and that's understandable. But what will happen next?"

"I don't know," said John. "I guess I'll be an old man."

"Yes," said his grandfather, "just like I am now, John. What will be the next step?"

John didn't know what to answer. The conversation came to a sudden end, for John had not thought yet about his own death.

Many things in life are uncertain, but there is one thing you can be sure of: you will die one day. The only thing you don't know about death is when it will come. Maybe you will die before this day ends; we never know. That is why you must be sure that all is well between you and the Lord. Your sins must be forgiven; you need someone who will carry your sins for you. Jesus is able and willing to do so! Ask Him today.

Do you know anyone who died before they were old?

Peter — Matthew 4:12–25

The Calling of Peter

And he saith unto them, Follow me, and I will make you fishers of men.
— Matthew 4:19

Simon Peter and his brother Andrew threw their fishing net into the Sea of Galilee. While they were busy with their work, Peter heard a voice. He turned around and saw the Lord Jesus standing on the shore. "Follow me," the Lord Jesus said to Peter. He did not have to repeat this command, for Peter immediately left his nets and followed his Master. When the Lord called, he had to let go of everything else. Peter was called to a different kind of work. He first had to learn from his Master and then he could tell others what he had learned. Now Peter became a fisher of men.

How does the Lord Jesus talk to us today?

Peter — Matthew 16:13–20

Peter is Right

And Simon Peter answered and said, Thou art the Christ,
the Son of the living God. — Matthew 16:16

The Lord Jesus was traveling with His disciples through the land of Canaan. The people talked about Him wherever He went. Jesus knew what they were saying about Him, but He wanted to hear it from His disciples. He asked them: "Whom do they say that the Son of Man is?" Some thought he was John the Baptist. Others thought of Him as Elijah, and yet others thought of the prophet Jeremiah. They told Jesus this. Jesus then asked, "What do you, my disciples, think of Me? Who am I really?" Simon Peter answered, "Thou art the Christ, the Son of the living God."

The Lord Jesus was very happy with this answer. Peter had not made this up himself; the Lord Himself had taught him this. Peter believed that the Lord Jesus was the promised Redeemer, sent by God. There would be others who, like Peter, would believe and make this confession and spread the Word. Only through faith in the Lord Jesus will you be blessed forever.

Who is the Lord Jesus to you?

Peter — Matthew 16:21–28

Peter is Wrong

But he turned and said unto Peter, Get thee behind me, Satan: thou art an offence unto me: for thou savourest not the things that be of God, but those that be of men.
— Matthew 16:23

The Lord Jesus told His disciples that He had to go to Jerusalem to suffer and die, but that He would also rise again. But Peter would not listen to this message. He was thinking, "That can't happen; nothing will come of His words. Can you imagine that the Master would let Himself be killed?" Peter would make sure that it would not take place. In fact, he even reprimanded the Lord.

Christ turned around, however, and said to Peter that he was a hindrance to the Lord's work. He had to suffer and die; otherwise Peter's sins could not be forgiven. No payment would have been made for your sins, either. Peter thought he was offering to do the best he could for his Master, but it was actually the worst. He did exactly what Satan wanted him to do.

Do you sometimes do something wrong even when you are trying to do your best? What should you do when you are frustrated in times like that?

Peter — Luke 22:31–34

A Warning

But I have prayed for thee, that thy faith fail not.
— Luke 22:32a

The Lord's Supper was celebrated with Jesus. It should have been a feast, but it turned into a sad occasion for the disciples. They did not understand so many things. Their Savior had warned Peter about Satan. Satan would try to drag Peter away from the Lord Jesus by making him commit a terrible sin. Satan wanted Peter to lose his faith; he wanted to sift Peter like wheat. In Bible times, wheat was laid on a large screen which was then shaken back and forth. The chaff would blow off the screen while the heavier kernels of wheat would stay on top to be stored away.

Peter thought that he loved the Lord Jesus so much that he would go to prison with Him—yes, he would even die with Him! But the Master knew that the future would be different. It was a blessed thing that the Lord Jesus knew Peter better than he understood himself. Before Satan began his attack on Peter, Jesus had already prayed that Peter would not lose his faith.

Which part of the Lord's Prayer does this verse remind you of?

311

Peter — Luke 22:54–62

Peter Denies Jesus

And the Lord turned, and looked upon Peter. And Peter remembered the word of the Lord.
— Luke 22:61

Danger had arrived and Peter had not been able to prevent it. The soldiers took the Lord Jesus captive and brought Him to the house of the High Priest. Peter followed them at a safe distance and went inside. He seated himself among the soldiers as if he belonged with them.

But then one of the maid servants recognized him. Peter was caught, but rather than admit it, he vehemently denied that he knew Jesus. But then another one pointed to him, "Hey, you were with them!" Again Peter denied his Master. An hour later, someone else recognized him as a disciple. For the third time, Peter swore with an oath that he had no idea who Jesus was. Before he finished speaking, the rooster crowed. Immediately, the Lord Jesus turned around and looked at Peter. One look from Jesus was enough to bring Peter to repentance.

One look from Jesus is all we need to show us our sins. God's children cannot resist so much love and mercy! A penitent Peter went outside and wept bitter tears.

Do you sometimes deny the Lord Jesus?

Peter — Luke 24:1–12

Disappointed

Then arose Peter, and ran unto the sepulchre; and stooping down, he beheld the linen clothes laid by themselves, and departed, wondering in himself at that which was come to pass. — Luke 24:12

The Lord Jesus had died and Joseph of Arimathæa had buried Him. It was too late for Peter to be reconciled with the Lord and to ask for forgiveness for his denial. On top of this, people like Mary Magdelene were saying that Jesus had risen from the dead. Peter did not believe it. Had Mary Magdelene seen angels at the grave? He had to go and see it with his own eyes. No angels were in sight; he only found a grave with the linen clothes that had been wrapped around his Master's body.

But Peter should have known better. The Lord Jesus had often mentioned that He had to suffer and die, but also that He would rise from the dead after three days. Peter had heard those words, but did not understand them.

We do not always understand Jesus' words either. That is why we have to ask the Lord to explain His Word to us. Bible reading and prayer always go together.

When you read about the Lord Jesus in the Bible, do you understand everything? If not, what should you do?

313

Peter — John 21:15–20

The Lord is All-Knowing

Lord, thou knowest all things; thou knowest that I love thee.
— John 21:17b

The Lord had risen and the disciples had seen Him with their own eyes. They had just finished eating with Him. After the meal, the Lord Jesus looked at Peter. Something had to be set straight. Jesus said to Peter, "Simon, son of Jonas." He did not use the name Peter, which means "rock," but his original name. "Simon, do you love Me more than the other disciples do?" The Lord Jesus asked this not only once, but three times. Peter became worried that the Lord was not believing his answer. Maybe it was his own fault because he had denied Jesus three times. He did not really belong to the disciples any longer.

"Yet, Lord, look at my heart! Thou knowest everything. In spite of my denial, I love Thee very much." Jesus did believe Peter. He commanded Peter to care for those who would soon believe in the Lord Jesus.

Can the Lord look into your heart? What will He see in your heart?

Peter — Acts 2:1–21

They Could All Understand

And they were all amazed and marvelled, saying one to another, Behold, are not all these which speak Galilaeans?
— Acts 2:7

It was very busy in Jerusalem. From near and far, the Jews had come to the temple. The hum of all the different languages could be heard in the streets. The disciples of the Lord Jesus were waiting in the upper room. They were praying for the coming of the Holy Spirit when, suddenly, they heard the sound of a rushing, mighty wind. They saw tongues of fire above each other's heads. Now they knew that the Holy Spirit, the Comforter whom Jesus had promised, had come.

The disciples went outside and started to talk to the people in their different languages. A surprised Egyptian was listening and wondered how these uneducated men could speak his language. Some of the crowd were frightened but others mocked them, saying they were drunk and making it all up.

Peter stood up and explained to them that what had happened had been prophesied by the prophet Joel. Peter preached his first sermon to them and his message was clear: you have to repent. Whoever will call on the name of the Lord will be saved. Peter was full of the Holy Spirit and his great desire was to speak of God's great deeds.

Do you have to be educated to talk about God's great deeds?

315

Peter — Acts 3:1–26

No Silver or Gold

*Then Peter said, Silver and gold have I none; but such as
I have give I thee: In the name of Jesus Christ of Nazareth
rise up and walk.*

— Acts 3:6

What a miserable sight! A crippled man was begging at the
beautiful door of the temple. He had never been able to walk,
so it was therefore impossible for him to work. That is why
his friends brought him to the temple every day; he had to
beg for money to buy his food. He sat at a good spot because
anyone who entered the temple had to pass him.

One day, Peter and John walked by and the crippled man
eagerly held out his hand for some alms. Would he get some
money? Peter told him to look up at him. The apostles did
not have silver or gold, but what Peter did have was worth so
much more! He had the power to heal the crippled beggar in
the name of Jesus Christ. And that is exactly what happened!
The crippled man jumped up and danced, following Peter and
John into the temple to thank God for this great miracle. Peter
was able to perform this miracle through the power of God.

*What is one thing that everyone has in common, whether
old or young, rich or poor, healthy or sick?*

Peter — Acts 5:1–11

Everything or Nothing

But Peter said, Ananias, why hath Satan filled thine heart to lie to the Holy Ghost, and to keep back part of the price of the land?
                                                        — Acts 5:3

"We won't give all our money, but we will keep some of it for ourselves. Don't tell the apostles; otherwise, they will think that we are not good Christians." Ananias was telling this to Sapphira his wife and she agreed with him.

But Peter was not happy when he received their money. He asked why Ananias had been filled with Satan. He had first deceived the apostles but also, and more importantly, he had tried to deceive the Holy Spirit. He did not have to sell the land and it was not wrong for him to keep some of the money. But he should have been honest to God. Because God hates lying, Ananias was punished with death. Some young men carried him away to bury him.

A few hours later, his wife, Sapphira, was also brought to the grave. She asked about her husband and also lied to Peter and the Holy Spirit. God knows whether we serve Him with our whole heart or whether we are keeping something back. The Lord wants everything or nothing.

What well-known psalm do you think of when reading this meditation?

Peter — Acts 9:32–43

A Twofold Miracle

And all that dwelt at Lydda and Saron saw him, and turned to the Lord.
— Acts 9:35

In Judea, Galilee, and Samaria, people were being converted every day. All around, new churches had started and Peter visited them to preach and to talk with the believers. He came to Lydda one day and was met by Aeneas. Aeneas was lame and had been confined to his bed for eight years. Peter said to him, "Aeneas! Jesus Christ can heal you. Stand up and make up your bed." Aeneas stood up immediately and was completely healed. Everyone who saw Aeneas marveled at the great power of God. The Lord used this miracle to convert them.

Shortly after this, two men came from Joppa and took Peter back with them. A sad event had happened in Joppa: Tabitha had died. She had done many good things for others, such as sewing clothes for poor widows. How distressing that this good woman had died! Peter went directly to Tabitha's house. The women there crowded around Peter, showing him the things Tabitha had made. Peter, however, wanted to be left alone. As he fell on his knees, he prayed to God for strength. Then he turned and said, "Tabitha, stand up!" Tabitha opened her eyes, looked at Peter, and sat up straight. She was alive! Through this great miracle, many more people believed in the Lord Jesus.

Why did Peter perform so many miracles?

318

Peter— Acts 10:1–20

Cornelius Joins the Believers (1)

What God hath cleansed, that call not thou common.
— Acts 10:15b

Peter was staying in Joppa. One day, he went to the roof of the house to pray and be alone with the Lord. After praying, he was hungry and asked if there was anything to eat. The food was not ready; it still needed to be prepared. While he waited, he saw a vision, which is a kind of dream. A great sheet came down from heaven, filled with unclean animals. The unclean animals could not be eaten by the Israelites. A voice told Peter to get up, kill the animals, and eat them. But Peter refused; he had never eaten unclean animals before. The vision was shown to Peter again. He did not understand it at all.

While Peter was reflecting on what he had seen, someone knocked at the gate. Three men asked Peter to follow them to Cornelius, their Roman officer. An angel had told Cornelius to call for Peter, for it was now God's time to spread the gospel to the Gentiles. The Lord knew that it would be difficult for Peter to go to an unclean Roman and minister to him; that is why He had sent Peter the vision. The vision prepared Peter to accept people who were Gentiles.

Is it very important for us to be kind to everyone, even people who are not like us. Do you know anyone who might feel left out? Think of a way to be especially kind to that person today.

319

Peter — Acts 10:38–48

Cornelius Joins the Believers (2)

Then Peter opened his mouth, and said, Of a truth I perceive that God is no respecter of persons.
— Acts 10:34

Peter had gone directly to the house of Cornelius, who was very happy to meet him so soon. Cornelius wanted to know more about God; he figured that a servant of God like Peter would be the best teacher. Now Peter understood his dream. God does not care what nationality you are: you could be a Jew, a Roman, or an American; it does not matter to the Lord because He looks at the heart.

Peter told Cornelius about the Lord Jesus. Peter himself had been present when Jesus had healed the sick, cast out the demons, and did good deeds to many. He had been crucified but had risen again. "I even ate with Him," Peter told Cornelius, "and now He has sent me to tell others about what I saw and heard." As Cornelius's company listened to Peter, the Holy Spirit worked in their hearts and they believed in Jesus. Cornelius and his household were baptized; now they were united with all the other believers.

Is there anyone you know who has not heard about Jesus? Plan to talk to them soon and tell them about the gospel. Pray that the Lord will give you a good opportunity to do so.

Peter — Acts 11:1–18

Not Only the Jews

Then hath God also to the Gentiles granted repent-
ance unto life.   — Acts 11:18b

The news that Gentiles had accepted the Word of God spread like wildfire throughout Jerusalem. Peter had visited a Roman officer and had baptized him! Some Jews did not understand Peter's actions; weren't they forbidden to associate with Gentiles? As soon as Peter returned to Jerusalem, he had to explain what had happened. He gladly described the vision he had seen and, following that, his visit to Cornelius. He told them that, during his sermon, the Holy Spirit had filled the hearts of the listeners in the same way as it had happened to them at Pentecost.

When God sends the Holy Spirit, nobody can stop Him. God was showing that the Gentiles had to hear the gospel, too; they would believe in the Lord Jesus. Peter knew that this was clearly the work of the Lord. The Jews gave God all the honor after they heard Peter's account, and were filled with gladness that the Gentiles were being converted.

Are you happy when you hear that the Lord has con-
verted someone?

Peter — Acts 12:3–19

Saved Through a Mighty Weapon

Where many were gathered together praying.
— Acts 12:12b

To do the angry Jews a favor, Herod had Peter locked up in prison. He had to stay there until after the Passover and he was rigorously guarded by four soldiers. Only one more night and Peter would be killed. Still, Peter slept peacefully because he knew that his life was in God's hands. Outside of the prison, his friends continually prayed for him.

Suddenly, an angel stood beside Peter and told him to follow him. Once outside, Peter realized that this was not a dream. He was free! He quickly walked to the house of his friends and knocked on the gate to be let in. From inside, Rhode cautiously looked out. She was so overjoyed to see Peter that she forgot to open the door and let him in! She ran to tell the others that Peter was standing outside, but nobody believed her. They did not believe that the Lord had answered their prayers for Peter's release. Peter kept on knocking until he was let in. He told them how the Lord had delivered him in a miraculous way. Don't you think that everyone in that house thanked the Lord?

Do you pray for your friends?

Peter — Acts 15:1–12

All of Grace

But we believe that through the grace of the Lord Jesus Christ we shall be saved, even as they.   — Acts 15:11

There was trouble in the early church and many of them gathered together to talk about the problem. Some converted Jews argued that the Gentiles who believed in God should be circumcised. If they refused, they would not go to heaven. But Paul and Barnabas completely disagreed. "We preach that faith in the Lord Jesus will save you, and nothing should be added to this." Some people agreed and others disagreed. Then Peter stood up and reminded them all that the Lord had very clearly sent the Holy Spirit to the Gentiles. Their hearts were made holy before God the same way as the Jews— through faith in the Lord Jesus.

What more do you need to do to be saved? There is nothing for us to do because the Lord Jesus has done it all. Salvation is possible completely through the grace of God. His grace allows you to have your sins forgiven and to be blessed forever.

Is it easy to be saved?

Peter — 1 Peter 1:13–25

A Letter from Peter

Be ye holy: for I am holy.
— 1 Peter 1:16

Peter was sitting at his table, writing a letter. The Jews who believed in the Lord Jesus were going through difficult times, so Peter was writing a letter to encourage them. They were being mocked and they found it difficult to live the way the Lord wanted them to. Peter wrote about how to live as a child of God, which we read in our Bible passage today. He also explained how believers ought to resemble God.

I am sure that you have been told at one time or another that you look like your mom or dad. Maybe you act like your dad, or you look just like your mom. In a similar way, a child of God has to resemble his heavenly Father. The heavenly Father is holy; therefore, you have to be holy, too. You have to listen to what He says in His Word, the Bible. Do not go your own way in life, but ask what God wants you to do. The other children of God are like your brothers and sisters. You have to love them, even if they are not always nice to you. This is difficult, isn't it? You can only be holy if the Lord Jesus has paid for your sins, bought you with His own blood, arose from the dead for you, and is now praying for you to His Father.

Can a child of God live a completely holy life?

Peter — 1 Peter 4:7–11

Love is Most Important

And above all things have fervent charity among your-selves: for charity shall cover the multitude of sins.
— 1 Peter 4:8

Real Christians, as children of God, will desire the best for each other. They are like brothers and sisters, for they love the same heavenly Father. They will look out for each other and will not discuss one another's faults. They will forgive each other after a quarrel and, when problems arise, they will try to help out.

The Bible talks about gifts, and each child of God has a gift or a talent—something they are good at. One is good at telling Bible stories, another loves helping out (think of Tabitha), and still another is very hospitable, welcoming everyone. All gifts were given by God in order to help others and to give God all the honor and praise due to Him, only for Jesus' sake.

How can you tell when someone is a child of God?

Peter — 2 Peter 1:3–21

A Lamp for Your Feet

We have also a more sure word of prophesy; whereunto ye do well that ye take heed, as unto a light that shineth in a dark place, until the day dawn, and the day star arise in your hearts.
                                                              — 2 Peter 1:19

When you go camping, one item you need for sure is your flashlight. What if you need to go outside in the middle of the night and it is pitch black? You will use your flashlight, shining it on the path by your feet.

Peter says that the Word of God is like a light shining in the dark. Due to sin, our hearts are pitch black and we go our own way. But when God's Word shines in our hearts, we see that we are on the wrong path, headed far away from God. We will start searching for the right path. We read in the Bible that the Lord Jesus is the way to God. He is the Way and the Light, and nothing in this world is as certain as God's Word, despite what very smart people might say. When we have His Word as a lamp to our feet and a light to our path, we will be able to travel safely through this world. We will be traveling to the city where there is no night because the Lord Jesus is the shining Morning Star.

How does the Word of God act as a light in your life?

Peter — 2 Peter 3:1–7

Mockers Walk Without a Lamp

Knowing this first, that there shall come in the last days scoffers, walking after their own lusts. — 2 Peter 3:3

God's Word is more solidly rooted than anything else on this earth. What the Lord has promised in His Word will surely happen. Peter warned against mockers who would go their own way and refuse to believe in God. They would try to lead people astray by luring them away from the right path. They would ask what was happening to the promise that God would make everything new, trying to make God seem unfaithful.

Abraham, Moses, and David all died without seeing the fulfillment of the promises, yet they still believed. Mockers do not use God's Word as a lamp and so they are blind to what has already happened. They forget that the flood really did occur. They don't realize that God, in His time, will burn up this earth and that they will have to appear before the heavenly Judge. They will be sorry that they did not use God's Word as a lamp, but followed their own dark path.

Do you sometimes forget what is clearly stated in the Bible? What can you do to remember it more often?

Peter — 2 Peter 3:8–18

No Delay, but Patience

The Lord is not slack concerning his promise, as some men count slackness; but is longsuffering to us-ward, not willing that any should perish, but that all should come to repentance.

— 2 Peter 3:9

Your classmate is sick and you think, "I should send him a card. I don't have time today, but tomorrow I will do it." The next day, it is freezing rain and you can't get out. Before you know it, your classmate is back in school. When you postpone things, they often don't happen at all.

In Peter's days, mockers thought that God was letting time slip away and that He would not fulfill His promises. Peter warned the Christians that this was a lie because God is not bound to our time. We cannot understand the high and holy God. The second coming of the Lord Jesus is not delayed. The Lord is patient because many people still have to be converted so that they will not be eternally lost.

Anybody who does not have a new heart can still receive one. And people who believe have time to learn more about the Lord Jesus. But hurry! No one knows when the Judge of heaven and earth is going to come. Hurry to save your life. The Lord Jesus is still the Savior, but soon He will come as the Judge.

Do you look forward to the second coming or are you afraid of it? Why or why not?

Philip — Acts 6:1–8

Too Much Work

Whom they set before the apostles: and when they had prayed, they laid their hands on them.
— Acts 6:6

Every single day after Pentecost, people were converted. Imagine hearing about people believing in the Lord Jesus every day. You, your parents, your family, your friends…it would seem like everyone was believing. The church would grow and grow so quickly.

That is what happened in this chapter of Acts. Because the congregations were growing larger, something went wrong. Some widows complained that they did not receive enough care and attention. So seven men were chosen to look after the poor. These men, called deacons, took over this special job from the apostles, giving the apostles more time to pray and preach. One of the chosen deacons was Philip. He was a wise man and full of the Holy Spirit. The apostles prayed with Philip and gave him the blessing of the Lord. Now Philip could work for the kingdom of God.

What work do the deacons in your church do?

Philip — Acts 8:1–8

Philip Preaches in Samaria

Then Philip went down to the city of Samaria, and preached Christ unto them.

— Acts 8:5

Matters were becoming dangerous in Jerusalem. Stephen had been stoned and the other Christians were also being persecuted. Many Christians left Jerusalem, and among them was Philip, the deacon. He had become an evangelist. When he arrived in Samaria, he immediately started to preach about Christ, God's Son. Soon things happened that had also occurred during Jesus' preaching. As a sign that Philip preached God's Word and not his own words, many lame and crippled people were healed. Demons were leaving the people they possessed against their will, crying and screaming.

Imagine how happy the people of Samaria were! Maybe they had heard of the apostles' miracles and their message before, but they had not seen any. Now they could see these great miracles and hear the gospel, the good news.

Why is the gospel called "the good news"?

Philip — Acts 8:9–24

Real and Counterfeit

Thou hast neither part nor lot in this matter: for thy heart is not right in the sight of God.
— Acts 8:21

Philip was not the first one who did miracles in Samaria. Simon the sorcerer also worked there. He performed miracles and he told everyone within hearing distance how special he was. Philip, however, never talked about himself; he only preached about the forgiveness of sins through the blood of Jesus Christ. When people believed his message, they were baptized.

Simon was so impressed with Philip that he had himself baptized and stayed with Philip. A little while later, Peter and John came to Samaria to see how the Lord was working. When Peter and John laid their hands on people's heads, they would receive the Holy Spirit. Simon saw that and thought to himself, "I want to learn how to do this trick, too." Simon asked the apostles if he could buy this ability from them. Peter became very angry because the gift of the Holy Spirit is never for sale. It is free and only available by grace.

Simon's heart was not upright before God. Is yours?

Philip — Acts 8:25–28

Philip Receives a New Task

And the angel of the Lord spake unto Philip, saying,
Arise, and go toward the south.
— Acts 8:26a

Philip was walking on the road from Jerusalem to Gaza. What was he doing on this rough, quiet road? There were no people around to whom he could preach. But Philip was following the command that an angel had given him. He obeyed, not knowing why he had to go.

Philip was alone, but not for long. In the distance, a chariot, pulled by horses, approached him. On the chariot sat a wealthy and important man. He was a chamberlain of Queen Candace of Ethiopia. He had worshipped in Jerusalem and was on his way home, back to Ethiopia. While riding, he was reading part of the prophet Isaiah's writings. Maybe he had heard part of this prophecy and wanted to read it again for himself. On this quiet road, nobody would disturb him. Or was there someone waiting for him?

Would you obey a command that came with no explanation?

Philip — Acts 18:29–31

Do You Understand
What You Read?

And Philip ran thither to him, and heard him read the prophet Esaias, and said, Understandest thou what thou readest?
— Acts 8:30

The chariot of the chamberlain came closer to Philip, and the Holy Spirit told Philip to walk beside it. When Philip drew near, he heard someone reading aloud. The words he heard were well known to Philip; the man was reading from Isaiah. Philip asked him, "Do you understand what you are reading?"

Surprised, the man looked up and honestly admitted that he did not understand it. He asked Philip to climb into the chariot and explain the words to him. To understand the Bible clearly, we often need someone to help explain it to us. It could be your minister, teacher, or parents. A good book can also be helpful, but the best teacher is the Holy Spirit, who can put His words into our hearts.

Are there parts of the Bible that you cannot understand? If so, pray about them and then talk to your parents or your pastor.

Philip — Acts 8:32–40

Philip Preaches and Baptizes

Then Philip opened his mouth, and began at the same scripture, and preached unto him Jesus. — Acts 8:35

As soon as Philip joined the chamberlain, the chamberlain began to read to Philip the prophecy that he found so difficult to understand. Isaiah was talking about a certain person who would be led as a lamb to the slaughter. That person was silent, like a lamb is silent when it is sheared. Who was Isaiah talking about?

Philip explained that the prophet was talking about the Lord Jesus. Jesus had to die on the cross because we have sinned. He had to carry the punishment and had to die the same way as sheep were killed as an offering in the temple. The Son of God came willingly to earth to suffer and die as a man.

The chariot was riding along a body of water and the chamberlain wanted to be baptized. Philip said he would only baptize him if he believed with his whole heart that Jesus Christ was the Son of God. The man did believe! After Philip baptized him, he was taken away by the Holy Spirit. The chamberlain traveled on alone but with great gladness. He was thankful for the greatest treasure we can possess: the Lord Jesus Christ.

Why were you baptized?

Philip — Acts 21:7–14

At Philip's House

And we entered into the house of Philip the evangelist,
which was one of the seven; and abode with him.
— Acts 21:8b

Paul had finished a tiring journey. He was staying at the house of Philip, the evangelist, to enjoy rest and to talk with the other apostles. Philip lived with his four daughters in Caesarea. They were a special family; the father was an evangelist and the four daughters were prophetesses. They spoke about the Lord and also about what would happen in the future.

After a few weeks of rest for Paul, the prophet Agabus came for a visit. He came to tell Paul that he would be cast into prison in Jerusalem. Everyone in the household was frightened and tried to stop Paul from going to Jerusalem. But Paul didn't want his friends to worry about him. He was ready to suffer and die for his Master. Nobody dared to argue with him; they placed the matter in God's hands and left it with Him. They knew that God's will always prevails.

How can you use your home in the service of God?

Paul — Acts 7:54–8:3

Saul Persecutes the Christians

As for Saul, he made havoc of the church, entering into every house, and haling men and women committed them to prison.
— Act 8:3

Saul was destroying the church. The Christians gathered together to listen to the disciples, but Saul despised the followers of the Lord Jesus and His teachings. He didn't go after the Christians because he hated God—no, far from it. Saul had studied the Bible and thought he was doing his best to help God. He even thought he was serving God by persecuting these men and women. He was blindly serving the Lord in his own way instead of in God's way.

The problem was that Saul didn't believe that Jesus was God's Son. Saul was a picture of the antichrist, which is what the Bible calls those who are against Christ and therefore against God Himself. How terrible it is to be against God! Ask the Lord to show you how to serve Him according to His will.

Would you still believe in God if that meant going to prison for your faith?

336

Paul — Acts 9:1-9

Saul Needs Help

And he trembling and astonished said, Lord, what wilt thou have me to do? And the Lord said unto him, Arise, and go into the city, and it shall be told thee what thou must do. — Acts 9:6

Saul suddenly didn't know what to do. Until now, he had been quite confident and knowledgeable. He knew he had to kill all the followers of Jesus and in that way help God. That was what he had thought all along, but now he was not so sure anymore. The Lord had stopped Saul on his way to Damascus and told him, "I am Jesus whom thou persecutest." Saul was puzzled and asked Jesus what he should do, which was the best question Saul could have asked.

When you experience things that you can't quite figure out on your own, the wisest thing for you to do is just what Saul did: ask the Lord what to do. Maybe you don't understand why some fellow students tease you at school, or you wonder why there is so much suffering and pain in this world. All your questions should be directed to the Lord. He answers you when you read your Bible; that is how the Lord speaks today. That is the right place to look for answers to all your questions.

Are you in the habit of bringing all your questions to the Lord?

Paul — Acts 9:10–22

Saul Speaking of Christ

And straightway he preached Christ in the synagogues,
that he is the Son of God.
— Acts 9:20

A great miracle happened in the life of Saul. A few days ago, we read in Acts 8 how Saul persecuted everyone who confessed Jesus to be the Son of God. Now he was doing the opposite! He was preaching in the synagogue that Jesus was God's Son. What changed him so dramatically? The Holy Spirit came into Saul's life, making him ask the Lord what he should do, just like you read yesterday. The Lord wanted Saul to tell anyone who would listen about His Son, Jesus Christ.

Just like Saul, you are called to speak well of the Lord. Have you ever told someone who doesn't know anything about who God is? It is important to ask the Lord to help you say the right words. We usually find it hard to talk about Jesus to others, maybe because it makes us feel embarrassed. You wonder what the other person will think of you. But it shouldn't be that way. It is a great privilege to tell others about Jesus, and the greatest gift you can possibly give them is a Bible. It is God's own Word.

Do you speak about Jesus to others?

Paul — Acts 9:23–31

Saul's Life is Changed

And after that many days were fulfilled, the Jews took counsel to kill him.
                                                    — Acts 9:23

Everything had changed in the life of Saul. People who used to be his friends were now his enemies. The Jews, who thought of Saul as an example of a good Jew, were now looking for ways to kill him. Saul used to throw in prison anyone who confessed Jesus to be the Son of God; now his own life was in danger. The only reason the Jews wanted to kill him was because Saul himself preached that Jesus was God's Son. Everything was turned upside down in Saul's life.

We will experience the same thing if the Lord speaks to us personally. If you listen to what the Lord tells you, you will act accordingly. That might mean that you have to let go of things that you loved doing. Or you might find yourself praying for that unfriendly boy in your class, even though you never wanted to before. There will be people who laugh at you, but do not let them discourage you. Never stop praying. Ask the Lord to give you strength to keep telling others about Him.

Do your friends believe in God? If not, pray for a chance to talk to them about Jesus.

Paul — Acts 11:19–26

Christians

And it came to pass, that a whole year they assembled themselves with the church, and taught much people. And the disciples were called Christians first in Antioch.
— Acts 11:26

Saul was with Barnabas in Antioch to tell the people there about the Lord Jesus. Barnabas was also a follower of Jesus. When the heathens in this city heard about them, they called them Christians because they were followers of Christ.

Maybe you are called a Christian sometimes. You must act like one; if you don't, you are putting the Lord Jesus to shame. We have to show in our conduct how important it is to follow Jesus. If someone is really important to you, you follow his instructions. Because of our sinful nature that can be hard to do. It is good to realize that we cannot obey in our own strength, for we need the Lord's help every single day to be a true Christian.

Do you want to be a true Christian?

Paul — Acts 13:1–3

Saul and Barnabas are Fasting

As they ministered to the Lord, and fasted, the Holy Ghost said, Separate me Barnabas and Saul for the work whereunto I have called them.
— Acts 13:2

We read about Saul serving the Lord while he was fasting. Fasting means that you eat nothing or only a little bit. Instead of eating anything you want, you deny yourself in order to think more of God. It shows that your food is not as important as having communion with God. Fasting is not as common today as it once was, but it is still a good thing to do.

There are other ways to show that serving the Lord is the most important thing in your life. For example, you could give part of your money to help others. There are a lot of poor people who would be very happy to receive some of your money as a token of God's love. You could also give some of your time. Visit someone who is lonely or sick instead of just playing on your day off from school. I am sure you could think of more ways to give back to the Lord. He gives you the incredible gift of His love. It will make you happier to show something of His love in your life to others who need it.

What are other ways you could show love to the Lord?

Paul — Acts 14:19–28

The Stoning of Paul

*And there came thither certain Jews from Antioch and Ico-
nium, who persuaded the people, and, having stoned Paul,
drew him out of the city, supposing he had been dead.*

— Acts 14:19

Saul's name had been changed into Paul, as you read in
today's passage. His Hebrew name was Saul and his Roman
name was Paul. Today's verse tells you about how people
stoned Paul. These people were encouraged to stone him
by the Jews of the cities where Paul had recently been. Of
course, he spoke of the Lord Jesus to whomever wanted to
listen. His teaching was the very reason the Jews hated Paul,
for they wanted to believe in their own ways, not what Paul
was telling them. They stirred up the people to stone Paul.

After they stoned him, they dragged his body outside the
city walls. They thought their job was done, for Paul seemed
to be dead. But Paul wasn't dead; the Lord took care of him.
The work that the Lord had prepared for Paul was not done,
so he could not go to heaven yet.

Do you experience the Lord's care over you in your life?

Paul — Acts 15:35–41

Paul Quarrels with Barnabas

And the contention was so sharp between them, that they departed asunder one from the other: and so Barnabas took Mark, and sailed to Cyprus.
— Acts 15:39

Maybe you didn't expect Paul to end up in an argument with his fellow preachers. A Christian shouldn't be quarrelling, right? No, indeed, the Lord commands us to love Him above all and our neighbors as ourselves. This event in Bible history shows us that the Bible is trustworthy, including even stories like this one. It would have been easy to leave this event out of the Bible. But the Lord wanted to show us that even people who love Him fall into sin. God didn't allow this to happen because He doesn't care about sin, but to warn us about the effects of sin. It shows us that, even when we sin, we can always go to Him to ask for forgiveness.

I am quite sure that you have been in an argument with someone at some point in your life. How did it end up? Did you talk to the other person to set things straight again, or did you just ignore them? Do you maybe even hate them? This is not the way the Lord wants us to handle our mistakes. Ask the Lord to help you solve your problems with others.

Do you apologize after quarrelling with someone?

Paul — Acts 16:1–10

Paul Goes to Macedonia

And after he had seen the vision, immediately we endeavoured to go into Macedonia, assuredly gathering that the Lord had called us for to preach the gospel unto them.
— Acts 16:10

One night, Paul received a vision. In that vision, he saw a man from Macedonia calling him to come to them. The Lord was showing Paul where he had to go next. Paul didn't hesitate; he went there immediately. The gospel (which means "glad tidings") was spread to more areas this way. The Lord took care to spread His Word, using men like Paul to accomplish the mission.

There are still people like Paul who tell the gospel to others, either in this country or in foreign countries. But there are still countries in the world where the people have never heard this message before. Preachers who work in foreign countries are called missionaries. Missionaries have a very hard task. It is so important that we ask the Lord to help them in their tasks.

Do you pray for missionaries? Remember to do so today.

344

Paul — Acts 17:10–14

Paul in Berea

These were more noble than those in Thessalonica, in that they received the word with all readiness of mind, and searched the scriptures daily, whether those things were so.
— Acts 17:11

Paul traveled from one city to the next, preaching the gospel of Jesus Christ everywhere. However, he was not welcomed with open arms everywhere; some people disagreed with his preaching. Paul also visited Berea, and our text for today says that the people there were "more noble." That doesn't mean that they were better than others, but it means that they were doing what they were supposed to do. They listened to what was being said about the Bible, and afterwards checked what they heard with the Scriptures. The people in Berea searched the Scriptures every day.

We should search the Scriptures every day just like they did. When you read your Bible every day, you begin to understand more of what it all means. The Lord is willing to change you in such a way that you will be able to listen to Him. The sermons you hear in church or elsewhere should lead you to search your Bible to check out whether what was said is really true. There are people who do not teach exactly what the Bible does. The Bible alone is the complete truth.

Do you pray before you read your Bible, asking the Lord to explain to you what you will read?

Paul — Acts 17:15–34

Paul Preaching the Unknown God

For as I passed by, and beheld your devotions, I found an altar with this inscription, TO THE UNKNOWN GOD. Whom therefore ye ignorantly worship, him declare I unto you.
— Acts 17:23

During one of Paul's missionary journeys, he arrived in Athens. While he walked through this great city, the many holy places caught his attention. The city was filled with many different altars, images, idols, and temples to worship different gods. Among these altars, Paul saw one that said, "To the unknown God." This altar was meant for a God they didn't know, so Paul took the opportunity to preach to them about God. The people listened closely to him, but after Paul told them that Jesus was risen from the dead they became angry with him. They couldn't believe it. They couldn't understand how this fact could be true, so they concluded it was a lie.

Do you understand everything you read in the Bible? Is it really possible that Jonah was in the belly of the fish for three days? How can it be true that water was changed into wine? God does not ask that we understand these things, only that we believe they are true. God is mightier than we are and nothing is impossible with Him.

Do you believe that God is almighty?

Paul — Acts 18:1–11

Paul Preaching to the Gentiles

For I am with thee, and no man shall set on thee to hurt thee: for I have much people in this city.
— Acts 18:10

There was no reason for Paul to be afraid when he started preaching. God had told him not to be afraid because He would be with him. Nobody would harm him, God promised, because the Lord had many followers in this city. This meant that the Lord already knew that many people in this city would believe in Him. The Lord had already chosen who would believe, so He knew that Paul was safe. It is beautiful to know the Lord's will for these people would really take place; they would receive faith in Him. Paul was used as an instrument in God's hand to tell these Gentiles about the Lord Jesus, leading them to believe in Christ.

We must all believe in Jesus. That is why ministers preach about God on Sunday. Maybe you say, "It says in the Bible that you cannot believe in your own strength." Yes, that is true, but that doesn't mean that you can sit back and do nothing at all, for the Bible also tells us to seek Him. God even promises that those who seek Him early will find Him! That is an amazing promise. If you search for God when you are still young, you will surely find Him.

Do you search for God?

347

Paul — Acts 19:13–23

God's Word Gives Strength

So mightily grew the word of God and prevailed.
— Acts 19:20

While Paul was in Ephesus, some miraculous events took place. Some of the Jews used the name of Jesus to cast out demons, but it didn't work because the Lord hadn't given them power to do so. The only reason these Jews wanted to do this was to show off, not to show the power of Jesus. Paul, on the contrary, cast out demons to show the power of God.

The people in Ephesus understood that they couldn't belong to Jesus and still hang on to sinful things, so they threw out all the sinful books they possessed. Right after that, more and more people believed in the Lord Jesus Christ, and their faith grew stronger. Their trust toward the Lord increased. That is what today's text is about.

The same thing will happen to us when we start to obey the Lord. Others will be able to see that the Holy Spirit gives us strength to trust in the Lord.

How does God's Word give you strength?

Paul — Acts 28:16–31

Paul in Rome

*And when they had appointed him a day, there came
many to him into his lodging; to whom he expounded
and testified the kingdom of God, persuading them
concerning Jesus, both out of the law of Moses, and out of
the prophets, from morning till evening.* — Acts 28:23

Paul arrived in Rome as a prisoner. The Lord still took care
of him, though, even in Rome; Paul received the privilege of
living in his own house. Paul could invite people to his house
and continue to tell them about the Lord Jesus. He tried hard
to persuade them to believe in Jesus; he tried to win them
for God's cause with all his might. Paul didn't have to make
his own sermons; he used the Old Testament and especially
the law of Moses and the prophets to teach. He was busy
speaking from early morning until late evening.

Today we read about the last part of Paul's life, and again
we read about how he preached about the Lord Jesus. You
could say his preaching was predictable. During his whole
ministry, you can see how much he loved the Lord. Can
others notice that the Lord is most important in your life, too?
If that is true of you, you are very rich for you have a treasure
in heaven.

What is the treasure in heaven?

349

Barnabas — Acts 4:32–37

Barnabas Sells His Land

Having land, sold it, and brought the money, and laid it at the apostles' feet.

— Acts 4:37

We will now look at the life of Barnabas. As you can read in the Scripture passage, Barnabas sold his land. You might wonder why selling land is such a big deal. Don't people sell land all the time? This sale of land was special because of what Barnabas did with the money he received. He laid it in front of the disciples' feet as a gift. It was meant to be used for the poor.

Perhaps you give money for mission work or you sponsor a child somewhere far away. Maybe that is how you give a part of what God has given you to help others. Do you realize that all you have is a gift from God? You should serve the Lord with all you have. This doesn't mean you have to give everything away, but you are called to give away part of it. Giving money to others doesn't make you poor, it makes you rich. That statement might sound strange to you, but the Bible tells us that it is better to give than to receive.

Have you ever experienced happiness after giving away something you really liked?

350

Barnabas — Acts 9:23–31

Barnabas Helps Saul

But Barnabas took him, and brought him to the apostles, and declared unto them how he had seen the Lord in the way, and that he had spoken to him, and how he had preached boldly at Damascus in the name of Jesus.

— Acts 9:27

Saul fled to Jerusalem after the Jews of Damascus tried to kill him. But the apostles didn't trust him. Although Saul claimed to be a disciple of Jesus Christ, they only remembered him as their persecutor. Barnabas, whose name means "son of comfort," helped Saul. Barnabas's real name was Joseph, but the other disciples called him Barnabas because the Lord had given him a special ability to comfort people with God's Word. Barnabas was a very friendly and patient man. In today's passage, we read how he told the apostles that Saul had seen the Lord on his way to Damascus. Saul had even spoken about the Lord Jesus in Damascus without fear. We read how this was a dangerous activity for Saul, for the Jews tried to kill him for preaching about Christ. After Barnabas explained all this, the disciples realized that Saul was really a different man. Through the help of Barnabas, the Lord made it possible for Saul to bring the gospel in Jerusalem.

Do you ask the Lord to make you a friendly and patient person?

Barnabas — Acts 11:19–26

The Good Man, Barnabas

For he was a good man, and full of the Holy Ghost and of faith: and much people was added unto the Lord.
— Acts 11:24

Acts 11:24 says that Barnabas was "a good man." Why does it say that? Doesn't the Bible teach us that no one is good by himself? The Bible tells us that Barnabas was a good man because he was filled with the Holy Spirit and with faith. He was not good because of his own abilities; his goodness came from the Lord.

I want to ask you a difficult question. Are you a good person? I imagine you answered that you cannot describe yourself in that way. But Barnabas didn't say it about himself, did he? What do you think the Lord would say about you? That is probably also a difficult question, but when you think about this carefully, you might admit that you do many things that the Lord doesn't want you to do. Barnabas was the same as you, even though he was a good man. The Lord forgave his sins and filled him with His Spirit and with faith. He was only good because of the good that the Lord had put in his heart.

Have you asked the Lord to send the Holy Spirit to live in your heart?

Barnabas — Acts 13:4–12

Barnabas Meets a False Prophet

And when they had gone through the isle unto Paphos, they found a certain sorcerer, a false prophet, a Jew, whose name was Bar-jesus. — Acts 13:6

Barnabas and Paul arrived on the island of Cyprus. Here they also preached the gospel of the Lord Jesus. While traveling around the island, they met a magician. Well, he wasn't really a magician, but rather a false prophet. A false prophet is someone who pretends to bring the Word of God. But you already understand that this false prophet didn't work for God. He spoke the word of the devil instead. The devil is God's enemy, always trying to prevent people from speaking about God's grace. He does everything to oppose this work, and he uses different methods to do it.

In today's story, Satan tried to keep the deputy of the country from believing in the Lord Jesus. That didn't work because the Lord is much mightier than the devil. But the devil doesn't give up; he also tries to keep you from having faith in God. For example, he tells you that God will not help you anyway, or that God doesn't even really exist. Don't believe these lies. Ask the Lord to help you to stay close to Him. Then the devil cannot harm you.

Have you ever noticed the devil's tricks to keep you from the Lord?

353

Barnabas — Acts 13:48–14:4

Barnabas Shakes the Dust off His Feet

But they shook off the dust of their feet against them, and came unto Iconium.
— Acts 13:51

Many of the people who heard Barnabas and Paul speaking about the Lord listened carefully and rejoiced in the message. They began to obey the Lord, and the Bible tells us that the gospel was spread in that entire region. The only ones who were unhappy with this development were the Jews, for now their religion wasn't the center of attention anymore. The message about Jesus was now the most important news. The Jews were jealous and tried to get rid of Barnabas and Paul, encouraging influential people to chase them from the area. Their plan worked out well. Barnabas and Paul did leave the area. "They shook off the dust of their feet against them." This means that they showed these Jews that they would not come back, for the Jews had rejected the gospel of Jesus.

The Lord often speaks to you in a sermon or when your teacher tells you a Bible story at school. When you read your Bible, it is the Lord who is speaking to you. It is God's desire that we listen to His voice and obey Him.

Do you think it's possible that if we continually refuse to listen to the Lord, He will not want to speak to us anymore?

354

Barnabas — Acts 14:5–18

Barnabas Explains that He is not God

And saying, Sirs, why do ye these things? We also are men of like passions with you, and preach unto you that ye should turn from these vanities unto the living God, which made heaven, and earth, and the sea, and all things that are therein.

— Acts 14:15

What was the excitement in Lystra all about? "Come, people, come; the gods have come to earth!" What had the gods done that so many people were worked up? Well, the people were amazed, for the gods had healed a paralyzed man, which could only mean that they really were gods. But Paul and Barnabas told the people that only the true God had healed this man, not another god as they imagined. The men explained to the people that they themselves weren't gods at all. "The power that is in us is not our own, but the power of the Lord."

That is how you should answer your friends when they're amazed at your skill in certain things. You are not talented because you're such a special person, but because the Lord is very good to you. He gives you the ability to be friendly to others, to learn well, and to do many other things. The Bible tells us that we can do nothing without God. We are capable of doing nothing, but God's strength enables us to do everything necessary.

Can you do anything without God?

Barnabas — Acts 15:35–41

Barnabas the Comforter

And Barnabas determined to take with them John, whose surname was Mark.
— Acts 15:37

Paul and Barnabas were back in Antioch. Once again, they preached about their Master. After staying for a while, Paul suggested it was time to continue their travels. Paul wanted to visit those who had listened to their message before. He would like to see how they were doing. Barnabas proposed bringing a man named Mark along on their journey. This Mark (not the Mark who wrote the Bible book of Mark) had accompanied them on one of their earlier journeys but had deserted them. Paul didn't want him to come along this time. That was the beginning of a quarrel. You read about this argument a few days ago when we talked about Paul's life. Paul and Barnabas argued because they were very different men. Barnabas was patient and wanted to forgive Mark his past mistakes. Paul's philosophy was that if you do something, you do it well.

God created us with different character traits. Paul and Barnabas are a good example of this. Maybe you see yourself in the patience of Barnabas. Or maybe you see more of Paul's restlessness in yourself. Whatever your character, the Lord expects you to trust Him for everything.

Do you trust in the Lord for everything, even when you have to wait for something?

Timothy — Colossians 1:1–18

Paul's Companion, Timothy

Paul, an apostle of Jesus Christ by the will of God, and Timotheus our brother.
— Colossians 1:1

We will look more closely at Timothy's role while he worked with Paul. Here in Colossians we can see that Timothy was Paul's helper. You can imagine that Timothy, just like Paul, wanted to speak well of the Lord. This time, he and Paul did so through a letter, written to the people in Colosse, where Paul visited when he was on his missionary journeys.

We can find a lot of letters in the Bible, but this letter is a beautiful one. In Colossians 1:14, you can read of the forgiveness of sins through Jesus' blood. You should take time to read through this letter; I am convinced you will find many more beautiful verses. Ask your parents to explain the things that you don't understand.

Is there a specific verse in the letter to the Colossians that is especially beautiful to you?

Timothy — 1 Timothy 1:1–11, 18–20

Timothy has to Fight the Good Fight

This charge I commit unto thee, son Timothy, according to the prophesies which went before on thee, that thou by them mightest war a good warfare.
— 1 Timothy 1:18

Paul called Timothy his son, but he didn't mean a natural son. He meant that he had taught Timothy many things regarding Jesus, just like a father tells his son about God. Paul also taught him how to deal with different people in the churches. Paul wrote this letter to remind Timothy of all the lessons he had learned from Paul, and also to give further instructions.

Paul said that Timothy had received special talents. He knew this because the Holy Spirit revealed it to him. When someone brings a message from the Lord, that person is considered a prophet and his message can be called a prophecy.

Timothy was encouraged to fight the good fight with his talents. He didn't need any weapons in this war against people who spoke wrongly about God and His Word. The fight could only be won through the power of God in him.

Do we have to fight people that oppose God and His Word?

Timothy — 1 Timothy 6:3–21

Be Content

And having food and raiment let us be therewith content.
— 1 Timothy 6:8

In this letter from Paul written to Timothy, we read that we have to be content with having food and clothing. Paul meant that, when we have enough to eat and wear, we lack nothing. Paul learned this from the Lord Jesus who said the same thing when He was still on earth.

The Lord wants us to be content. Maybe that is difficult for you, just like it was for many people in Paul's time and still today. We often want more and more. For many people, it is most important to have a lot of money, but Paul warns that having a lot of money can be dangerous. How can having money be dangerous, you wonder? Isn't it handy to have a lot of money? It is fine to use your money to buy things that are necessary in life, but the danger is that we forget the Lord and are never satisfied with what we have. Are you generous, letting someone else have the first choice? If you end up getting less than the others, are you still content and happy? Do you complain when the biggest piece of cake isn't on your plate? Search your heart to see if you are content.

Do you think that having a lot of money will make you happier?

Timothy — 2 Timothy 1:1–14

Timothy's Calling

Who hath saved us, and called us with an holy calling, not according to our works, but according to his own purpose and grace, which was given us in Christ Jesus before the world began.
— 2 Timothy 1:9

Timothy had been called by God, as you've read in today's passage of Paul's letter. He was called by the Lord just like Samuel. He was given a holy calling, which means that he was called to live his whole life in special service to God. God did not choose Timothy because he was such a good person or because he had a godly mother and grandmother, although this was a blessing in Timothy's life. Timothy was called by God's grace; he was allowed to serve God although he didn't deserve to do so. His calling was already part of God's plan for his life before he was born—even before the world began. We may not be able to understand this amazing truth, but we must believe it because it is from the Lord. That is why Timothy could trust that the Lord would help him in the upcoming task.

Do you think the Lord has a plan for your life as well?

Timothy — 2 Timothy 2:1–13

Jesus Christ is Risen from the Dead

Remember that Jesus Christ of the seed of David was raised from the dead according to my gospel.
— 2 Timothy 2:8

Paul reminded Timothy to keep in mind the resurrection of the Lord Jesus Christ. He would then have courage to speak boldly about his Lord and not be ashamed. The risen Lord was from the family of David. Timothy must realize this important truth for it means that Jesus was a human being. Timothy would be raised from the dead in the future, just like his Master. The fact that the Lord was born out of the lineage of David was a sure reminder that God's promise in the Old Testament had been fulfilled. When we read about the prophecies of Jesus' sacrifice, we know that the gospel is true. The Lord is now alive and lives in heaven to pray for His own people. Ask the Lord often to pray for you, for God the Father will surely listen to the prayers of His own Son.

Why is it so important to know that the Lord conquered death and is alive today?

361

Timothy — 2 Timothy 3:10–4:5

Timothy's Upbringing in the Word

And that from a child thou hast known the holy scriptures, which are able to make thee wise unto salvation through faith which is in Christ Jesus. — 2 Timothy 3:15

When Timothy was still a young boy, he was already exposed to the Word of God—not the Bible as we know it; just the Old Testament. It is very important to listen to and learn from God's Word. It can make us wise unto salvation, like you have read today. This means you will read how to obtain forgiveness of sins in your Bible. You already know that the blood of the Lord Jesus cleanses you from your sins. But it is not enough to know it; you also have to believe it, and, because we cannot believe it by ourselves, we need Christ Jesus. Christ is the answer to all your questions. Timothy had to ask Him for forgiveness of sins, just like you need to do.

We are even more blessed than Timothy because we have not only the Old Testament, but also the New Testament. The New Testament is a treasure, telling us about the life of the Lord Jesus. Read it often!

What does it mean to become "wise unto salvation"?

Timothy — 2 Timothy 4:9–22

Paul's Best Wishes for Timothy

The Lord Jesus Christ be with thy spirit. Grace be with you. Amen.
— 2 Timothy 4:22

Paul, the writer of this letter to Timothy, expressed the wish that all would go well with Timothy. Paul didn't say this in a shallow way like we often do when we wish someone all the best, meaning that all will go smoothly and well at school or that they will be healthy. No, Paul hoped that the very best would happen to Timothy—that the Lord Jesus Christ would go with him. Paul not only wished this grace to be true for Timothy, but for Timothy's congregation, too. Paul knew how badly this grace was needed, probably more than any other person could. His well-wishing was to encourage Timothy in his challenging work, but it also encouraged the members of his congregation.

These words are also written to encourage you. You need the Lord's grace in everything you do, too. Maybe you don't realize that very often, but it is true. We cannot move one finger if the Lord doesn't give us the strength to do it. We couldn't even take a breath without Him! I hope that you will experience the Lord Jesus Christ being with your spirit, and that it will make you tell others about Him.

What did the grace of God do for you today?

Elisabeth — Luke 1:5–17

Our Hearts are Known to God

And they were both righteous before God.
                                    — Luke 1:6a

Can you tell that certain people love the Lord? Can you see it by the clothes they wear? Outward appearance is not enough. Elisabeth's life clearly showed that she lived a holy life devoted to the Lord. It was her desire to serve God with an upright heart. "Lord, what wilt Thou have me to do?" was her daily prayer. By her holy walk, she was an example to her neighbors.

Elisabeth and Zacharias were both righteous before God, as we read in God's Word. Both were descendents of a priestly race. This does not mean that if your father is a priest, minister, or elder, you are automatically a child of God. You only become His child when the Lord gives you a new heart. Elisabeth received a new heart and therefore loved the Lord and His service. She placed all her troubles and worries in His hand.

Being a child of God does not mean that there will be no sorrow. God's Word says, "Ask and it shall be given unto you." But the Lord will give in His own time and way. Elisabeth experienced sorrow in her life. She did not have a child even after many years of praying for one. Still, the Lord kept her from becoming rebellious.

Do you tell the Lord all your troubles?

Elisabeth — Luke 1:18–23

Will God Forget to be Gracious?

For thy prayer is heard.
— Luke 1:13b

Zacharias and Elisabeth had no children, which was very sad for them. Usually the Lord blesses a marriage with the birth of a child. But sometimes He does not, having His own wise reasons for this. When Zacharias and Elisabeth were younger, they often prayed for a child. Now they were old, reaching the age of a grandfather or grandmother. At this age, they could not have children anymore. Would Elisabeth still have prayed for a child? Or would she have said, "Lord, Thy will be done and make me agreeable to Thy will"?

One day, Zacharias came home from serving in the temple. He had so much to tell Elisabeth! He wanted to tell her, but could not. Because of his initial unbelief, the Lord had sealed his mouth and he could not talk. But he was still able to bring her the message he had received from the angel Gabriel. By grace, Elisabeth would receive a child and his name would be John. He would be a child with a special calling. In God's own way and time, their prayer had been answered.

When your prayers have not yet been answered, do you stop praying?

Elisabeth — Luke 1:24–25

The Almighty Makes Everything Well

Judah, thou art he.
— Genesis 49:8a

What sin did Elisabeth commit so that the Lord did not bless her with a child? This was the common question among the people around Elisabeth. Elisabeth sensed this every time the women talked about their children. She could not join in those conversations.

Elisabeth's mother came from the tribe of Judah and the women of this tribe had a special promise. The Lord Jesus, the Redeemer, would be born from Judah. But Elisabeth was left out and the shame she endured was painful until the promise of the birth of John was brought to her. Elisabeth believed the promise, for she said, "Thus hath the Lord dealt with me." The Lord was so good to her by giving her a child, a son. No, it was not the Son of God, the Redeemer; yet he was still a child that would be used by the Lord. The child would be filled with the Holy Spirit and his preaching would be blessed. John would point the people to the Lamb of God who takes away the sins of the world. Under John's ministry, people would repent of their sins.

It was a miracle for Elisabeth. She did not deserve to have a child from the Lord at her age—and then a child with such a special calling! God be praised for His unspeakable gift.

Ask God if you may become a child who is useful to Him.

Elisabeth — Luke 1:34–37

Observe the Miracles

For with God nothing shall be impossible.
— Luke 1:37

If you hear some news, you can quickly get on the phone and tell someone else what has happened. In Elisabeth's day, this was impossible. They would send messengers to bring their news. A messenger came to Mary one day—not sent by Elisabeth, but sent by God. It was Gabriel, the same angel who had visited Zacharias and had told him about the coming birth of John. His wife, Elisabeth, was old but would have a child.

Gabriel had another message: a child for Mary, a young woman who was not yet married. No man was needed for the conception of this child, but only the Holy Spirit. This child was God's own Son, the long-promised Redeemer. Mary had to call Him Jesus, meaning "He will save His people from their sins." What was once impossible would now be possible; people could be saved because God would become man! Gabriel told Mary that, as surely as her cousin was expecting, so surely these things would happen.

Miracles still happen. People whom the doctors have given up on are healed, and perhaps you could add a story that you've heard. But the greatest miracle is that the Lord will watch over sinful people like you and me.

> *Have you ever thought to yourself, "There is no hope for me; I cannot be saved"? Always remember that nothing is impossible for God! Pray for what you think is impossible.*

Elisabeth — Luke 1:39–45

Believe His Word

And blessed is she that believed.
— Luke 1:45a

As soon as Mary was expecting, she wanted to talk to Elisabeth. The Lord had done so many miracles in both their lives. She traveled from Nazareth to the hill country of Judea. It would have taken her four days if she walked this distance.

When Mary finally greeted her cousin, something wonderful happened: the Lord caused the child in Elisabeth's womb to leap for joy. Elisabeth began to prophesy and everyone could hear her words: "What a miracle that the mother of my Savior has visited me! It is such a blessing that the Lord chose Mary from among the women, and that He will be born of her." Mary believed Elisabeth and was blessed by her because both of them were certain that, whatever the Lord had promised, He would do.

The Lord Himself did not directly go to them, but had sent an angel, a messenger. Today, God sends His pastors to bring us God's Word. "For God so loved the world, that he gave his only begotten Son, that whosoever believeth on him, should not perish, but have everlasting life" (John 3:16).

Do you believe the messages that God sends you?

Elisabeth — Luke 1:57–58

Rejoice in the Lord

And thou shalt have joy and gladness; and many shall rejoice at his birth.
                                                    — Luke 1:14

Mary and Elisabeth often discussed the great works of the Lord. They rejoiced in the Lord because Elisabeth's sorrow had changed to joy. How did this news affect the neighbors? Did they perhaps tell Elisabeth not to rejoice too soon, but to wait until the child was actually born? Did they caution her that many things could go wrong with her or the child because she was so old?

Maybe they did, but what the Lord has promised would be fulfilled. You can be sure of that! At the time appointed by God, the child was born. How wonderful is the new life of a child—a child born from two different people! This is always very special and a great miracle each time it happens. The neighbors and family rejoiced with Elisabeth and Zacharias when they saw God's mercy displayed at John's birth.

John was already a child of God before his birth. He didn't realize this himself, for he was just a baby, but Gabriel had told his parents.

Is joy a mark of a child of God? Why or why not?

Elisabeth — Luke 1:59–64

Obedient in Faith

Not so; but he shall be called John.
— Luke 1:60b

Eight days after the birth of John, the family and neighbors all went to the home of Zacharias and Elisabeth. The baby John was going to be circumcised and given an official name. The circumcision in their days and our baptism today is a sacrament. Everyone could witness it, for the Lord speaks to us through the sacraments in a visible way. Zacharias was still unable to speak, so Elisabeth was in charge. She repeated what the angel Gabriel had told Zacharias: the baby's name would be John, which means "the Lord is gracious." The family members agreed with the meaning, but it was a custom to name the child after his father! They assumed Zacharias would want this. To their surprise, Zacharias wrote down that his name would be John. At this moment, the Lord opened Zacharias's mouth and he could speak! The first words he spoke were praise to God for all of His goodness and grace.

Do you obey the Lord regardless of what others think?

Anna — Luke 2:22–38

Confession of Faith

And spake of him to all.
— Luke 2:38

The temple square was a busy place. Animals for the offerings were sold to people who came from far away. You could exchange your foreign money, which was not a bad thing, but the moneychangers made quite a profit. Thus the temple was changed into a market. Was there nobody who showed reverence to the Lord and His service? Did the people still come to pray?

Yes, some did. An old man was standing there with a baby in his arms. It was Simeon, who was praising God for being able to see his Savior. An old woman walked towards them and also confessed that this baby was the Messiah. Who was this woman? It was Anna, and she was eighty-four years old. Her husband had died after they had been married for seven years. She was a God-fearing woman and every day she was in the temple, praying and fasting. She longed for the Messiah and now she knew for sure that this child was the long-promised Redeemer. How did she know? The Holy Spirit revealed it to her; that is why she was called a prophetess. She wanted to share what the Holy Spirit had told her. She told everyone who was also looking for the Redeemer that He had come to save His people from their sins.

Are there prophets in your church?

Tabitha — Acts 9:36–42

Stand Up!

*The hour is coming, and now is, when the dead shall hear
the voice of the Son of God: and they that hear shall live.*
— John 5:25

Tabitha had died! She was a woman who feared the Lord
and had done many things for the widows of the small
congregation of Joppa. And now she had passed away. When
her friends heard that Peter was in Lydda, they asked him to
come right away. They had heard of so many miracles; could
he, with God's help, do something? In Tabitha's house, the
widows were waiting for Peter and wept as they showed him
the clothes Tabitha had made. They told him how good she
had been in sewing for them.

Peter sent them out of the room and knelt down. He
asked for help from God because he could do nothing. God
had to show His power. Then a miracle happened—Peter
brought Tabitha back to life! Many who saw it believed in the
Lord. Today is the last day of the year. At a program, I heard
this song:

*If Jesus comes back tomorrow,
I have one day left.*

But what if He comes today? Just as Tabitha was raised
from physical death, so also you and I need to be raised from
our spiritual death.

*What would happen if Jesus came back today? Are
you ready?*

ath = 293 metres